Crafting a Valley Jewel

Architects and Builders of Woodland

For Diane, Emily & Rose

Architecture is frozen music.

— *Goethe*

Architecture is visible history.

— *Vincent Scully*

Civics as an art has to do, not with imaging an impossible [utopia] where all is well, but with making the most and best of each and every place, and especially of the city in which we live.

— *Patrick Geddes*

Crafting a Valley Jewel

Architects and Builders of Woodland

by David L. Wilkinson

Yolo County Historical Society

Published by the Yolo County Historical Society
Post Office Box 1447
Woodland, California 95776

Design: Ruth Santer

Front cover:
Background; apartment building by Jacob Witzelberger, photo by Roger Klemm. Left; Stephens House by John Hudson Thomas, photo by Robert Campbell. Center; Porter Building by William H. Weeks, photo by Roger Klemm. Right; Gable Mansion by Edward Carlton Gilbert, photo by Roger Klemm.
Back cover:
Gus Keehn at City Planing Mill, courtesy Joe T. Keehn

Contents

Acknowledgements

Many people contributed to the creation of this book, whose genesis was in 1989 when I worked on the *Walking Tour of Historic Woodland* booklet. Ron Pinegar, Woodland City Planner, has been a long-time colleague, inspiration and major resource for the book. I fondly remember the many hours we spent in the basement of City Hall thumbing through dusty tax assessment books while together researching Woodland houses and buildings for the various walking tour publications. Ron is a selfless, dedicated public servant with a strong vision and commitment to Woodland's historic preservation. His steady, determined presence as the city liaison with the Historic Preservation Commission and his early involvement with the success of the Stroll Through History are exemplary — elevating historic preservation into Woodland's mainstream planning policies in the 1990s.

When a book began to materialize in the late 1990s from several years of sporadic research and writing on the architects and builders, Bob Campbell, of the Yolo County Historical Society, generously read a very rough manuscript and gave many helpful suggestions for prospective publication. As the chairperson for the Publications Committee that eventually shepherded the book through the publication process, Bob has devoted many hours to the completion of the book, including several diligent re-readings that have greatly improved the text. I am very grateful for his encouragement and efforts. Thanks also to Richard Berteaux and Marion Tuttle of the Publications Committee for their careful editing, helpful suggestions, and overseeing publication. With deep gratitude, I thank the Board of Directors of the Yolo County Historical Society for their underwriting of this book.

Two friends merit special attention, for they have been instrumental in enhancing the quality of the book. Roger Klemm, a professional architect and colleague, has teamed with me for many pleasurable Woodland Stroll Through History walking tours. My architectural knowledge has been sharpened by his keen observations. In addition, his excellent photography adds greatly to the book's impact and I am indebted to him for his artistic contribution. Robert Becker, a professional writer and editor, has provided, along with constant encouragement and inspiration, effective language, frameworks and organizing patterns. His many contributions make the book eminently more readable and cohesive. Everyone should have such good friends and patient experts when faced with the daunting task of publishing.

Along the way, many people assisted me with research and I wish to thank them: staff and volunteers at the Yolo County Archives and Records Center, including Marylin Thompson, Shipley Walters, Virginia Isaacs, Mel Russell, and Howard Moore; Betty Marvin and Gail G. Lombardi at the City of Oakland, Cultural Heritage Survey; William W. Sturm, City of Oakland Public Library; Dennis Andersen for the gift of a scholarly book on Seattle architects and Jeffrey Ochsner, Department of Architecture, University of Washington; Steve Franks, Spokane Public Library; Don Napoli, Sacramento-based historian, for his careful and thoughtful reading of the manuscript; Joseph Keehn and Josephine Motroni Gillette and many others who generously offered the use of their photo collections for publication; the Yolo County Archives and Records Center and the Yolo County Museum for use of their photo collections; Mary Goetz and Jim Smith at the *Daily Democrat* for publication of excerpts from the draft manuscript; Marcel Berteaux for his skillful scanning of many photos; Ruth Santer, graphic designer, for the creative design and layout of the book; Robert Campbell, Virginia Isaacs, Jeanie Sherwood, and Roberta Stevenson for preparing the index; and finally, my gratitude to Penny Adams, Bruce Ahlquist, Kevin Bryan, Clare Childers, Don Cox, Nancy Crippen, Robert Dunn, Gary A. Goss, Martha Gutierrez, Debbie & Dennis Housen, Richard Landucci, Teri Laugenour, Justine Morrell, Anthony C. Newman, Ron Noble, Joan Seear, Tom Stallard, and Barbara Woolsey.

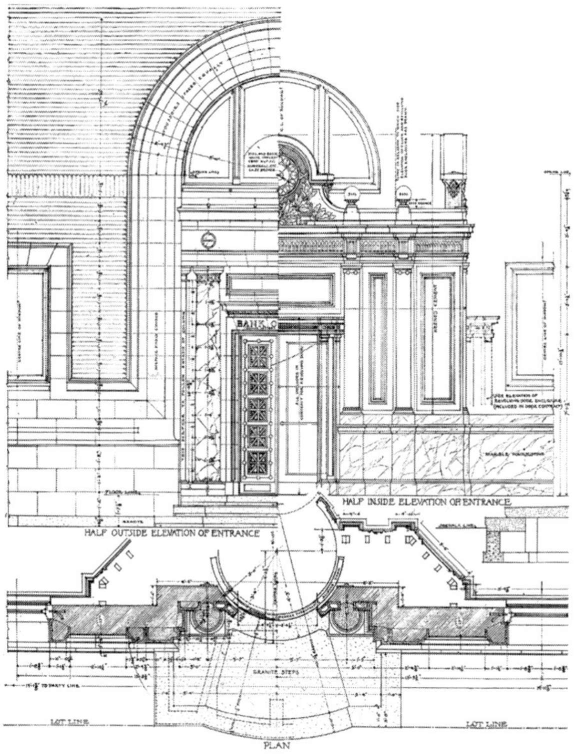

Entrance detail, Bank of Yolo

Preface

Woodland contains more quality home styles in better condition across a wider time period than any comparably sized California city. Within a small, concentrated residential area, you can walk street after street and view classic homes representing most major California styles, including Gothic-Revival, Italianate, Stick, Queen Anne, Shingle, the Revival styles — Colonial, Mission, Cape Cod, Monterey — and Bungalow, Prairie, Art Deco, and Ranch. Some experts liken Woodland's historic neighborhoods to a "museum" of styles. Equally impressive is Woodland's stock of vintage commercial and public buildings that include fine examples of Gothic Revival, Richardsonian Romanesque, Spanish Colonial Revival, Mission Revival, and Renaissance Revival, to name a few. How did this veritable feast of architecture in a small Sacramento Valley town come to be?

Laying the foundation for this exceptional architecture were the prosperous pioneer farmers and rich grain barons whose hard work and entrepreneurship transformed Woodland from a small trading post beginning about 1860 to a very wealthy agricultural community. In fact, by 1888, according to the *Pacific Coast Commercial Record*, Woodland was calculated to be the richest US town in proportion to its population.[1] The wealth extracted from Yolo County's fertile soils supported a merchant class that supplied financial capital, dry goods, hardware, and services. This affluent business class built pricey custom homes and Victorian mansions in the latest styles, conspicuously adorned with stained glass and layers of gingerbread trim that bespoke an owner's high social standing.

In response to the steady demand for upscale houses, locally owned and operated *planing mills* (machine shop for milling and shaping lumber) sprang up in Woodland, headed by inventive builders. These craftsmen shaped the raw lumber into the intricate balustrades, spindles, brackets, finials, cornices and other architectural elements of the Victorian era. They also constructed sophisticated houses, often relying on architectural *pattern books* or house catalogues for design ideas. These special master builders brought skill, creativity, and hard work to their profession.

In addition to its broad, wealthy business class, Woodland, the Yolo County seat of government, attracted a well-paid class of attorneys, judges and clerks who could afford architect-designed houses. Similarly a medical industry developed in Woodland in the early 1900s, headed by a group of doctors whose houses revealed a keen appreciation for progressive architecture.

Historical changes were also afoot. The 1906 San Francisco earthquake attracted a wave of Italian artisans to the Bay Area to help rebuild, and several talented builders left their unique mark on Woodland. Finally, Woodland over many years had ample resources to import talented architects noted for competence, experience, and originality from Sacramento or the Bay Area to erect high quality public buildings, banks, churches, schools, and beautiful homes.

Early in its history, Woodland became self-consciously proud of its prosperity, entrepreneurship, and tradition of fine homebuilding. Its stylistically diverse

---

[1] Shipley Walters, *Woodland City of Trees* (Woodland: Yolo County Historical Society, 1995), p. 40.

houses were photographed and used in public relations publications to promote these ideals. For example, a 1920 publication boasted that Woodland was the "Gibraltar of the West," with the following description of its culture and values framed by photographs of four architecturally distinct houses of the period:

> *As the wealthiest city per capita in any agricultural community in the world, Woodland, the county seat of Yolo, has gained more than ordinary fame; and as an educational center and the city of wonderful people and attractive homes it is likewise booming along to recognition. Populated by some 5500 people and surrounded by as fertile and productive lands as are to be found anywhere, Woodland is fast expanding and coming to be known as one of the most forward cities of California. Money, people and land make up the winning combination for the Yolo County seat... Imbued with a spirit characteristic of the west, particularly California, Woodland people are of the kind who accomplish things. They'll take a risk or a venture, and nine times out of ten make good.* [2]

It took imagination and money, born out of natural wealth and a hard-working opportunistic people, to craft Woodland, a jewel of California's Central Valley. Significantly, the means and resources to develop such an exceptional town were guided by an appreciation and cultivated taste for fashionable architecture by Woodland's movers and shakers. They were inspired to create a beautiful town and they sought out local and regional designers and builders to deliver the goods.

This history is an introduction to the significant architects and builders who seized the economic opportunities Woodland offered and produced its exceptional architecture. Entrepreneurship, opportunism, and craftsmanship — born of an exceptionally steady demand for upscale buildings — are the amalgam of Woodland architecture. The 63 illustrated profiles describe the careers and works of individual architects and builders or, in several cases, partnerships that made significant contributions to Woodland's built environment. Three general essays describe the evolution of Woodland's remaining planing mill, the history of Beamer's Woodland Park, and the development of East Street Court, an imaginative historic preservation project.

Why Woodland Architects and Builders Deserve a History

Why a book on Woodland architects and builders? The dual objectives are to honor genuinely historic achievements — providing the built environment of our special community — while defining critical, ongoing opportunities and directions. The story of the artists and artisans behind Woodland's treasures has never been brought to light, and this story needs telling to better appreciate and understand the architecture itself. But there is certainly a practical motive relative to contemporary planning policy. A deeper knowledge of the qualitative factors that define our historic neighborhoods becomes a crucial benchmark

---

[2] Woodland *Daily Democrat*, *Yolo in Word & Picture*, 1920. pp. 28-29.

for evaluating what gets built in the future — and how to preserve our sense of place. Moreover, the better we understand and appreciate Woodland's exceptional architectural heritage with its talented cast of creators, the more likely this legacy will be celebrated by enhanced preservation policy and actions, motivated by a larger awareness that these historic resources distinguish the community from its economic competitors.

This book evolved from my exposure to several key architects and builders while co-authoring the *Historical Downtown Woodland Walking Tour* (1992) and *Walking Tour of Historic Woodland* (1989, 1997). Unknown architects and builders were discovered by researching the story behind certain houses and structures in Woodland. Many Victorian-era builders and designers, particularly hardy, Woodland-based "blue-collar" talents who made little or lost it all during the hard times, were long forgotten — visible to me only as names in old newspaper articles. I wanted to know more about these forgotten souls who gave Woodland such an enduring legacy. Further, several of the architects profiled are well known for work done outside of Woodland, particularly in larger cities, but their work in Woodland had not been documented.

Of note, most of the architects and builders completed their projects in Woodland prior to 1960 and are no longer living. Although conceived as essentially an "historical" guide, the book profiles a few contemporary firms to establish continuity between Woodland's illustrious past building traditions and the present. Ironically, Woodland did not have a local licensed architect until 1956 when Robert Crippen set up shop. The firm he founded in Woodland is still in existence, although Crippen left Woodland in 1968. He and his successors deserve profiles because of close association with Woodland during the last forty-plus years.

Significantly, many of Woodland's Victorian-era "architects" began their careers as carpenters and along the way acquired design and drafting skills. Typically, these were general contractors who designed and built homes and buildings for their middle- and upper-class customers. The designer-builder tradition of Woodland home building, so prevalent throughout the twentieth century, continues today. Thus, firm distinctions between architect-designer-builders in Woodland's history present an unnecessary, even misleading portrayal. Given that successful construction requires all of these skills and artisans, the book examines a wide range of integrated building professionals — designers, architects, and builders — who made significant contributions to Woodland's built environment.

Examining the lives and works of the builders — as distinguished from architects — is a way of honoring the backbone of Woodland's architectural fabric: the tradition of *vernacular* buildings. These are the nondescript, less stylish buildings that mark the historical periods of Woodland's development and house the vast majority of the population.

Woodland's History is California's History

The story of Woodland's architects and builders, particularly during the early years, reflects California's formation as a land of adventurous and creative entrepreneurs. Many builders arrived with little or no money or assets, but were resourceful, tenacious, and risk takers. Some were speculators and self-promoters, while others were steadier and more conservative in their real estate ventures and business practices. Some were well-seasoned builders before they arrived in Woodland, while others evolved into master builders by developing their skills and talent as opportunity presented itself. They worked hard and prospered during the boom times, only to eke out a living or start over during the hard times.

In short, builders converged on prosperous Woodland and crafted a beautiful and gracious small town. Of the 63 profiles in the book, nineteen were immigrants from Australia, Italy, Germany, Sweden, Denmark, England, Ireland, Scotland and Canada. The American-born builders arrived from a variety of states, including New York, Pennsylvania, Indiana, Ohio, Iowa, and Texas.

Structure of this Book

The Introduction summarizes the major periods in the development of Woodland architecture. This sweeping summary, hardly complete, provides a general context for the individual essays on the architects and builders.

Each essay presents a summary of an architect's or builder's life and career with emphasis on major works completed in Woodland. The lengths of profiles vary, reflecting the wide variation in primary information from histories, architectural guidebooks, archives, newspapers, obituaries, death certificates or interviews with knowledgeable people. Hopefully, this initial inquiry will inspire other historians or architectural buffs to dig deeper into the past. Since my list of architects and builders in the appendix is hardly exhaustive, there are surely other stories waiting to be told.

The essays are illustrated with photographs, etchings, or sketches of key buildings described in the text. The use of historical photographs was preferred, but contemporary images have been substituted when necessary.

The Epilogue evaluates Woodland's architectural tradition today, what the community can distill and learn from this legacy, and how the best elements of that tradition can inspire a more beautiful future. An Appendix lists dates of construction and locations of documented Woodland area buildings by each architect and builder profiled in the book.

Gothic Revival at 704 Second Street, 1873
photo by Roger Klemm

Introduction *A Historical Overview of Architecture in Woodland*

As we start this millennium, Woodland is a medium-sized city of 50,000 people with steady growth on its southeastern border expected for years to come. From the vantage point of Interstate 5 on the northern part of the city, Woodland looks like many Sacramento Valley towns — with a wide array of fast food restaurants, big box retailers and monotonous tract housing and apartments with sound walls hugging the freeway. Some of Woodland's highway-oriented development — a Denny's Restaurant stationed at each of three off-ramps and an inland sea of warehouses, some of monstrous proportions — provides the only identification Woodland offers to the passing motorist. In fact, Woodland's special historical resources remain a mystery even to the bulk of shoppers who flock to the County Fair Mall from outlying regions. Only those who venture into Woodland's historic core area or walk or drive its tree-lined streets, filled with well kept and restored historical homes, are rewarded in discovering the "real" Woodland.

Although regional recognition of Woodland's exceptional historical architecture has been slow in coming, by the late 1980s the outside world began to take notice. A *Sacramento Bee* writer and old house enthusiast, smitten by what he saw, described Woodland as a "house museum." In 1989 Woodland history buffs began celebrating their good fortune with a festival named the Stroll Through History. This annual event draws both tourists and locals to downtown Woodland each September for walking tours of historic neighborhoods, open houses, entertainment, antique shows and carriage rides.

Further, Woodland public policy has evolved in recent years to reflect growing community interest in preserving Woodland's historic resources and small-town identity while facing tremendous growth pressures. In 1992 the city completed a Downtown Woodland Specific Plan, emphasizing the preservation and enhancement of Woodland's historic commercial buildings and other enhancements to attract pedestrians to Main Street. A crowning achievement came in 1998 when Downtown Woodland gained listing on the National Register of Historic Places, drawing deserved attention to old town Woodland's special character. A Caltrans sign on I-5 now alerts motorists to Woodland's historic district, as do directional and monument signs placed by the city on East Main Street.

Despite this expanding awareness, Woodland still struggles to retain its special character under the strain of a generation of cookie-cutter subdivisions and bigger and blander commercial strip centers. Such "modernization" reflects steady population growth, coupled with a long-standing laissez-faire attitude among civic leaders towards community design. In response, enlightened city planners and community activists, no longer content with the monotony and dullness of much of Woodland's late 20th century development, are increasingly looking creatively to Woodland's pedestrian-oriented, architecturally-diverse, tree-lined historical neighborhoods as a model and source of inspiration for shaping Woodland's future.

Brick Storefront
photo by Roger Klemm

Brick and the Early Years

Woodland was born as a community in 1853 when Henry Wyckoff erected a small wooden building at what is now 323 First Street. In 1856 Wyckoff built a second commercial building with a clapboard facade near the corner of Sixth and Court streets. The trading post and saloon was called "Yolo City" and served local farmers and travelers on the trail between Sacramento and Cacheville (Yolo).

In 1857 Frank S. Freeman, a '49er who settled in Yolo County to become a farmer, purchased Wyckoff's store. Building a wooden-gabled house just north of the store at 1037 Court Street (still standing), he acquired 160 acres of surrounding government land which he envisioned becoming a prosperous town. Freeman established the post office in 1861 in the town's first brick commercial building at First and Main streets. His wife, Gertrude, named the new town "Woodland," inspired by the Valley Oak trees that dotted the landscape. In 1862, after serious flooding in Washington (West Sacramento), the county seat of government was shifted to Woodland.

As Woodland started to develop in the 1860s, simple brick row buildings sprang up on Main Street forming a commercial center. A common wall with the adjoining building still connects many of these brick commercial buildings. These vernacular brick structures form the nucleus of downtown's look and charm, anchoring the taller buildings. They are built to a comfortable human scale and have housed innumerable small businesses, supplying essential goods and services to Woodlanders for several generations.

Brick was also used in early home construction. Pioneer houses in Woodland, like the Gibson Mansion and Beamer Ranch House, were humble brick dwellings dating to the late 1850s, later remodeled into Greek and Monterey Colonial Revival styles as families prospered. The use of brick reflected the masons who settled in Woodland, started construction businesses, and built many early commercial buildings, churches, and the foundations and chimneys for houses.

Due to the clay deposits in the local soils, enterprising builders could manufacture bricks with crude kilns. Brick was favored for commercial buildings for its durability and fireproof qualities. Al Hiatt, City Engineer from 1950 to 1983, sited locations of clay pits from knowledge handed down by long-time residents and engineers who worked in Woodland in the early 1900s. Hiatt also produced the city's first contour map about 1950 that identified pits excavated for brick making in the otherwise flat terrain. The clay pits located near the northwest corner of Walnut and Oak streets, and northwest corner of McKinley and Oak streets, have been filled in. Another pit on the southeast corner of East Street and Lemen Avenue is still visible.

Levi Craft, one of Woodland's early entrepreneurs, settled in Yolo County in 1857 and developed a brick-making operation on the outskirts of Woodland shortly thereafter to supply the building trade. Many of Woodland's oldest buildings are constructed from bricks manufactured locally at Craft's kilns. Craft was also a general contractor, constructing buildings large and small, including Holy Rosary Catholic Church on Main Street in 1869.

Harrison Ervin was another Woodland brick mason noted for his large brick kiln that produced millions of bricks annually. Between 1880 and 1900, Ervin constructed many of the brick buildings in downtown Woodland, including the Beamer Block at 708-712 Main Street and the picturesque Jackson Apartment Building at First and Bush streets.

In 1863 Freeman offered Yolo County Supervisors an entire city block bounded by Court, North, Second and Third streets as the site for the first Yolo County Courthouse. Albert Bennett, a prominent Sacramento architect who worked on the California State Capitol Building, was selected as the architect. Built of brick, this handsome Italianate style public building was completed in 1864. The Yolo County Courthouse and Hesperian College (1861), a tall structure built just south of Main Street near what is now Bush Street, were Woodland's first prominent buildings.

Brick was the predominant building material for nonresidential construction in Woodland well into the 1900s. Concrete walls appeared for the building shell of the new Yolo County Courthouse in 1917 and reinforced concrete was introduced shortly thereafter. Brick industrial warehouses were constructed in the downtown area as late as the 1940s. Several of these early brick buildings have been rehabilitated, stripping away added-on facades and layers of paint, to reveal the warmth and charm of the original natural brick surface; others have deteriorated and await seismic reinforcement and refurbishing.

Planing Mills and Mansions

William Winne and James Sibley established the first planing mill in Woodland in 1869, the same year that the railroad arrived in Woodland and connected the growing town to lumber suppliers. Woodland prospered and grew steadily throughout most of the Victorian period, although economic depressions, particularly the severe downturn signaled by the Panic of 1893, stalled the construction industry at times. Yet Woodland's general prosperity across decades and eras fueled steady demand for upscale houses and buildings. Significantly, several artisans opened planing mills to manufacture a range of wooden building materials, became general contractors, and then designed custom homes to fit all budgets.

As architectural book publishing expanded, Woodland's architects and builders had ready access to a wide array of trade journals and pattern books that advertised house designs. Pattern books were essentially house catalogues containing drawings and descriptions of house plans published by architects to advertise and sell their designs. Such noted architects as George Barber of Knoxville, Tennessee, Samuel & Joseph Newsom in San Francisco, and many others scattered across the United States published pattern books. Not only did contractors and house buyers rely on these catalogues to learn the latest styles, they also purchased complete sets of building plans, which stimulated the creation of specific, up-to-date houses customized to the owners' desires.

By the 1880s local builders Winne, Samuel Caldwell, William Henry Carson, Glenn & White, and the Keehn Brothers all operated planing mills that churned out Victorian gingerbread, turned columns, brackets, siding, window sashes, and cabinets for the new construction. All Victorian house styles spanning the period from 1870 to 1893, largely fashioned out of abundant, virgin redwood, are well represented in Woodland, including Gothic Revival, Italianate, Second Empire, Stick, and Queen Anne.

Some, truly magnificent, were to become state landmarks. In 1885 a local entrepreneur, Edward Carlton Gilbert, designed and built the Gable Mansion for a wealthy farming family. The impressive scale and considerable cost of the mansion symbolized, as nothing before, Woodland's ascent as an exceptionally prosperous community. By now Woodland had several resident millionaires and banks to provide capital for sustained economic growth.

The *nouveau riche* merchant class of farmers, grain merchants, and shopkeepers flaunted their wealth by the houses they built. The Porter Mansion, built for banker, real estate developer and philanthropist A.D. Porter, by Glenn & White in 1886 at Main and Walnut streets, rivaled the Gable Mansion in size and opulence. Although the Gable Mansion survives, today restored and listed as a California Historical Landmark, the Porter Mansion met its demise in the 1930s. The Ritchie and Hershey mansions, long-time landmarks built on Main Street near the Porter mansion, were destroyed in the 1970s.

Local craftsmen erected many other large Victorian houses that survive to the present day, including outstanding examples of the Italianate and Queen Anne styles. Other prominent Victorian buildings constructed during this period but since destroyed were the Byrns Hotel (1883), Holy Rosary Academy (1884), YMCA Building (1886), Yolo County Hospital (1892), and first City Hall (1892).

Propelling the expanding architectural range in Woodland was the great fire of 1892, which wiped out a major section of downtown. However, rebuilding was swift and by 1894 three sandstone-clad Richardsonian Romanesque buildings, all designed by Joseph Hall, were erected at Second and Main streets, including the landmark Farmers and Merchants Bank dressed in red Arizona sandstone. Across the street, the Julian Hotel replaced the fire-damaged Exchange Hotel. The Woodland Opera House, originally constructed in 1885 from plans drawn by noted San Francisco architect, Thomas Welsh, was rebuilt and opened to the general public in 1896. Due mainly to the economic problems besetting the country, housing construction was slow from 1893 to 1900.

The Bay Area Connection: A Continuing Mainstay of Ideas

During the early part of the twentieth century, several top-flight architects from San Francisco and Berkeley were commissioned to design beautiful and interesting houses, bank buildings, meeting halls, schools, and a grand hotel. In 1903 Bay Area architect William Henry Weeks designed the Romanesque Yolo County Savings Bank at College and Main — the first of many outstanding buildings Weeks would create in Woodland.

His Woodland masterwork is the 1917 Yolo County Courthouse, funded by a local bond measure. This remarkable Renaissance Revival building is a splendid example of inspired architecture sculpted with terra cotta ceramic tile. Artisans employed by Gladding, McBean in Lincoln, California crafted and shipped tens of thousands of individual pieces of terra cotta from the factory to Woodland by train where tile setters grouted the pieces together like a giant puzzle.

In 1928 the town celebrated the grand opening of the Hotel Woodland. Weeks not only designed the gracious Spanish Colonial Revival building, he was a major owner of the tourist hotel. The architectural style of the Hotel Woodland had wide appeal to Anglo-Californians in search of historical connections with its largely romanticized Spanish and Mexican periods. Beginning with the remodel of the Corner Drugstore about 1900 from a Victorian to a Mission Revival style of building, Spanish style architecture became the rage in Woodland. The Woodland Public Library (Dodge & Dolliver, 1904), Odd Fellows Hall (1905), Northern Electric Train Depot (Arthur D. Nicholson, 1912) and the Primary School (Weeks, 1915) are good examples of the style. Later renditions include the United Methodist Church (Rollin Tuttle, 1925), Old *Daily Democrat* Building (Dean & Dean, 1925), Kraft Bros. Funeral Chapel (Dean & Dean, 1927), Woodland City Hall (Dean & Dean, Harry Devine, Sr. and Schaefer-Wirth 1932-1936-1976), Woodland Post Office (1935) and Disciples of Christ Christian Church (Dragon, Schmidts & Hardman, 1949).

Of special interest, the School of Architecture at the University of California in Berkeley was founded in 1903, attracting bright young designers and artists whose brilliance and novel ideas spread far and wide in California, thus enriching small and big towns alike. As the first academic program in northern California to educate and train professional architects, its presence was crucial in elevating the quality and variety of architecture in northern California.

The UC program founder, John Galen Howard, hailed from the East Coast, had studied in Europe, and brought innovative experiences working with top-flight firms as well as the brightest, most creative East Coast architects. Howard proceeded to design several new buildings for the Berkeley campus and attracted talented young people inspired by modern ideas in architecture. The quality and number of Howard's apprentices would eventually contribute to the shaping of a distinct "Bay Area" style of architecture, today still concentrated in the Berkeley and East Bay hills.

Unlike their carpenter-architect predecessors, whose ideas for Victorian styles were transmitted by pattern books with replicated designs in countless variations, the intellectual Berkeley group had a broader, more visionary view of architecture shaped by first-hand experiences abroad or from academic courses. These young architects adapted modern architectural innovations to northern California geography, climate, and lifestyles, using local materials and craftsmanship to produce expressive, more humanistic structures.

Affluent Woodland homeowners, merchants, and churches sought out these talented architects in their own quest for quality and originality. Five architects or firms associated with Berkeley left their creative marks on Woodland's built environment. Ira Hoover designed the modernistic Bank of Yolo in 1907 with inspiration from the great Chicago architect, Louis Sullivan. In 1912 William Hays crafted the rustic Gothic Revival St. Luke's Episcopal Church. John Hudson Thomas, the bold and artistic architect of hundreds of interesting East Bay homes, designed three exciting houses on First Street in Woodland between 1916 and 1927. Dragon, Schmidts & Hardman, an offshoot of the Weeks firm, created the aerodynamic Streamline Moderne Yolo Grocery in 1937 and the picturesque Mission Revival Christian Church in 1949. Finally, Joseph Esherick, the great architect of Cannery Row and Monterey Bay Aquarium fame, contributed a Ranch Style house at 303 Gibson Road in 1958.

The Italians: New Skills, New Hands

Lured by economic opportunity and encouragement from the American government, countless skilled Italian artisans immigrated to San Francisco following the 1906 earthquake. Fedele Costa and Eugenio Ricci were already expert craftsman, steeped in the renowned Italian building tradition, before they hit American shores and made their way to Woodland. In 1912 Costa crafted the short-lived Holy Rosary Catholic Church in stone. Ricci remodeled his humble house on East Street into a showcase of Italian-style masonry that became a local landmark.

Though Joseph Motroni was young and unskilled

when he immigrated, hard work, masonry training, and ambition made him the most prolific builder of quality homes in Woodland's history. Between 1920 and 1950 Motroni built over 200 houses and buildings, including many in the Mediterranean style, today celebrated for their exceptional craftsmanship and durability.

The Craftsman Period

In 1910 the Keehn Bros. built Woodland's first Craftsman Bungalow at 754 College Street for Woodland physician, Fred Fairchild, inspired by the designs of Gustav Stickley, publisher of the *Craftsman* magazine. Influenced by the English Arts and Crafts Movement, particularly the writings of John Ruskin and William Morris, Stickley's designs rebelled against the boxy floor plan of the Victorians; instead, new ideas favored living areas that flowed smoothly into each other, thus reflecting the way people lived. Comfort and simplicity of style and form came to the fore over Victorian ornamentation and compartmentalization of spaces. Natural building materials, such as cobblestones, clinker bricks and wooden shingles, were used on the exterior of the houses, while interiors emphasized built-in cabinets, inglenooks, cozy fireplaces and crafted Mission style furniture. The natural and relaxed feel of the house was often enhanced with vine-covered trellises and informal cottage style gardens.

Chester Fairchild, brother of Fred, built a similar looking house in 1913 at 914 First Street designed by Olin S. Grove. In this variation of the organic Craftsman style, the chimney and base of the house were constructed of rusticated concrete blocks that mimic stone. The Fairchild brothers also built a small Craftsman cottage at 744 Second Street in 1910 that integrates cobblestone into the natural feel of the design. Several Craftsman Bungalows were constructed in Woodland from 1910 to 1920, including superior examples on Pendegast Street between College and Elm streets and the 600 block of Elm Street across from Dingle School. Southern Pacific Railroad architects even adapted Craftsman style architecture for commercial purposes when they built the Woodland Train Depot in 1913.

Beamer Park and the 1920s

In 1913, Bay area entrepreneur Hewitt Davenport subdivided Beamer Park, an upscale residential enclave of Woodland, assisted by noted landscape architect, Mark Daniels. Several local builders began constructing homes in the Park in 1914. William Fait, a designer-builder who arrived in Woodland in 1912 from Spokane, was very active in Beamer Park, crafting an assortment of Bungalows both before and after World War I. He and Joseph Motroni, who built more houses in this section of town than any single builder, were both residents of Beamer Park.

Architectural tastes in the 1920s were eclectic and period revival homes became popular. Tudor, Colonial, and Mediterranean Revival houses were built in tree lined neighborhoods beside aging Victorians. Some Victorian estates covering whole city blocks were cleared and subdivided. The John Stephens estate, bounded by Cross, Craig, First, and College streets, was subdivided and named Craig & Riser Park. Between 1917 and 1935, a wide assortment of houses, ranging from the wooden shingled Bay Area style to the California Bungalow to the Cape Cod Revival, filled these lots.

Similarly, the Laugenour-Reith Victorian mansion, which stood for fifty years on the south side of Cross Street between Second and Third Streets, was taken down in the 1920s and the land filled in with an assortment of cottages and bungalows. "Oaks Park" in northwest Woodland, bounded by Cleveland-West-Court-North streets, was yet another large subdivision of this era that supplied homebuilders with new lots to meet the housing demand of a growing population.

The simplicity and charm of the Tudor Revival home was particularly attractive to Woodlanders in the 1920s. C. Carleton Pierson, a Woodland resident who worked by day for the State Architect's office in Sacramento, designed several good examples of the style, including the home at 902 Elm Street. Dean & Dean, an accomplished Sacramento firm that designed many of the lovely homes in the Fabulous 40s of East Sacramento, was also active in Woodland. The consistent high quality of their work is evident in the Mission Revival house at 904 First (1924), Kraft Bros. Funeral Chapel (1927), a Monterey Colonial Revival at 750 Second Street (1936) and a storybook French Cottage at 714 W. Keystone (1936). Dean & Dean also designed the first phase of Woodland City Hall (1932).

The Depression Years

After the stock market crash in 1929 and during the Great Depression that followed, home building slowed considerably for several years. Motroni, Brown & Woodhouse, Del Fenton, Anton Paulsen and other local builders constructed a few houses each year until the late 1930s when the housing market rebounded. At this time Motroni began filling in West Keystone Avenue in Beamer Park with an assortment of houses, including his own dream house in the shape of an airplane, at 524 W. Keystone Avenue in 1937. This was a very productive period in Motroni's career as his design talent and stature as a trusted builder and successful businessman rose to a peak.

From 1938 to 1941 Brown & Woodhouse built many upscale homes in their own subdivision in the southwest part of Woodland along the 100 and 200 blocks of Bartlett, Marshall, and Hays. Several of these single-story, rectilinear homes are good examples of the Ranch Style, influenced by the popular designs of California architect Cliff May featured in *Sunset Magazine*.

During the depths of the Great Depression, federal dollars were pumped into the economy to help fund public works projects and reduce unemployment. In 1935 a new Mission Revival style Post Office was constructed at 720 Court Street through the federal Works Progress Administration (WPA). In 1936, with 45% matching WPA funds, an eastern addition to Woodland City Hall was completed under the supervision of Sacramento architect Harry Devine, Sr.

By 1937 Woodlanders could escape the worries of the Depression and oppressive summer heat in the refrigerated air-conditioned Art Deco movie palace, the State Theatre. Other Art Deco commercial buildings appeared including the Streamline Moderne style: Mulcahay Building at 443 First Street (1936)

Art Deco at 930 Second Street, 1938
photo by Roger Klemm

and the Yolo Grocery at 534 Bush Street (1939). Devoid of exterior ornamentation, both of these buildings have aerodynamically-rounded corners and horizontal banding reflecting the "less is more" philosophy of the era. A striking residential version of the style was built at 930 Second Street (1938).

Post World War II

Woodland's boundaries expanded steadily after World War II to meet the housing demand of young families and steady population growth. Large chunks of land on Woodland's south and western borders were subdivided, and a new era of mass produced tract housing began. In 1946 about fifty parcels were approved for building permits along Homewood Drive, Rosewood Way, and Coloma Drive. Klinkhammer Construction and other local builders were active in the late 1940s in the new South Land Park subdivision on Buena Tierra and Fremont Streets. The Klinkhammer subdivision, a new addition to Woodland in the early 1950s, was located in the southwest corner of the city bounded by Gibson and West Streets and included Eunice Drive, named in honor of Gerhard Klinkhammer's wife.

Two beautiful new churches were constructed in 1949. Holy Rosary Catholic Church, a contemporary Romanesque style design of Harry Devine Sr., was constructed at 301 Walnut Street with a 108-foot tall bell tower. The California Mission period is captured in the design for the Christian Church, Disciples of Christ at 509 College Street by Dragon, Schmidts & Hardman.

Robert Crippen, Woodland's first academically-trained architect, opened his own firm in 1956. For the next twelve years he kept busy designing modest and functional churches, banks, and government buildings for the steadily growing town.

While tract housing, offering affordable home ownership to many new families, became the dominant housing product in post-World War II Woodland, a relatively small number of architect-designed houses with some originality and flair were built in scattered locations. Because Woodland grew relatively slowly prior to World War II, stylistic changes in architecture marking different historical eras are clearly visi-

International Style House, 1962, 321 Bartlett Avenue, Gus Reedy
photo by Roger Klemm

ble and obvious. With large tracts of production housing obscuring designer houses, a clear continuum between the 1940s residential architecture and the styles that followed became difficult to discern.

Still, with a little searching, interesting houses are to be found. In 1956 the noted Sacramento firm of Dreyfuss & Blackford designed an artistic home for the Leiser family at 409 Casa Linda Drive. The interior design for the house follows the "great room" concept, featuring a large central room with a copper-plated fireplace. The great Bay Area architect, Joseph Esherick, teamed with equally talented landscape architect, Thomas Church, to craft a spacious and gracious Ranch Style estate for Dan and Bernice Best at 303 West Gibson Road in 1958. Woodland architect Gary Wirth began his career in Woodland about the time that Charles Moore's Sea Ranch condominiums on the northern California coast were published in 1965. Beginning with his own house at 4 Sequoia Place built in 1969, Wirth incorporated "shed" shapes into houses, schools, and commercial buildings off and on during the next thirty years.

The modern, rectilinear single-story Ranch style house, with open interior plans, modern kitchen conveniences and prominent attached garages, lured some established residents and many newcomers to suburban Woodland. These practical houses were economical to heat and cool and designed for a casual lifestyle. The more adventurous, particularly younger people undaunted by the challenge of old house restoration, bought aging Victorians, attracted by their irreplaceable craftsmanship and voluminous living space. Interior designer Howard Terhune, a New Jersey transplant, opted for history and purchased the 1870s Italianate Victorian at 648 College Street in 1953. Terhune's successful rehabilitation of the historic home marked the beginning of an embryonic historic preservation movement in the old residential neighborhoods that would flower in the 1970s.

By the late 1950s Downtown Woodland languished. Victorian-era structures had begun to show their age and very few new buildings were being constructed. Parking was considered inadequate in the compact downtown area originally designed for pedestrians and horses and buggies. Gradually, the commercial sector spread west along Main Street, where land was cheaper and ample room was available for strip commercial development. Woodland's first automobile-oriented shopping center, costing over one million dollars to develop, was built on the site of the venerable Holy Rosary Academy in 1957. The modern shopping center prompted J.C. Penney's to move from its smaller downtown location to join F.W. Woolworth.

Live Oak with Ranch House, 220 Bartlett Avenue
photo by Roger Klemm

By 1960 Downtown Woodland was a mere shadow of its glorious past and city leaders searched for ways to reinvigorate and "clean up" the area. Woodland's first attempt at redevelopment in 1961 was partially underwritten by the Federal government. The resultant "urban renewal" plan, typical for the time, viewed historic buildings as old and useless, opting instead for a four-block area in the heart of downtown to be razed and redeveloped into a new "pedestrian mall." The commercial viability of the mall was to be enhanced by limiting (and in some

Jaqueline Payne Harlin House, 1992, 710 Fairview Lane, Leslie Leonard
photo by Roger Klemm

cases, down zoning) commercial property outside of the project area.

Woodland's foray into urban renewal met stiff community resistance, perceived by some as heavy-handed government intrusion bordering on a "Communist plot." After much public debate, the Redevelopment Agency was disbanded. There was no serious discussion about government-sponsored revitalization of downtown Woodland for almost thirty years until another Redevelopment Agency was created in 1988, overseen by a citizen's advisory committee.

Public Investment and Preservation

In response to federally sponsored public works and urban renewal programs and private commercial and industrial development that had destroyed significant American historical resources (and for a time threatened downtown Woodland), Congress enacted the National Historic Preservation Act in 1966 and established the National Trust for Historic Preservation. State Historic Preservation Officers were appointed by governors to oversee the nomination of significant historical resources to the National Register. These properties were afforded some level of protection from demolition or alteration by Section 106 of the Act, which mandated the adverse impacts of historic properties be evaluated and mitigated when approving development projects receiving federal funding. The Secretary of the Interior also began making grants to state governments for the preservation of properties listed on the National Register. In 1976 the Federal Historic Preservation Tax Credit was created to spur private investment in the preservation and adaptive reuse of commercial and industrial properties for contemporary uses.

By the 1970s a preservation ethic and consciousness had emerged in Woodland. Several aging Victorians and other vintage homes, including the Gable Mansion, were acquired at bargain prices by enterprising do-it-yourselfers and brought back to their former glory. Now over thirty years strong, the preservation movement here has restored hundreds of Woodland homes, the result of a remarkable, sustained, and private grassroots effort without government assistance.

Downtown historical buildings also began to receive more attention from both the public and nonprofit sectors as cultural resources to be preserved and rehabilitated for community uses. The Yolo County Historical Society purchased the Opera House in 1971, saving it from the wrecking ball, and began fundraising for its restoration. The city attempted to save the Farmers & Merchants' Bank next to the Opera House, but absent a Redevelopment Agency, could not offer financial assistance to a would-be developer. In 1970, faced with a dangerous building and no means to fix it, the city had the red sandstone landmark destroyed. The city did manage to expand and remodel City Hall into a unified Mission Revival design in 1976 under the supervision of Woodland architects, Schaefer and Wirth.

A new generation of private investors, with a belief in the historical integrity of downtown and an appreciation for quality architecture, began to purchase and restore aging downtown buildings, many of which could be purchased at bargain prices in the 1970s and '80s. Financial incentives, provided by the Federal Historical Preservation Tax Credit Program, aided the creative efforts of several Woodland entrepreneurs who transformed run-down buildings into attractive and unique spaces. The Jackson Building, housing Morrison's Restaurant, the Alge House professional offices, Beamer Block with Steve's Pizza, Odd Fellows Building, the Excelsior Building with Woodland Travel, and other commercial buildings, were rehabilitated and adapted to new uses during the 1980s, thus bringing both jobs and more foot traffic to downtown.

A new Yolo County Administration Building with an inviting atrium, creatively designed by architect Dean Unger, was sited in the heart of downtown, as was a new *Daily Democrat* newspaper building. In 1986, captivated by Woodland's architectural history, a local attorney and entrepreneur, Tom Stallard, recreated the Mission Revival style Northern Electric Train Depot for use as a commercial building. The structure was originally built in 1912 but demolished in the 1960s. The Woodland community, increasingly aware of the value of historic buildings and the need to protect civic buildings downtown, wisely approved a $2.5 million bond measure for the restoration and expansion of the Woodland Public Library. The restoration of the Opera House was completed in 1989 with the assistance of large federal and state grants.

In 1990 one million dollars in public funds were invested in a streetscape beautification project along Main Street and for the construction of Heritage Plaza, adjacent to the Opera House. With the adoption of the Downtown Specific Plan in 1992, the community forged a strong pedestrian-oriented vision for the future of downtown, with a strong emphasis on historic preservation and well-designed infill commercial and public buildings.

The three-story brick Globe Rice Mill and warehouse at Court and East streets was transformed into an interesting bohemian mixture of artist housing and commercial uses in 1992. The corrugated metal warehouse was divided into two buildings separated by a courtyard, housing live/work studios, while the main brick structure was converted into professional offices with an independent bookstore as the anchor tenant.

A local non-profit group of railroad buffs, the Sacramento Valley Historical Railways, saved the Woodland Train Depot from demolition by agreeing to Southern Pacific Railroad's condition — to move the 1913-built structure from the main rail line

Woodland Train Depot, 1913
photo by David Wilkinson

to the corner of Sixth and Lincoln streets. In 1992 the depot was moved and placed on a new foundation, as a federal Transportation Enhancement Activity grant enabled the group to install a new shake roof and begin restoration.

In one of the most visible redemptions, and a shining example of the result of the Downtown Specific Plan, the Woodland Redevelopment Agency aided private developers in 1996 with the restoration of the Hotel Woodland. William Henry Weeks' 1928 Spanish Colonial Revival landmark building, blighted before the city stepped in to facilitate a transfer of ownership, benefited greatly from a talented Yolo County housing and commercial development team. The stunning restoration, under the direction of Woodland architects Wirth & McCandless, was heartily celebrated by the community, proudly reclaiming the ornate lobby and gracious courtyard as a gathering place for important public and private events.

East Street, a long-time, blighted transportation corridor in Woodland, with run-down motels and mobile home parks, desolate railroad switching yard, and old warehouse district, officially began its facelift with the adoption of the East Street Specific Plan in 1998. Attractively designed in-fill development is scheduled for East Street to transform the old railroad yard and state highway into an interesting mixed-use district. Even before the plan was adopted, the Woodland Redevelopment Agency partnered with Blue Shield in 1993 on the development of a new office building at Lincoln and Sixth streets. Designed by Wirth & McCandless, the long, voluminous building has Craftsman features and massing reminiscent of its neighbor, the Woodland Train Depot. A new police station and a transformation and upgrade of the trailer parks along East Street by Community Housing Opportunities Corporation of Davis also promise to renew this key area in the heart of the community.

The Future

In 1993 visionary architects founded the Congress for the New Urbanism, dedicated to designing new neighborhoods and towns that assure a high quality of life for the residents. Today, this "New Urbanism" school of planning, with 2,300 members nationwide, seeks to reverse the late 20th century trend of sprawling housing tracts and strip commercial centers devoid of any community orientation. Walkable neighborhoods and access to public transit are awarded equal footing with the omnipresent automobile. New Urbanism developments are inspired by traditional town plans similar to Woodland's historic core area: a mixture of housing sizes and types, attracting an economically diverse cross-section of the populace; high quality architecture and attractive streetscapes based upon neighborhood design guidelines, with schools, stores and offices, parks and other public spaces within walking distances from neighborhoods. Regional versions of New Urbanism were developed in the 1990s in Laguna West south of Sacramento, Aggie Village in Davis, and Suisun City.

As Woodland begins a new century of growth and development, New Urbanism planning concepts and "Smart Growth" in-fill strategies provide genuine, positive ways to promote compact development and preservation of open space. The Spring Lake Specific Plan, shaped and re-shaped by unprecedented public input and innumerable intensive study sessions by planners and developers, is Woodland's version of the New Urbanism. Thousands of new housing units, schools, commercial and office buildings, and public spaces will be designed and built during the 15-year phasing period of Spring Lake on the southeast side of Woodland. Regional and local architects and builders, working within design guidelines inspired by the Woodland and American building traditions that nurtured livable communities and enhanced the urban experience for its citizens, will be instrumental in shaping the future look of a place called Woodland.

"Old Urbanism": Two Small Second Street Bungalows
photo by Roger Klemm

Albert A. Bennett

Sacramento Architect Who Defined Woodland's Early Public Face

Albert A. Bennett
California State Library Collection

What do the magnificent California State Capitol and Yolo County's first Courthouse and hospital have in common? The answer is: Albert A. Bennett (b. 1825), the premier architect in the Sacramento region during its early settlement period. Born in 1825 into a Quaker family in Schoharie County, New York, he apprenticed as a carpenter and designer for five years until he moved to Montgomery, Alabama in 1846 to work on the State Capitol. Bennett's stay in Alabama was abbreviated by the lure of the Gold Rush and vision of major building opportunities out West. In 1849 he landed in San Francisco after a 102-day trip by boat from Panama. The 365 passengers aboard the ship included Colis P. Huntington, who would later make his fortune in the Golden State as one of the "Big Four' builders of the transcontinental railroad. In 1850 Bennett settled in Sacramento where he rose to prominence before relocating to San Francisco in 1876.

Bennett served as State Architect under Governors Haight and Irwin and collaborated with other leading architects on the construction of the monumental California State Capitol building. He also worked on modest buildings, including the oldest remaining commercial building in central downtown Sacramento, Pioneer Hall at 1009 7th Street, where he maintained his basement office. As one of the first professionally trained architects in the Sacramento region at the dawn of the great settlement period in California, Bennett was recruited to design important public buildings in emerging towns in the Central Valley and Gold Country.

By the early 1860s Yolo County officials began to build substantial government buildings to support growing county operations. In 1861 Frank Freeman secured a U.S. Post Office and Woodland gained its official name. In 1863 Freeman sold land to the county for the first Yolo County Hospital.[1] A small wooden building, modest in size and cost, the hospital started at what is now 121 North First Street, still in use as a residence *(fig. 1)*. Albert Bennett received $25 from the Yolo County Board of Supervisors to develop the plans and specifications for the hospital building, serving the general population until a larger, more modern facility was built in 1892 at Cottonwood and Beamer Streets.

In addition, in 1863, the same year that Freeman filed the town plat for Woodland, he offered county supervisors an entire city block bounded by Court, North, Second and Third Streets as the site for the first Yolo County Courthouse. Albert Bennett was retained by the Board of Supervisors to design this early landmark building *(fig. 2)*. Completed in 1864, the two story brick Italianate building cost a substantial $27,858 to construct.[2]

1. Yolo County Hospital, 1863, Albert A. Bennett
photo by Roger Klemm

[1] Shipley Walters, *Woodland City of Trees* (Woodland: Yolo County Historical Society, 1995), p. 25.
[2] Ibid.

2. Yolo County Courthouse, 1864, Albert A. Bennett
from *Illustrated Atlas and History of Yolo County*, 1879, *Shields Library, U.C. Davis*

3. Courthouse Square. The Courthouse (left) faces Second Street and Hall of Records (1889) faces Court Street.
courtesy Yolo County Archives

Significantly, the Courthouse was the first public building in Woodland and benefited from being designed by a professional architect. Most trained Gold Rush-era architects, like Bennett, came from the eastern United States, where they were schooled and steeped in New England culture and building traditions. Bennett's sophisticated design for the building was classical with Italianate influences. In 1864, Woodland was still a small village with a few scattered wood frame dwellings, Hesperian College, and a small grouping of vernacular commercial buildings. This stylish building, no doubt, created a civilizing effect, marking a big step in Woodland's transformation from a frontier trading post to a small American town.

The Yolo County Courthouse faced Second Street near Court Street. In 1889, after the County Hall of Records was built south of the Courthouse facing Court Street, these two imposing institutions formed the center of county government known as "Courthouse Square" *(fig. 3)*. The first Yolo County Courthouse functioned for 37 years until condemned in 1911. Its replacement in 1917, the extant Beaux Arts Romanesque building designed by William Henry Weeks, today graces Courthouse Square.

Nathaniel D. Goodell

Noted Governor's Mansion Architect Designs Upscale Hotel

Local entrepreneur David Barnes settled in Yolo County in 1856 where he farmed for a few years until commercial opportunities in Woodland presented themselves. He invested in the Woodland Winery, a warehouse, and built one of the early hotels, the American Exchange, at the northeast corner of Second and Main streets (now the site of Heritage Plaza and the *Daily Democrat* Building). This was a small two-story hostelry that needed remodeling by 1882 to keep up with the growth and prosperity of the town. Barnes sought out Sacramento architect, Nathaniel Dudley Goodell (1814-1895), to design an enlarged three-story structure.

Like Bennett, Goodell was an established Eastern architect who immigrated to the West during the Gold Rush. According to Harold Kirker, Goodell "acquired an education in carpentry in Amherst, Massachusetts, built the city hall at Belchertown, and an entire mill town before the lure of gold brought him to Sacramento in 1849."[3] Goodell was a prominent professional architect, with a well-established reputation and portfolio that included the lavishly ornate Governor's Mansion built on the corner of 16th and H Streets in Sacramento in 1878.

The remodeled "Exchange" Hotel became an early downtown landmark and destination spot, costing a substantial $25,000 to construct. Its builder was local contractor, William H. Winne. The Masonic Lodge used the third story of the building as a meeting hall. Lasting just ten years, the hotel was destroyed in July 1892 by a large fire that also wiped out the Opera House and all the commercial buildings between the Exchange Hotel and Third Street. Barnes never rebuilt the hotel, although the Julian Hotel, developed by Dr. George Jackson, rose in its place in 1894.

Levi Craft

The Art and Craft of Brick Making

A native of Pennsylvania, Levi Craft (b. 1819) came west in 1850 during the Gold Rush, settling for a period in Sacramento where he operated a mercantile business. Sensing opportunity in the emerging farming community of "Yolo City" (Woodland), Craft moved across the river in 1857 and, shortly thereafter, established a brick manufacturing plant.

Brick served as both a basic material and key stylistic theme forming the face and color of early Woodland. Many of Woodland's oldest extant buildings

[3] Harold Kirker, *California's Architectural Frontier* (Salt Lake City: Gibbs M. Smith, Inc., Peregrine Smith Books, 1960), p. 48.

4. Detail of Town Hall, 1882, Levi Craft
photo by Roger Klemm

were constructed of bricks manufactured at Craft's brickyard. Levi Craft was also a brick mason and building contractor, engaged in 1869 to erect a brick church building for the Holy Rosary Catholic Church in Woodland. Located on the north side of Main Street near Walnut Street, the church was very short-lived. Only three years after its completion, the structure became unstable due to a weak foundation and was demolished.

In 1882 Richard H. Beamer contracted with Levi Craft to construct a two-story brick building used by the City of Woodland for about ten years as a Town Hall and Fire Station *(fig. 4)*. Still standing at 702 Main Street, the exterior of the building was stripped of its bay windows and most of its Victorian detail many years ago.

The Lowe and Hollingsworth Block (1883), constructed by Craft at 411-425 Main Street, exemplifies a row of brick commercial buildings developed as one "business block" by local investors to meet the growing demand for commercial rental space as downtown expanded. Over the course of time, all but one storefront, 413 Main Street, were remodeled.

In 1884 Levi Craft sold the brickyard to his business partner, contractor William H. Winne. Craft, now 65 years old, may have retired after 25 years in the Woodland building industry, but not before leaving a permanent mark on the structure and feel of downtown.

Harrison Ervin

Brick Entrepreneur and Prolific Builder

Harrison Ervin (b. 1839) was a second important brick mason settling in Woodland during the time of enormous commercial downtown growth. By the 1860s substantial brick and mortar commercial buildings began to house Woodland's emerging business community. Born in Warsaw, Hancock County, Illinois, Ervin crossed the plains and mountains and arrived in California in 1864, where he married N.J. Pennington, with whom he had six children.

Ervin developed a contracting business in Woodland, specializing in brick and stonework. He also owned a brick kiln, manufacturing his own bricks. A newspaper self-promotion in the January 1, 1892 *Yolo Weekly Mail* declared him

> *the builder of all the principal brick buildings which have been erected in this city within the last decade, and has never failed to give entire satisfaction, both in point of workmanship and quantity and quality of materials used. He burns his own brick, which amount*

to several millions annually, and which are pronounced by experts as first-class in every particular.

By all published accounts, Ervin had a thriving brick-making business. The August 20, 1890 "local brevity" column in the *Woodland Democrat* noted Ervin "is burning a kiln of 1 million bricks."

1891 was a busy year for Ervin who constructed a two-story brick and stone building designed by San Francisco architects Gould and Colley for Marshall Diggs' hardware business at 514-516 Main Street. He also did the brick work for the landmark Jackson Apartment Building, developed by Dr. George H. Jackson, with architectural plans also provided by Gould and Colley *(fig. 5)*. In 1892 Ervin erected the Beamer Block at 708-712 Main Street, developed by Richard H. Beamer. Thomas J. Welsh, a noted San Francisco architect, provided the inspired design for this distinguished building.

Erwin's business scope likely extended beyond commercial construction to the housing industry. Though most late Victorian period houses were constructed of redwood, foundations and chimneys required brick masons. No doubt Ervin was kept quite busy with these smaller contracts as well, especially during the boom times of the 1880s and early 1890s.

In a 1904 City Directory Harrison Ervin's residence and business address was listed at 1252 Main Street, near Johnston Avenue (since demolished). While the exact location of his brick kiln is unknown, his bricks still make up the foundation and the structure of important buildings.

Harrison Ervin
from *Yolo Weekly Mail*,
January 1, 1892
Woodland Public Library Microfilm Collection

5. Arched Brick Windows, Jackson Building, 1891,
Harrison Ervin
photo by David Wilkinson

William H. Winne

The First Planing Mill Comes to Woodland

Born in Amsterdam, New York, William Henry Winne (1840-1933) was apprenticed at age 16 as a carpenter and builder, working at the trade until the Civil War. He joined Company B, Thirty-second New York Volunteer Infantry as a 20-year old and after two years was honorably discharged in 1863. He then joined the engineering corps until the Civil War ended when he was again honorably discharged, having participated in most of the battles of the Army of the Potomac.

In 1867 the Civil War veteran, well versed in building, landed in San Francisco looking for a fresh start in peacetime America. After a short stint in the Bay Area and Sacramento, he moved to Woodland in 1868 and immediately started a contracting business. One of his first projects was Woodland's first public school near the southwest corner of Main and East Streets in 1868.

In 1869 "Captain" Winne, as he was respectfully known around town, built the first planing mill in Woodland with partner James Sibley. The planing mill was located on First Street near Bush Street, the pres-

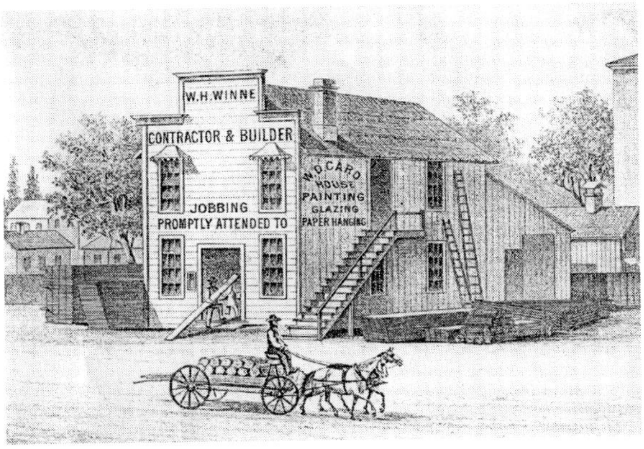

6. Winne Planing Mill on west side of First Street near Bush Street.
from *Illustrated Atlas and History of Yolo County*, 1879
Woodland Public Library

ent site of the Jackson Apartment Building *(fig. 6)*. By this time lumber, particularly redwood, was becoming more popular and available as a building material. This was also the same year that the first railroad arrived in Woodland, connecting local builders to readily available sources of lumber.

The significant presence of a planing mill, providing a steady supply of building materials, improved building efficiency, saved costs, and offered local builders (and owners) greater flexibility for creative choices. Winne owned the planing mill only for a couple of years before selling out to partner Sibley; in 1874 the mill property and machinery were acquired and converted into a machine shop by local inventor Byron Jackson, whose centrifugal pump refinements helped revolutionize agricultural irrigation.

Winne constructed the first Episcopal Church (1887) and the German Lutheran Church (1892), destroyed by fire in 1934. Woodland's oldest remaining church, the old Congregational Church at 450 First Street (1874), is also attributed to Winne *(fig. 7)*. Captain Winne's impact covered large commercial projects in Woodland, including the Julian Hotel in 1894 at Second and Main Streets, which replaced the Exchange Hotel which he had constructed and which

7. Congregational Church, 1874, William H. Winne
photo by Roger Klemm

8. Steiner House (1888) and First Street Panorama, William H. Winne, builder
courtesy Yolo County Museum

burned in 1892. Winne also won the bid to rebuild the Woodland Opera House in 1895.

Two good residential examples illustrating Winne's skill as a fine homebuilder are the Stick style Holcom house at 715 First Street (1886) designed by Thomas Welsh and the Eastlake style Steiner house at 632 First Street *(1888, fig. 8)*. He also built houses on a speculative basis that were sold or rented to the growing population. William H.Winne died in 1933 at the age of 92 at his home at 440 First Street (now the site of the Yolo Grocery Building, facing Bush Street).

John C. Pelton, Jr.

San Francisco comes to Woodland — Eastlake Style meets Row House

Between April 1880 and January 1882, the *San Francisco Evening Bulletin* newspaper published a series of house plans and specifications by a young architect, John Cotter Pelton, Jr. (1856–c.1912). The newspaper was dramatizing the proliferation of badly designed houses constructed in the poor, working class neighborhoods developing on the outskirts of San Francisco. The goal of the newspaper series, *Cheap Dwellings,* was to provide carpenters a set of free house plans, specifications, and cost estimates for poorer families to construct well-designed homes for well under $2,000, the "minimum" appealing to an architect working for a standard 5% commission.

9. Pelton's Eastlake Cottage Perspective
from *Cheap Dwellings* (San Francisco Bulletin Company, 1882), *Foundation for San Francisco's Architectural Heritage*

Pelton was born in San Francisco. His father, John C. Pelton, Sr., was a well-known educator and social reformer from Massachusetts who settled in San Francisco in 1849 where he and his wife, Amanda, established the first free public school. John C. Pelton, Jr. apprenticed for several years as a draftsman in San Francisco before starting his own firm about 1880. His interest in improving working-class housing was likely shaped by the social consciousness of his parents. Only twenty-four years old, he was just beginning to make his mark in the architectural profession when the *Cheap Dwellings* propelled his career.

Controversy helped, pushed by nervousness of established designers fearful of losing fees. The *Cheap Dwellings* series was harshly criticized by James E. Wolfe, the editor of *California Architect and Building News*, published monthly by the San Francisco chapter of the American Institute of Architects. Wolfe's diatribe focused on what he considered ugly design and unrealistically low cost estimates provided by Pelton. However, Wolfe's ulterior motive was professional jealousy — and the prospect that Pelton's proposals would reduce commissions for local architects. Wolfe's attacks notwithstanding, Pelton's house plans grew in popularity with each publication.

In total, twelve house designs were published in the *Cheap Dwellings* series. About half of the plans incorporated progressive Eastlake design elements in larger homes targeted for the more sophisticated and affluent middle class *(fig. 9)*. Beyond simply improving the quality of low income housing, Pelton's creative mission was to develop a new style of domestic architecture synthesizing the new Eastlake design elements introduced on the East Coast with the established San Francisco vernacular wooden row house. The popularity and demand for Pelton's house plans was so great that the San Francisco Bulletin Company published all the plans as an 1882 pattern book.

10. Welges House, 1881, John C. Pelton, Jr.
courtesy Yolo County Archives

Pelton's drawings were quite influential, certainly thanks to a successful public relations campaign. Consequently, his firm stayed busy with commissions during most of the 1880s. As early as 1881, when Pelton's plans were being circulated, Woodland physician, Dr. George Lorenzo Welges, contacted him to design a two story home at the northwest corner of Second and Court Streets. One wonders to what degree Dr. Welges hired this 25 year old architect because of his Bay Area celebrity. Welges' choice of architect is intriguing and revealing, especially because several experienced Woodland architects were available to design his house. However, an important historical trend was forming, specifically for affluent and inspired Woodland home owners/builders to seek out "big city" architects. This tendency efficiently brought new, even pioneering ideas to the Central Valley, with great impact on the range, options, and sophistication of Woodland's development.

The design for Dr. Welges' house was Italianate, with a two-story bay window, bracketed eaves and rectangular, hooded double-hung windows. Instead of the traditional small portico typically specified for Italianate homes built in Woodland in the 1870s, the Welges house included a veranda extending along most of the width of the front facade. Although borrowing heavily from the Renaissance period, the house exemplifies what Pelton called his "American Style," characterized by not using wood to mimic Italian stone houses, functional verandas, and window hoods. Welges' house was built for a substantial sum of $4,250 — not exactly a workingman's cottage *(fig. 10)*.

While Dr. Welges used his large house for both his office and pharmacy, in its later years, Yolo County used it as a detention home. By 1950 the house had fallen into a state of disrepair and the Board of Supervisors solicited bids to have the building razed. The Yolo County Administration Building was constructed on this site in 1984.

Pelton's progressive Eastlake style of home design,

introduced in the *Cheap Dwellings* series, influenced regional builders. This style showed up in Woodland about 1885 as local architects moved away from the more heavily ornamented Italianate style. Many four- and five-room country cottages were built in Woodland during the boom times of the late 1880s. Distinguished by their functional verandas, tall ceilings, hipped roofs, bay windows, and standard five-room floor plans, these homes considerably resemble Pelton's new plans.

Afterwards, John C. Pelton, Jr., the social reform-minded architect whose work encompassed the entire socio-economic spectrum of clients, had a checkered career as an architect. Affected, like his peers, by the boom and bust building cycles of the era, he bounced between San Francisco and Los Angeles following the flow of development. By the time of his death about 1912, Pelton was experimenting with poured concrete houses. Today, many modest houses erected in the historically working-class Mission and Portrero Hill districts of San Francisco indicate Pelton's optimistic *Cheap Dwellings* designs gave hope to the immigrant masses in pursuit of the American Dream at the height of the Gilded Age.

Bryan J. Clinch

Prolific, Distinguished Designer of Landmark Catholic Academy

In 1884 the Holy Rosary Academy, a three-story, stately Victorian boarding school operated by the Catholic Church was constructed on the south side of Main Street west of Cleveland Street (site of the Woodland Shopping Center). The Academy was a major landmark and regional educational institution, drawing students from several western states. Bryan James Clinch (1843-1906), an architect based in San Francisco, designed this venerable campus — thus providing another example of a major local building enhanced by a distinguished outsider.

Born in Ireland, Clinch graduated with highest honors from Queen's College before immigrating to the United States about 1866. In San Francisco Clinch's intellectual gifts blossomed and he led a prominent life as an architect, scholar, and writer. As an architect he designed and supervised the construction of many noted Catholic churches in northern California, including the landmark Cathedral of the Blessed Sacrament located at 11th and K Streets in downtown Sacramento (1887). He also designed St. Joseph's (Bishop's) Cathedral in downtown San Jose and other Catholic churches in Los Gatos, Santa Clara, Gilroy, Alameda, Berkeley, Mill Valley, and Santa Rosa.

In keeping with the rural location of the institution, Holy Rosary Academy was constructed of wood. Clinch designed the three-story building in the Italianate style with a central tower rising above the roof *(fig. 11)*. A long balustrade veranda spanned a good portion of the width of the front of the school. Woodland contractor, Samuel Caldwell, constructed the building. From 1904 to 1907 there were major expansions to the original campus.

Holy Rosary Academy was a noted, idyllic academic institution, educating students in Woodland for over 70 years. The building caught fire in 1952, was partially destroyed, but was used for a few more years. The entire building was demolished in 1956 to clear the site for the Woodland Shopping Center.

In 1891 Clinch drew the plans for a new rectory for Father Hynes, apparently the pastor of Holy Rosary Church. The rectory was located on the north side of Main Street between Elm and Walnut Streets next to Holy Rosary Church and was either relocated or demolished in the late 1940s.

In addition to architectural work, Clinch was a noted author and essayist with readers on both sides of the Atlantic. In 1904 he published an authoritative two-volume work, *California and Its Missions.* Bryan Clinch died in 1906 shortly after the shock and devastation of the great San Francisco earthquake and fire left his beloved city in ruins.

11. Holy Rosary Academy, 1884, Bryan J. Clinch, architect, Samuel Caldwell, builder
courtesy Holy Rosary Church Archives

Samuel Caldwell

A Top-Notch Victorian Builder of Townhouses

A Canadian by birth, Samuel Caldwell (1847-1896) lived in New York for a short period before arriving in San Francisco via Panama in 1867. Caldwell spent three years in San Francisco as a carpenter honing his skills and learning the trade. Searching for greener pastures, he moved to Woodland in 1870. In 1873 Caldwell married Tena Beamer, daughter of prominent Woodland pioneers Richard L. and Rebecca Beamer, and sister of Richard H. Beamer. The couple had four children, Ella May, Forrest, Irene and Neil.

In 1876 Caldwell formed a partnership with machinist and inventor Byron Jackson to set up a general contracting and planing mill business. Within a couple of years, Caldwell and Jackson went their separate ways, with Jackson concentrating on his agricultural pump inventions and Caldwell building his own machine shop, the Yolo Planing Mill, near the southwest corner of Main and Fifth Streets. By 1879 Caldwell had also built himself a picturesque home near the northeast corner of College and Laurel

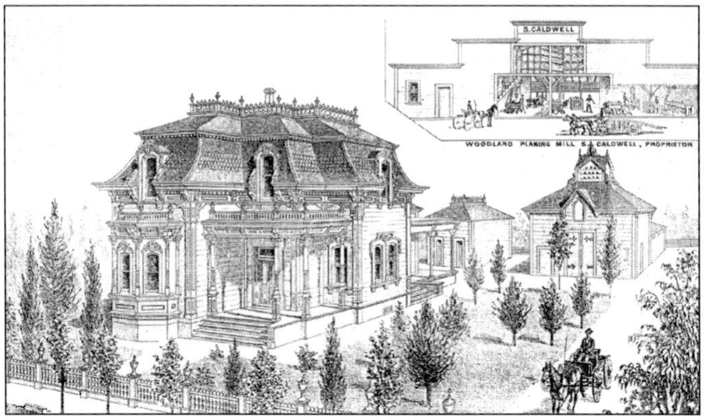

12. Samuel Caldwell House and Planing Mill, c1870s
from *Illustrated Atlas and History of Yolo County*
Woodland Public Library

14. Three Townhouses, 1886, Samuel Caldwell
photo by Roger Klemm

Streets. This large two-story house was designed in the Second Empire style with a French mansard roof *(fig. 12)*.

13. Queen Anne Cottage with Ship's Prow Bay Window, 1886, Samuel Caldwell
photo by Roger Klemm

His mastery of the Victorian Italianate style of architecture, so prominent in San Francisco, is exemplified by several of the prominent buildings he constructed in Woodland. In 1884 Caldwell was the low bidder for the Holy Rosary Academy, a three-story, stately Victorian boarding school designed by Bryan J. Clinch of San Francisco. Caldwell built the school for $15,585.

The single-story Italianate house at 547 First Street (1882) constructed by Caldwell originally had iron cresting above the square bay window, the portico and the widow's walk on the roof. A square portico was also replaced by the present rounded one. An ornate fence surrounded the property. A picturesque Victorian cottage at 163 Second Street built by Caldwell (1886) has a unique "ship's prow" bay window that projects from the main body of the house at a 45 degree angle *(fig. 13)*.

Sam Caldwell created San Francisco imagery in Woodland when he constructed three row houses at 165-169 College Street (1893-*fig. 14)*. Known today as the "Triple House," the complex was originally known as the "Caldwell Apartments." These housing units were actually townhouses, an innovation for Woodland, with urban-style street frontage. Caldwell probably rented the properties and today each townhouse is broken up into a lower and upper rental unit.

15. House at 326 Lincoln Street, c1900,
Joseph Caldwell (attributed)
photo by Roger Klemm

The latter part of Sam Caldwell's life was apparently marred by severe health and personal problems. According to a newspaper obituary in 1896, illness "left him dependent, homeless and in broken health."[4] The official cause of death at age 49 was tuberculosis.

The Caldwell family produced several generations of builders in Woodland. Sam's brother, Joseph Caldwell (died in 1927), was also a Woodland builder *(fig. 15)*. Lester J. Caldwell, son of Joseph Caldwell, perpetuated the Caldwell family building tradition, constructing many Woodland homes during his career. Today, Thomas Caldwell, a descendant of Samuel Caldwell, operates a general contracting business in Woodland.

William Henry Carson

Affordable Victorian Cottages and Luxury Hotel Accommodations

Like many Woodlanders of his generation, William Henry Carson (1824-92) was a transplanted Midwesterner who designed and built many Victorian homes and commercial structures during a fifteen-year period. Born in Ohio in 1824, he migrated to California in 1852 where he met and married Harriett B. Hanson of Mariposa County in 1863. William and Harriett Hanson Carson settled in Woodland in 1877. Following several enterprising competitors, Carson mustered up enough capital to equip the Woodland Planing Mill, located on the north side of Main Street near Sixth Street.

Several of the single-story Victorian cottages that Carson designed and built are still standing and some have been restored by their owners. These modest custom homes, typically built for Woodland's middle class for about $2,000, were designed to stay cool during Woodland's hot summer months. The ceilings in these homes are typically twelve feet high, with rather tall attics providing very good air circulation. Carson-built Victorian cottages are recognizable by his basic floor plan and the scale of the house. Featuring two or three chambers (bedrooms), a cozy front porch with room enough for people to sit and enjoy the weather and passers-by, the style was typical of "cottage domestic architecture" advertised in architectural trade publications of the 1880s. He customized his homes to reflect his clients' tastes, adding exterior embellishments, such as gables or hipped roofs, jigsaw-designed frieze decoration, and carved brackets, to create formal Italianate or more casual Stick styles of Victoriana. A good example of this style of house is the Eastlake cottage at 745 First Street (1885), with board and batten stick work on the cut-away gable *(fig. 16)*.

William Henry Carson was more than competent as a designer, responsible for houses both large and

[4] *Woodland Daily Democrat,* September 12, 1896

16. Eastlake Cottage at 745 First Street, 1885, William Henry Carson
photo by Roger Klemm

small and several commercial buildings. He designed a venerable Woodland landmark, the Ritchie Mansion (1886), which stood at the southwest corner of Cleveland and Main Streets until demolished in 1975 to make way for a bank *(fig. 17)*. Italianate in style, the large house was constructed for prosperous farming family, John and Elizabeth Ritchie, who emigrated from Germany. On October 30, 1886 the *Yolo Weekly Mail* described the house at its creation:

> *The new residence of Mr. J. Ritchie just being completed on the corner of Main and Cleveland streets is one of the many handsome buildings lately erected in this city. It covers about 35 feet front by 50 feet depth,*

17. Ritchie Mansion, 1886, William Henry Carson
courtesy Yolo County Archives

and is two tall stories high, adorned on the north, east and west by capacious double bay windows. Its style of architecture is a compromise between the modern county style and the city fashion of building, and is just the kind of home in which a hardworking farmer like Mr. Ritchie has been may retreat to in his well kept age and amply saved fortune, and settle down to a life of ease and comfort... This house will cost not less than seven thousand dollars, and to finish the improvement he contemplates on his home, Mr. Ritchie will expend hardly less than $10,000... The outside of the house is painted a medium drab, relieved by red trimmings, after the liking of the owner.

In 1883, one year after the Exchange Hotel was completed across from the Opera House, Woodland businessmen John Byrns, A.D. Porter, and Thomas M. Pryor approached Carson with a vision for a three-story, upscale hotel to be situated on the corner of Main and College Streets (on the current Hotel Woodland site). Built at a substantial sum of $60,000, the Byrns Hotel was designed to be the region's showcase hotel attracting overnight travelers with luxury in mind. The brick structure featured a turret with portholes cresting above the roofline and looming tall over the intersection of College and Main Streets *(fig. 18)*. The hotel was named after one of its developers, John Byrns, who, alas, did not live to see the building completed.

The building, no doubt, became an instant downtown architectural icon and a beacon luring train travelers from the eastern end of Main Street. In its day the Byrns Hotel was promoted as one of the finest hotels in northern California outside of the Bay Area. The Byrns served the traveling public for about thirty of Woodland's formative years. By the time the building was demolished in 1927 to make way for the Hotel Woodland, the Byrns' allure had faded. The once gracious hotel was used as a flu "hospital" during the epidemic of 1918 and shortly afterwards was condemned.

In 1889 Carson was commissioned by town promoters to design the upscale, elegant three-story Georgian Revival brick hotel in the new rural town of Esperanza (Esparto). The syndicate that developed the hotel for $30,000 included Charles F. Thomas of Woodland and Wolf Levy, the major partner in the Levy & Schwab dry goods business located across the street from the hotel. The hotel, diagonal to the new train depot and built to capitalize on the tourist trade, was constructed shortly after the Vaca Valley and Clear Lake Railroad was extended from Madison through the Capay Valley in 1888. The hotel was razed in 1935.

One year later in 1890, Woodland businessmen George Armstrong and Richard Alge sought out Carson to design the handsome brick and stone Italianate building at 604-606 Main Street in Woodland for their growing meat packing company *(fig. 19)*. Upstairs was used for professional offices. Carson may also have designed the similar building adjacent to the Armstrong & Alge Building for Selig Hyman. The

18. Byrns Hotel, 1883, William Henry Carson
courtesy Yolo County Archives

19. Armstrong & Alge Building (with bay window), 1890, William Henry Carson
photo by Roger Klemm

new look of these buildings was a major enhancement for downtown Woodland. The August 4, 1890 edition of the *Woodland Democrat* noted that the Armstrong & Alge building "will present a very pretty appearance. It is the only front of its kind in town, being faced up with Winters sandstone, Vallejo pressed brick and lined with black mortar."

William Henry Carson's career as a distinguished Woodland architect reached its pinnacle late in his life, and he died in Woodland in 1892. His 15-year career as an architect, contractor, and planing mill owner from 1877 to1892 coincided with a building boom period in Woodland when capital was plentiful and growth blossomed across town and region. Shortly after Carson's death in 1892, an economic depression beset the country. The "Panic of 1893" sent real estate prices plummeting and once-prevalent, investment capital dried up. Other Woodland developers and architects, whose fortunes were tied to the real estate market, saw their dreams and promising careers wrecked or, at the least sidetracked, after 1893.

Edward Carlton Gilbert

The Meteoric Rise (and Fall) of the Master Builder of The Gable Mansion

Edward Carlton "Carl" Gilbert (1858-1934) was the principal of the Woodland contracting firm of "Gilbert & Sons," which began designing and constructing impressive buildings in Woodland about 1880. Born in Catskill, New York, in 1858, Carl Gilbert and his brother, Frank, apparently came west to Alameda County as young men in 1876 and moved to Woodland a few years later in search of opportunity. For the short period Gilbert resided in Woodland — he moved to Oakland in 1894 — he was very active as a developer, real estate speculator, architect, and general contractor. Full of youthful drive and ambition, Gilbert made a big splash in Woodland during the boom times of the 1880s.

Carl Gilbert's most noteworthy commission and enduring legacy is the outstanding architectural showpiece, the Gable Mansion at 652 First Street, constructed in 1885 when Gilbert was only twenty-seven years old *(fig. 20)*. Gilbert designed and built this local landmark for $16,000 — a princely sum for a "rural" residential contract and undoubtedly the most expensive home built in Woodland in this era. The house was built for Amos and Harvey Gable, two brothers who succeeded as '49ers-turned-ranchers and then combined fortunes to build the mansion that both Gable brothers called home.

Like most contractor-builders of his era, E.C. Gilbert probably had no formal training as an architect. His design expertise was probably acquired through on-the-job training as a builder, by observation, and by studying published building designs and technical manuals of the era. Perhaps he was trained by his father for he adopted the family business name of "Gilbert & Sons," which he used throughout his Woodland career. A person by the name of A.J. Gilbert also lived in Woodland and was affiliated with Gilbert & Sons, but it is unclear how he was related to Carl Gilbert.

The design and construction of the Gable House epitomizes Gilbert's creative skill as a designer and craftsman. The eminent art historian and former U.C. Davis Art History Professor, Joseph Baird, described the Gable Mansion as an outstanding example of "Stick Vernacular" architecture, meaning a locally unique variant of the Stick style of Victorian architecture in vogue in the 1880s.

Although Gilbert's design for the Gable Mansion was original, like most builders he had access to published pattern books and trade journals to keep abreast of the latest fashions in architecture. For a short period of time, Gilbert was a frequent contributor to the *California Architect and Building News* (CABN), a trade journal of the San Francisco chapter of the American Institute of Architects (AIA). Between 1884-1892 he contributed short articles and architectural renderings to the *CABN* describing and promoting his projects in Woodland.

20. Gable Mansion, 1885, Edward Carlton Gilbert
photo by Roger Klemm

An elevation of the Gable Mansion and first floor plan was published in the October 1887 edition of the *CABN*, revealing similarities in massing with a design for a large home (or villa) previously published in *CABN* in 1881. The first floor plan of the Gable Mansion has an impressive central "stair hall" with a curved stairway visible from the front entrance vestibule. The second story of the home was laid out with seven bedrooms, and the third story was a ballroom. Robert McWhirk purchased the Gable Mansion from the Gable estate in the early 1970s and spent twenty years rehabilitating the structure. Today the building is a registered California Historical Landmark and symbolizes the high point of the *nouveau riche*, landed gentry of Woodland's formative years.

One year before the Gable Mansion was constructed, Gilbert built another landmark house in Yolo County. From plans furnished by San Francisco architect Harold Mitchell, Gilbert's construction company, Gilbert & Sons, built the handsome Victorian farmhouse now known as "Yolanda" for farmer and inventor Byron Jackson in 1884. It cost $10,000 to construct the large house, located on the corner of Roads 99 and 25A south of Woodland.

Another landmark building of the Victorian era designed by Gilbert was the picturesque YMCA Building (1886) constructed near what is today 433 Second Street (Garden Court Office Building) just south of Main Street *(fig. 21)*. This beautiful building (actually three individual buildings with a unified design) further illustrated Gilbert's talent as a designer — and promoter. Gilbert was apparently one of the key investors in the YMCA project, built at a pricey cost of $25,000. At the time the YMCA project was built, Carl Gilbert served as Secretary to the Woodland YMCA and in 1889 was elected president of the Board. Gilbert applied his promoter and builder skills and his insider position with the YMCA to materi-

21. YMCA Building, 1887, Edward Carlton Gilbert
courtesy Yolo County Archives

alize his dream of creating a state-of-the-art showpiece.

As described in an August 15, 1887 article in *CABN* (presumably written and submitted by Gilbert), the YMCA "Block" was 70 feet wide with a height of 75 feet six inches, making it among the tallest buildings then in Woodland. The project consisted of the central YMCA building featuring a French mansard roof, flanked by two smaller buildings designed to be structurally independent of the main building. Each building could be "sold separately or as a whole." The building to the right of the main structure, described as "Eastlake style in finish," was rented to a doctor as a residence with the first floor "arranged especially for Turkish and Russian baths, after the famous Hammam of San Francisco. This enterprise will give Woodland what few towns of its size East or West can boast of first-class, scientifically arranged and managed steam baths" (p.105).

The building on the left side of the YMCA block, according to the *CABN* article, is "suggestive of the Italianate style," arranged "for a private residence and has been rented to one of Woodland's enterprising merchants." Visitors entered the elegant YMCA building in the center of the complex through a spacious recess under a large arch. There were baths, a bowling alley, and gymnasium on the first floor. The main hall, library, and secretary's office (i.e. Gilbert's office) were on the second floor, and the third floor offered "class rooms, ladies' central committee kitchen, rooms for boys' branch, and quite a number of lodging rooms for young men." Carl Gilbert also had his business office within the building.

At the close of the *CABN* article Gilbert — the architect, builder, YMCA administrator, and real estate speculator all rolled into one — concludes with a fine bit of self-promotion and salesmanship, touting both moral and economic imperatives of investing in the "Y" building:

> *The probable cost of the block will be $25,000 when finished, and will be a credit to the enterprising builders. The Association is fortunate in getting the second Association building erected on this coast, and no doubt its usefulness will be increased a hundred-fold when it gets into the new building. Surely the business men cannot invest their money in anything where it will do as much good and bring larger returns than in the Young Men's Christian Association.*

The YMCA Block was admired for its beautiful design and was noteworthy for being the second "Y" building on the entire West Coast. Although Gilbert was initially able to attract business tenants to the building, including McCraes' Business College in 1889, the cash-flow on the real estate venture began to dwindle after a few years. By about 1893 the YMCA moved out of the building, probably squeezed by high rent and shrinking dues precipitated by depressed economic times. Gilbert and his associates were eventually forced to sell the building to Reuben

Cranston, who used it primarily as a boarding house known as the Windsor House. About 1917 the building was taken down.

In June 1886 in a letter to the editor of *CABN*, Gilbert explained that in laying the cornerstone to the new Methodist Episcopal Church South on the southwest corner of Second and Court streets *(fig. 22)*, a small casket of items was buried in a time capsule. Among the items buried, he indicated, was a May 1886 edition of the *CABN*. Then Gilbert waxed philosophical in concluding his letter to the editor:

> *Let us work and work well, while the day lasts, and be ready when the great Architect of the universe has need for us, and hope that our bodies may rest as secure and peaceful as the volume in the corner-stone, while our spirits and good influence will ever on.*

By 1888, Carl Gilbert could reflect on his life and feel a sense of pride in completing several admired buildings, including his own YMCA project. He had become a well-known and respected pillar of Woodland society, and the future must have loomed as his to conquer. Perhaps realizing the dream of any ambitious and inspired architect, Gilbert spent part of 1888 traveling in Europe and his return was celebrated in a January 3, 1889 notice in the *Yolo Democrat:*

> *Carl Gilbert returned yesterday from his long European tour, and has been undergoing the hearty greetings of his friends for hours . . . says there is but one California. The skies and fruits of Italy bear no comparison with our own. The grapes of the Rhine are small and insignificant beside our luscious fruit.*

In 1890 Gilbert's business expanded to the Bay Area, where he was hired to design the four-story Juanita Hotel at Eighteenth and San Pablo in Oakland. Considered by the *Oakland Enquirer* as "one of the handsomest structures in Oakland," the $45,000 building was developed by William Hatfield. Although larger in scale, the design of the Juanita Hotel in Oakland was very similar to the smaller Byrns Hotel, designed and built by W.H. Carson in Woodland in 1884.

In a January 2, 1892, the *Woodland Daily Democrat* reprinted an article from the *Oakland Tribune* featuring the architecture of Gilbert & Sons. In addition to publishing the elevation for the Juanita Hotel, the newspaper also ran drawings of large, Romanesque style houses built in Oakland for restaurateur Richard Stege, realtor N. Holoway, and a front elevation for a home built at 804 First Street in Woodland for Superior Court Judge Nicholas A. Hawkins *(fig. 23)*.

22. Methodist Episcopal Church South, 1886
Edward Carlton Gilbert
courtesy Yolo County Archives

Next to the lengthy newspaper article concerning Gilbert & Sons' Oakland projects was Gilbert's twelfth "Annual Building Report" summarizing the building for the year in Woodland and surrounding Yolo

23. Hawkins House, 804 First Street, 1892,
Edward Carlton Gilbert
courtesy Yolo County Museum

County. Gilbert was not only a marketing expert and self-promoter *par excellence*, but has proven an architectural historian's godsend, recording for posterity who was building what in Woodland during the golden period leading up to economic depression in 1893.

Gilbert's Annual Building Reports, published locally, varied between objective tallying of the year's construction statistics and praise of noteworthy projects to outright self-promotion of the architect's profession. Here is a sample from the 1887 building report, published on January 3, 1888 by the *Yolo Democrat,* with the heading, "Mr. Gilbert makes an exhaustive statement-Better houses and more of them:"

> *As a rule, we too often accept the apparent, and entirely ignore the real and its most important mechanical adaptations; in this way many splendid appearing buildings are splendid shams. And while we are forced to acknowledge that decorative ornamental construction is no doubt the essence of much that is beautiful and pleasing in architecture, but, like many other good things, this, too may be overdone. Now, at this most important point, the services of a skilled artisan become almost indispensable- to equalize and adjust harmony, remove obstacles and overcome difficulties.*
>
> *It costs less to build a house and pay for plans, details and working drawings than to work without them. The mistakes and blunders in construction, the cost in attempting to correct them, the waste of time and material, and worse than all, at the end you only have a shoddy, crippled building, inconvenient and unsaleable. All this you have as an offset for the small amount of architect's fees.*

In 1892 Gilbert won a design competition sponsored by Yolo County for a Queen Anne style General Hospital to cost $12,000. This new institution replaced the original county hospital built in 1863 at 121 First Street (still a residence). The new county hospital was located on the northwest corner of Cottonwood and Beamer Streets, now the site of the Yolo County Employment and Social Services building. A lithograph of the front elevation of the building was published in the *California Architect and Building News* in April 1892 *(fig. 24).*

The Victorian-era hospital was designed with a two-story central building used by the warden and attendants and for physician's offices and a dispensary. A wide veranda with arched moldings spanned the main building that housed two large patient wards. The two turrets at each end of the main building accommodated insane patients in one and the nurse in the other. The 1892 vintage Yolo County Hospital was in service for over fifty years until replaced by the existing county medical facility (now a clinic) constructed in 1944 directly across the street at 8 N. Cottonwood. The 1892 building was torn down several years after the new hospital came on line.

Believing Woodland's residential area would continue to expand as it had throughout the 1880s, Gilbert speculated in other real estate as well. The E.C. Gilbert subdivision, bounded by Cross, Pendegast, Fifth and Sixth streets, was annexed to the city and settled by Mr. Gilbert. His house, now demolished, stood near the southeast corner of Cross and Fifth streets.

Gilbert's meteoric rise to affluence and prominence

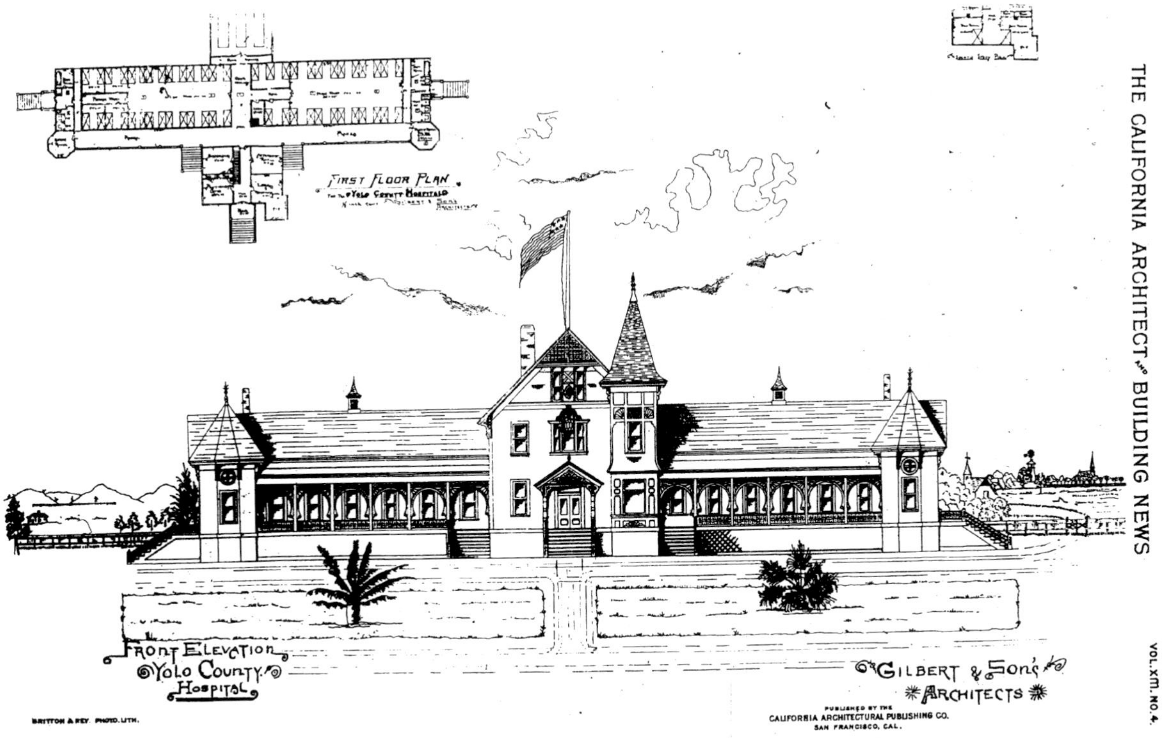

24. Yolo County Hospital Rendering, Edward Carlton Gilbert
from *California Architect and Building News,* April 1892, *Bancroft Library, U.C. Berkeley*

in Woodland began to unravel in 1893. A series of events, both personal and financial in nature, hastened his leaving Woodland as a young man. In 1889 he married May Dexter, a Woodland schoolteacher in a large, publicized wedding. In a newspaper article the groom was described as "an energetic and efficient man in church and business, as well as in all benevolent enterprises." After a few years of marriage, however, May Dexter Gilbert sued for divorce in 1893. The couple had no living children, having suffered through the trauma of a stillborn child. Court records housed at the Yolo County Archives indicate that, at the time of the divorce proceedings, Mr. Gilbert was "heavily in debt and owed $6,000 on real estate." Moreover, he was "unemployed at the time, with few prospects for work."

His economic woes were indicative of the sharp "boom and bust" building cycles of the time. Gilbert was heavily leveraged in real estate at the same time credit was being tightened by banks as the nation entered a deep economic depression. After lengthy court hearings, May Dexter Gilbert was granted a divorce with a settlement of $200. After the break-up with Gilbert, May Dexter went on with her life in Woodland, distinguishing herself with a long career as an educator. She was appointed Yolo County Superintendent of Schools in 1906, re-elected in 1910, and served until 1914.

His marriage dissolved and investments gone sour, Carl Gilbert moved to Oakland in 1894 at the seasoned age of 36 to begin life anew. There, according to local directories, he engaged in the building trade for many years as a carpenter and small contractor, his daring entrepreneurial days apparently behind him.

His brother, Frank Gilbert, lived with him in Oakland until moving to Sacramento in 1909.

Carl Gilbert remarried and he and his wife, Anna Jones Gilbert, had three children. For most of his Oakland years he resided at 604- 34th Street near Telegraph Avenue. This house was demolished many years ago to make way for a freeway and urban park.

Edward Carlton Gilbert was a man who seized the moment in Woodland to bestow his entrepreneurial skill, artistry, and boundless ambition — only to see those youthful dreams dashed by an unhappy marriage and financial woes. He lived to be 76 years of age, passing away in Oakland in 1934. His creative spirit, however, manifested in several Victorian landmark buildings which helped shape the enduring image of Woodland as a prosperous and architecturally rich agrarian community, lives on.

25. Byron Jackson House "Yolanda", 1884, Harold D. Mitchell, architect, Edward Carlton Gilbert, builder
courtesy Yolo County Archives

Harold D. Mitchell

An Englishman Designs the Gracious "Yolanda"

Harold D. Mitchell
from *California Architect and Building News,* March 1884, *Bancroft Library, U.C. Berkeley*

In 1884 Woodland farmer and inventor, Byron Jackson, decided to build a large picturesque ranch house two miles south of Woodland on the corner of Roads 99 and 25A. Here, Jackson could experiment with and perfect the centrifugal pump he invented a few years earlier at his machine shop in downtown Woodland. By the time his beautiful country house was erected, the success of Jackson's pumps had enabled him to open a large factory in San Francisco. Perhaps it was during the course of his business dealings in San Francisco that Jackson became acquainted with architect Harold D. Mitchell.

Mitchell (b. 1854) was from Manchester, England where he attended the Royal Institute of Art. These studies led to an interest in architecture and a desire to travel. As a young man he sailed to San Francisco in 1870. He learned the architectural trade by working in the offices of Wright & Saunders, a large, prominent firm, for eight years. Confident of his skills as a designer with excellent training on two continents, he opened his own practice in 1878. Mitchell was still a young man of thirty when he crossed paths with Byron Jackson, who commissioned him to design his Woodland home *(fig. 25).*

The two-story house is constructed of wood with minimal ornamentation, thus creating a relaxed, informal setting. A jerkenhead gable extends well over the roof supported by elbow brackets. Stoop porches on the north side of the home have bracketed roofs. This picturesque country home is clad in three different textures of wood siding, including fish scale shingles and board and batten. There is a generous amount of stained glass windowpanes and a two-story veranda with a decorative balustrade. Gilbert & Sons of Woodland constructed the house at a cost of $10,000.

In 1893 Jackson hired German immigrant, George H. Hecke, a trained horticulturist who studied at the Royal Botanical Gardens, at Kew, near London, England to run his farm. A few years later Jackson sold the ranch to George and Elizabeth Hecke and moved permanently to the Bay Area. The house and lush grounds became a focal point for the state agricultural community in 1919 when the governor appointed Hecke to be the first director of the State Department of Agriculture. Hecke renamed the house and ranch "Yolanda," a poetic and fitting name for this beautiful residence that graces the farmlands of Yolo County, just south of Woodland.

Thomas J. Welsh

S. F. Sophistication Comes to Woodland in an Opera House and Public Buildings

Thomas J. Welsh from *Commercial Encyclopedia of the Southwest* (Berkeley, 1911) by E. Davis, ed. *California History Section, California State Library*

Born in Australia, Thomas J. Welsh (1845-1918) became one of the most prolific and reputable architects of San Francisco before the 1906 earthquake. He grew up in San Francisco and attended Jesuit schools. As a student, he developed a love for the study of ancient Rome, Greece, and Egypt. He began his career as a carpenter before mastering architecture in the well-known San Francisco firm of Farquharson, Kenitzer, and George Bordwell.

Welsh began his forty-year solo career in San Francisco in 1870. He left a legacy of some seven hundred buildings concentrated in San Francisco, but also many scattered over several small towns, including Woodland. By the time Welsh was approached by the Woodland business establishment to design a cultural showplace for the prosperous small city, he had a solid reputation in San Francisco. No doubt his impressive track record of designing prominent churches, schools, and houses in the Bay Area gave rural Woodlanders confidence that Welsh, another big city architectural name, would deliver a slice of urban sophistication to Main Street within budget.

The first Woodland Opera House, designed by Thomas J. Welsh (1885), was constructed for a significant sum of $28,000 *(fig. 26)*. While the style for the Opera House was upscale and classical, its two-story size and second story balcony did not overwhelm surrounding buildings. Set back from the corner of Second and Main, the Opera House had an angled corner tower and second story bay window that gave the building street presence. The builder for the project was Woodland contractor, William H. Curson.

At the time the Opera House was being built, J.J. McIntyre hired Welsh to design a two-story brick commercial building near the Opera House on the north side of Main Street between First and Second Streets. Tragically, both of these substantial downtown buildings were destroyed in the July 1892 fire that started in Dead Cat Alley behind the Opera House and wiped out most buildings on the north side of Main between First and Second Streets.

Another Woodland landmark of the Victorian period designed by Welsh was the Yolo County Hall of Records building (1889, *fig. 27*). With a central tower facing Court Street, this handsome structure was erected adjacent to the first Yolo County Courthouse completed in 1864. These two public buildings comprised Courthouse Square. The cornerstone for the Hall of Records was laid on February 9, 1889 in a public ceremony. The style of the building was Romanesque with first-class materials specified by Welch as described in the *Yolo Democrat*:

> *The style of the architecture will be of that character that prevails largely in the Eastern cities at the present time, and what is styled the Romanesque... The exterior is pressed brick with stone trimmings. The cornices of galvanized iron... the ceiling is formed by a system of arches, the material being terra cotta - this is the first of the use of terra cotta for the ceilings of any public building in the*

26. Woodland Opera House, 1885, Thomas J. Welsh, architect, William Henry Curson, builder
courtesy Yolo County Archives

27. Yolo County Hall of Records, 1889, Thomas J. Welsh
courtesy Yolo County Archives

state, and was molded especially from the drawings made by Mr. Welch (sic), architect of the building.

The terra cotta architectural tile used on the building, including a nine-foot long "Hall of Records" casting, was manufactured at Gladding, McBean in Lincoln, California, which is still in operation today.

One month earlier, as the Hall of Records construction commenced, Thomas Welsh was on the job site in Woodland to assure the taxpayers in his self-confident manner that the people would soon be enjoying a top quality building — as reported in the *Yolo Weekly Mail* on January 12, 1889:

> *Mr. Welch (sic) takes no small degree of professional pride in the structure, and is watching its construction with keen interest; and with unqualified confidence he assured a representative of this paper that the people of Yolo County were getting a structure upon which he was entirely willing to state his professional reputation for all time to come.*

The Hall of Records was indeed a special building in which the community could take considerable pride. The building was rather short-lived, however, for by 1916 the Hall of Records and the Courthouse were razed to clear the site for another splendid building, the extant Yolo County Courthouse constructed in 1917.

The only known house in Woodland designed by Welsh is a picturesque Victorian Stick home located at 715 First Street (1886, *fig. 28*).

In 1892 Welsh was retained by Woodland developer Richard H. Beamer to draw up architectural plans for the "Beamer Block" at 708-712 Main Street. This large two-story commercial building had Italianate detailing with four upper-story square bay windows and a mansard roof. The street level storefronts featured iron columns. This ornate Victorian facade was destroyed in 1948 when the building was remodeled. In 1983 Woodlander Tom Stallard rehabilitated this prominent Main Street building.

Although the vast majority of Welsh's S. F. buildings were destroyed in the earthquake and fire of 1906, several restored Victorian houses and one prominent church, Sacred Heart Church (1898) at Fillmore and Fell Streets, survive to the present day, according to San Francisco Heritage Foundation records. After the earthquake of 1906, Welsh formed a partnership with John Carey. From 1906 to 1914 the firm of Welsh and Carey were responsible for rebuilding several churches and other buildings.

During his long career, Welsh designed many Catholic churches, convents and schools in northern California. Active in the Catholic Church, he served as President of St. Patrick's Mutual Alliance and Knights of St. Patrick. He was also a member of the Knights of Columbus and the Society of St. Vincent de Paul.

28. Holcom House, 1886, Thomas J. Welsh, architect, William H. Winne, builder
photo by Roger Klemm

Thomas Welsh was elected architect for the San Francisco School Board and designed many early public schools in San Francisco. The Irving M. Scott School, located on Tennessee Street in San Francisco, is the only surviving nineteenth century public school designed by Welsh, now designated a San Francisco Historical Landmark. Welsh was active in business affairs, serving as president of the San Francisco Mutual Building and Loan Society. He was also a member of the American Institute of Architects. Thomas Welsh died in 1918, having led a rich life as a very significant contributor to the cultural history and material advancement of northern California, including Woodland.

Glenn & White

Their Porter Mansion Rivals the Gable Mansion

In 1880 the general contracting firm of Glenn & White began designing and building custom homes and commercial buildings in Woodland. Partners George Kyler Glenn (b. 1842) and Charles G. White formed the company. William Samuel White (1848-1936), brother of Charles, also worked for the firm for a few years. Like their fellow Woodland builder, Sam Caldwell, the White brothers were natives of Canada (New Brunswick).

In addition to their contracting business, Glenn &

29. Porter Mansion, 1886, Glenn & White
courtesy Yolo County Archives

30. Charles G. White House, 1888, Glenn & White
photo by Roger Klemm

White operated a planing mill. Located along an alley near the west side of Elm Street, just south of Main, the planing mill is shown on 1886 and 1889 Sanborn Maps as "Glenn and Wright's (sic) Planing Mill." Prior to establishing this machine shop, the White Brothers & Crane built an earlier mill in 1877 on the north side of Main Street near what is now Sixth Street. It was sold to William Henry Carson by 1879, when the mill shows up in an etching in Gilbert's *The Illustrated Atlas and History of Yolo County.*

Glenn & White built several houses on the western side of Woodland in the vicinity of their planing mill operation. The largest house they designed and built was a $12,000 mansion for Adelbert and Elizabeth Porter (1886) located on the southwest corner of Walnut and Main *(fig. 29)*. William White was the superintendent of construction for this large project. The Porter mansion rivaled its cross-town neighbor, the Gable Mansion, in scale, being one of the larger homes in the Sacramento Valley. The style for the mansion was described as "French Renaissance" by the *Daily Democrat* in August 6, 1886.

After A.D. Porter's death in 1911 the mansion was vacant for about nine years until rented to a nurse who converted it into a boarding house. Although the house was demolished in the 1930s to make way for a gas station, the carriage house at 435-37 Walnut Street survived. In 1921 White remodeled the Porter carriage house into a dwelling that today is used as a duplex. In 1892 Glenn & White constructed a single story Victorian home for William A. Porter, son of A.D. and Elizabeth, at 427 Walnut Street, across the street from his parents' mansion.

In 1888 Charles G. White built his personal residence at 554 Elm Street *(fig. 30)*. This Victorian cottage incorporated abundant gingerbread trim and a large rounded sitting porch gracing the corner lot. In 1891 Glenn & White was hired by Phillip J. Laugenour to build a large Shingle style house on the northwest corner of Main and Walnut Streets directly across from the Porter Mansion. Designed by the noted San Francisco architectural firm of Shea & Shea, this beautiful home cost a substantial $8,600.

About 1900 Charles White moved to Berkeley and went to work at the Cavan & Day Planing Mill on Shattuck Avenue and Glenn & White's Woodland operation was dissolved.

Shea & Shea

The Shingle Style Arrives in Woodland

Frank T. Shea
from *Commercial Encyclopedia of the Southwest* by E. Davis, ed., 1911
California History Section, California State Library

In 1891 an interesting Shingle style house was built for Phillip and Kate Laugenour on the northwest corner of Main and Walnut Streets on the western edge of downtown Woodland *(fig. 31)*. The architecture for the home was progressive, reflective of current urban and national trends in house design. A large triangular-shaped gable formed the front of the house with a small bay window flanked by two small double hung windows on the second story facade. A bay

31. Laugenour-Hershey House, 1891, Shea & Shea, *courtesy Yolo County Archives*

window and enclosed porch were beneath the gable. The Walnut Street elevation had twin dormer windows projecting from the sweeping roof and a Queen Anne style "witches hat" turret. The Shingle style, with major emphasis on the steep-pitched triangular gable facade, developed on the East Coast and spread to other parts of the country through published drawings by architects Bruce Price, McKim, Mead and White, and other trend-setting design firms.

The architect for this interesting home was the San Francisco firm of Shea & Shea, comprised of brothers Will D. and Frank T. Shea (1860-1929). A native of Bloomington, Illinois, Frank Shea was only six years old when the family moved to San Francisco. His architectural training involved eight years of work with prominent San Francisco architects, Bugbe & Sons and P.R. Schmidt. He also spent two years traveling in America and Europe studying ecclesiastical architecture. In 1889 Frank Shea entered private architectural practice. At different times during his career he was associated with his brother.

Between 1891 and 1906, three different Laugenour brothers owned the Woodland house: Henry and Sarah Laugenour were the second owners, then William and Irma Laugenour. In 1906 the home was sold to David N. and Ella Hershey, the same family that was instrumental in the re-building of the Woodland Opera House.

The Hershey family owned the home for two generations. Davidella and Florence Hershey, daughters of David and Ella, lived there until the 1960s when they moved into a retirement home. The house sat vacant and steadily deteriorated until condemned by the city. In 1970 a demolition permit was issued and the city planned to burn the structure. Arsonists beat the city to the task on February 1, 1970 when an early morning blaze destroyed the venerable landmark.

The Shea brothers designed the Laugenour house in Woodland early in their career. The firm eventually became well established and distinguished in the Bay Area. One of their prestigious commissions included the dome of the old San Francisco City Hall, destroyed in the 1906 earthquake. Frank Shea was also associated with John O. Lofquist during part of his career. Shea was noted for the many interesting and varied Catholic Churches he designed throughout northern California, including the following extant churches in San Francisco: Star of the Sea, Nuestra

Senora de Guadalupe, St. Vincent de Paul, St. Brigid's, and St. Paul's. Frank Shea also designed St. Thomas Aquinas Catholic Church in Palo Alto, St. Rose in Santa Rosa and the Norman-English half-timbered style St. Anselm's Church in San Anselmo.

In 1911 Shea & Lofquist were retained by Father Michael Wallrath to develop a preliminary design for a new Catholic Church in Woodland. A sketch of Shea & Lofquist's proposed design for the church was published in the November 4, 1911 edition of the *Daily Democrat* and also converted into a postcard *(fig. 32)*. The design was Gothic, with a central tower facing Main Street crowned by a ten-foot statue of the Queen of the Rosary standing on a ball 100 feet off the ground. The press release noted that:

> *Around the statue will be an elliptical halo of 53 white and 6 red electric lamps, with a cross string of lights representing the beads of the Rosary, illuminating the white statue. The building will no doubt be an ornamental attraction to Woodland.*

Ultimately, this extravagant design had to be abandoned due to economic constraints and an Italian builder, Fedele Costa, was selected by Father Wallrath to build a more modest church in 1912.

32. Artist's Rendering of Shea & Shea's Proposed Holy Rosary Church, c1911
courtesy Yolo County Archives

Fedele Costa

Italian Artisan Builds a Catholic Church

On March 1, 1912 ground was broken for a new Catholic Church in Woodland on the northeast corner of Walnut and Main Streets. This was the fourth in a succession of Catholic Churches erected in Woodland. The third church, built in the early 1870s was moved north to the corner of Court and Walnut Streets to make room for the new church. Father Michael Wallrath, pastor of the Woodland's Holy Rosary Catholic Church, participated in the groundbreaking ceremony, as did the architect and builder of the church, Fedele Costa, and about thirty parishioners.

This must have been a gratifying moment for Father Wallrath. Economic realities had recently forced him to give up his original dream of building a monumental church designed by the big-city architectural firm of Shea and Lofquist. His vision was dashed by the cost of such an undertaking. Changing course, he selected a relatively unknown Italian artisan and builder, Fedele Costa (b. 1863), to modify the final design for the project and to erect the building *(fig. 33)*.

In 1910 Costa proved himself to be a skilled church builder by completing St. Joseph's Catholic Church in Auburn much to the satisfaction of the local building committee. After completing the Auburn project, Costa was presented with a diamond ring and locket as tokens of gratitude. With the strong recommendation of Auburn church officials, Father Wallrath must have felt confident in choosing Costa as the man to fulfill his dream for a new Woodland house of worship.

Born in Bioglio, Italy, Fedele Costa was trained as a builder by his father. Starting as a day laborer, he worked his way up to superintendent for large construction firms in Italy before starting his own contracting company. Like many skilled Italian artisans, he immigrated to San Francisco shortly after the 1906 earthquake to help rebuild the city. Costa represents another major theme in the development of Woodland's architectural heritage, one of many talented emigrant artisans whose creations embellished the character of the city.

It appears that Shea & Lofquist's original design was adapted as a starting point by Costa for his plan for the Woodland church. According to newspaper accounts, the seating capacity for the church was the same as on the original plan. The building was constructed of reinforced concrete and the walls were faced with granite blocks per the original plan.

The main modification to the Shea & Lofquist plan was the facade facing Main Street. As originally proposed, the bell tower was to be a monumental, cascading Gothic edifice towering over the main entrance to the church. In Costa's design the bell tower was pushed to the corner of the building and became a more restrained single pointed steeple. Shea & Lofquist's idea for a large statue of the Queen of the Rosary was retained by Costa but, instead of crowning the bell tower, was placed on the roof parapet above the front entrance.

Holy Rosary Church records reveal that tempers flared on several occasions during the course of construction. Reportedly, Wallrath took exception to Costa's crew relaxing on the job, which led to arguments with Costa who, more than once, walked off the job — only to return a few days later as if nothing had happened! All parties ultimately survived the stresses and strains of the construction project and Father Wallrath's vision for a new, beautiful church was realized when the Holy Rosary Church was dedicated on June 2, 1913.

Unfortunately, as was the case with the second Catholic Church erected in 1869 by Woodland brick mason Levi Craft, Costa's church developed structural problems as the ground underneath the church shifted and settled due to the tremendous weight of the structure. These problems grew so severe that by 1943 the church had to be abandoned — unsolvable structural problems threatened to split the church in two.

In 1946 the church and the rectory property on Main Street were sold to auto dealer Layton Knaggs for $35,000 and torn down for use as a car lot. In 1949 the fifth and present Holy Rosary Catholic Church was built north of the old site on Court and Walnut Streets.

33. Holy Rosary Catholic Church, 1912, Fedele Costa
courtesy Yolo County Archives

Gould & Colley, Colley & Lemme

Innovators of the Stylish Jackson Building

In 1891, wealthy Woodland physician and investor, Dr. George Jackson, conceived of the idea of developing an upscale apartment building with commercial shops at a prominent location on the corner of Bush and First Street. Designed by the San Francisco architectural firm of Gould & Charles J. Colley (c.1849-1928), the composition of the building is an eccentric mixture of Romanesque, Frontier, and Queen Anne styling *(fig. 34)*. The architects started with a basic brick structure and added a dazzling roofline for eye-catching effect. Large dormers protrude from the steep-pitched slate shingle roof, with a tall, bullet-shaped turret placed on the corner. A second-story balcony wraps around the building. Local brick mason, Harrison Ervin, constructed the shell of the building at a cost of $25,000.

The local economy was still dynamic in 1891 and the future of the city appeared bright. Seizing the opportunity, hardware dealer Marshall Diggs commissioned Gould & Colley to draw plans for another Woodland building: a large two-story brick and stone mid-block building for his expanded business. This building, known as the Diggs Block, was the most prominent building on the south side of Main Street between College and First Streets (514-516 Main Street). The impressive front facade of the building had second-story arched stone windows. Carl Gilbert, Woodland architect and town booster, in his January 2, 1892 annual report published in the *Daily Democrat*, praised the building:

> *M.Diggs' next to Mr. Ball's is one of the best, if not the finest, brick and stone structures on Main Street. The architects, Gould & Colly [sic], deserve much credit*

34. Jackson Building, 1891, Gould & Colley architects, Harrison Ervin, brickmason
photo by Roger Klemm

for the taste displayed in the arrangement of this stylish front, and Mr. Diggs is to be congratulated on having the finest hardware store in Northern California.

Unfortunately, this grand facade has been covered with stucco and today is buried in the past.

In 1892, Woodland's first publicly-funded City Hall and Fire Station was built at First and Court Streets *(fig. 35)*. Charles J. Colley designed this picturesque building with a different partner, Emil S. Lemme (c.1863-1921). The firm of Colley & Lemme was noted for its design of the Sutro Baths, a San Francisco landmark of the era featuring Roman-style public baths located near the Cliff House along the Pacific Ocean.

Colley & Lemme designed the Woodland City Hall in the Romanesque style with medieval features. Like the Jackson Building, City Hall displayed a compelling roofline with enormous corner turrets with "witches hat" roofs and tall central clock tower facing First Street. A giant arched window overlooked Court Street. A sketch of the building was published in the August 1892 edition of the *California Architect and Building News*. The plan for the Main Floor of the building reveals that county offices such as the Tax Collector and Assessor, the School Board Superintendent, and the court system used the building. The basement of City Hall was used by the Fire Department.

35. Woodland City Hall & Fire Station, 1892,
Colley & Lemme
courtesy Yolo County Archives

The Jackson Building and City Hall were commanding bookends on First Street. The dramatic, extroverted buildings engaged the public in the power and pleasure of imaginative architecture.

By 1919 City Hall developed structural problems so severe that the city hired architect William Henry Weeks to compare the cost of condemning and destroying the structure versus rehabilitation. Weeks recommended substantial improvements to the building that added several more years of use by the fragile structure. By 1931, however, City Hall was rated structurally unsafe and was demolished to make way for the present City Hall.

The Jackson Building, however, has survived and was rehabilitated by a local investment group in 1985-86 headed by Marcus Ullrich. The attic, virtually unused for nearly one hundred years, was converted to a restaurant. Today, the building remains an enduring landmark of the Sacramento Valley, adding significantly to the special architectural character of Woodland.

Joseph Johnson Hall

English-Born Rambler Brings High Style to Public & Private Buildings

On July 2, 1892 a wind-swept fire that started in Dead Cat Alley destroyed most of the business block on the north side of Main Street between First and Second Streets, including the original Opera House and the Exchange Hotel. Catastrophic events, such as fires and earthquakes, often create major opportunities for the building profession. Joseph Johnson Hall appears to have seized this opportunity and parlayed his move to Woodland into several large architectural commissions that replaced buildings destroyed in the fire. He also designed in 1892 two houses that were architectural showpieces.

Little is known about architect Joseph J. Hall. Born in 1834 in England, Hall became an American citizen in 1856 in Ohio. The date of his arrival in California remains a mystery and his career in Woodland was very short. Records at the Yolo County Archives indicate he registered to vote in Woodland in August 1892 and moved on to San Jose by 1896 when building slowed in Woodland. An architect of considerable skill with a solid grasp of modern trends in design, Hall set up shop above the New York Store (now Corner Drugstore) at First and Main Streets. There, he quickly established a clientele of several of Woodland's movers and shakers anxious to rebuild after the conflagration. In 1892 the economy was still on an upswing and the future looked bright.

A few months after the fire, a Woodland investment group, headed by local entrepreneurs Richard H. Beamer, Marshall Diggs, David N. Hershey, and Dr. George H. Jackson, hired Hall to design the Farmers & Merchants' Bank *(fig. 36)*. The three-story bank building was to be prominently sited on the corner of Second and Main Streets in front of the destroyed Opera House, which would be rebuilt two years later in 1895.

Hall designed the bank in the progressive Richardsonian Romanesque style constructed with elegant Arizona red sandstone. The architecture was inspired by the work of the great nineteenth century American architect, Henry Hobson Richardson, whose East Coast stone masonry buildings of the era formed the basis of a nationwide Romanesque Revival movement.

36. Farmers & Merchants' Bank, 1894, Joseph Johnson Hall, architect, Daniel McPhee, builder
courtesy Yolo County Archives

A large arched entrance on the corner of Second and Main emphasized the bank's corner location. For many years the Masonic Lodge owned the third story of the building. In fact, Hall's original plan for the building was a two-story structure, but the Masons evidently became enamored with the idea of a modern, prestigious meeting facility on the top of Woodland's new signature building after plans for the building were announced. So, a third story was added, increasing the scale and presence of the building. The *Woodland Daily Democrat* was effusive in its praise of the Farmers & Merchants' Bank building when the doors opened and business commenced on January 2, 1894, exactly one and one half years after the fire:

> *It is built after plans made by J.J. Hall of Woodland, an architect of acknowledged ability of a high order, and in beauty of design, is not surpassed by any other building in California.*

The building was not only beautiful and designed in the latest style, but also unique, as Woodland's first commercial building clad entirely of stone. In his *Annual Building Review* report for Woodland published in the *Woodland Daily Democrat* on December 30, 1893, fellow Woodland architect and town booster, Edward Carlton Gilbert, heaped praise on the Farmers & Merchants' Bank:

> *A few of the most important improvements will crown the record of the year and deserve special mention. First comes the Farmers & Merchants' Bank, which is, without a doubt, the finest structure of its kind on the coast, outside of the largest cities; and we have never yet seen a city of the same size as Woodland, and many that are larger, with as fine a building as this one, except, perhaps, some of those buildings erected by the State . . . It is the first of any importance to be built in this place of stone, and we think the managers made a very wise selection when the red sandstone of Flagstaff, Arizona, was taken. The building is lighted throughout with the incandescent light, and when all three of the floors are lit up at night, it is a thing of beauty.*

The Farmers & Merchants' Bank graced Downtown Woodland for about seventy-five years. During this time the bank went through several changes of ownership and name changes, including First National Bank and Home Savings Bank. By the 1960s the building's poor condition reflected deferred maintenance and age. Inspections by the city determined the parapet walls of the building were weak and posed a threat to pedestrians. Eventually the city assumed ownership of the building and, unable to find a buyer to rehabilitate the structure, had the building demolished in 1970. The site stood vacant for twenty years until it was redeveloped into the Opera House Intermission Garden by the Woodland Rotary Club in 1990.

Hall also designed two buildings adjoining the Farmers and Merchants' Bank: one at 619-21 Main Street developed by Marshall Diggs and another at 617 Main Street developed by Dr. George H. Jackson and the Michael Bros. These two buildings, also erected in 1893, each have Richardsonian Romanesque style stone facades. Hall designed the bank and two adjacent commercial buildings to complement each other in design, symmetry, and contrasting colors of sandstone. The Diggs Building, constructed of brick with a brown Ventura sandstone facade, was designed for three shops with offices above. In 1977 Woodland architects Robert Schaefer and Gary Wirth, who used a large portion of the second story for their offices, restored this handsome building.

The Jackson-Michael Building at 617 Main Street is very similar to the Diggs-Wirth Building differing only in width, color — a Winters graystone was used — and the arched window treatment on the second floor. This building originally had a storeroom on the first floor with an upstairs boarding house. Today it is a commercial building.

Hall also had a hand in the Julian Hotel, developed by Dr. George H. Jackson and named in honor of his wife, Lizzie E. Julian *(fig. 37)*. Located on the northeast corner of Second and Main across from the Farmers and Merchants Bank, the Julian Hotel replaced the Exchange Hotel destroyed in the 1892 fire. The architecture for the Julian Hotel was apparently a collaborative effort. A conceptual design for the build-

37. Julian Hotel, 1894, Wood, Lovell & Claflin, Joseph Johnson Hall, architect, William, H. Winne, builder
courtesy Yolo County Archives

ing appeared in the *California Architect and Building News* periodical in October 1893. The Bay Area firm of Wood, Lovell & Claflin is cited as the architect submitting this conceptual design for the Julian Hotel — which matches the design of what was actually built. However, local newspaper reports at the time of construction of the Julian Hotel in 1894 cite J. J. Hall of Woodland as the architect. Apparently, George H. Jackson chose Hall to supervise the construction of the hotel by local contractor, William H. Winne.

The Julian Hotel was also of Romanesque design but, unlike its rusticated sandstone cousin buildings, was clad in smooth brick. The corner entrance to the building, where the post office was located for many years, featured an arcade with large arches constructed of a lighter colored material — perhaps terra cotta — which complemented the darker brick color of the remainder of the building. The third story of the Julian Hotel burned in 1920 and was never replaced. The Julian Hotel was also a victim of the wrecking ball, meeting its fate in 1967. Today the location is the site of Heritage Plaza and the *Daily Democrat* Building.

Joseph J. Hall's architectural talent was further exemplified by his designs for two of Woodland's most picturesque Queen Anne homes, both constructed in 1892. These homes were very extroverted in appearance, with superb street appeal, reflecting the economic standing of their merchant owners. A two-story Queen Anne was built on the southeast corner of College and Laurel Streets for prosperous businessman, Marshall Diggs and his wife, Georgia *(fig. 38)*. The exuberant roofline of the house had many gables and dormers of varying sizes and heights and a dramatic Roman vaulted turret rising more than twenty feet above the second story. The front, wrap-around porch was decorated with splayed arch moldings and elaborately carved double doors were set back from an arched vestibule. Tragically, this home was badly damaged in a 1972 Christmas day fire that started in the chimney. The house was taken down and replaced by a new home that incorporates the old carriage house into the design.

38. Diggs House, 1892, Joseph Johnson Hall, architect, Samuel Caldwell, builder
courtesy Yolo County Archives

An equally impressive cottage version of this style of home, rendered by Hall for a grocer, T.S. Spaulding, was also built in 1892 at 638 First Street *(fig. 39)*. This lovely home is a *tour de force* in fine home building. It too features an assortment of gables, dormers and a balcony with a horseshoe opening. An amazing variety of moldings and surface textures decorate the front facade of the home. Grid-style moldings and rounded openings grace the wide sitting porch. This home was also severely burned by a fire in 1981 at a time when the home was run-down and used as a boarding house known by locals as Gilbert's Gables. The fire destroyed the entire second story.

Luckily, Woodlanders Judy Boyer and Joe Johnson saved the house from demolition and spent several years meticulously restoring the house, using historic photos to guide them. Their heroic restoration efforts were recognized in 1992 when the couple was awarded the National Trust for Historic Preservation's grand prize for the Great American Home Awards.

And what became of Joseph J. Hall? He left Woodland in 1896 destined for San Jose, once more a rambler. Whether or not he ever again practiced architecture is unknown. There are no known buildings of his in San Jose. An enigmatic figure, Hall had a few good years in Woodland capturing a slice of the California dream. He was a major figure in the revitalization of downtown Woodland. His architectural ideas were well received by a community that possessed a strong desire to develop a beautiful town and had the money and motivation to materialize those dreams.

39. Spaulding House, 1892, Joseph Johnson Hall, architect, William Henry Curson, builder
photo by Roger Klemm

William Henry Curson

An Immigrant, Builder, Commander, and Civic Leader

William Henry Curson
from *Woodland Daily Democrat*, May 16, 1922

William Henry Curson (1845-1922) — not to be confused with William Henry Carson! — was born in Lincolnshire, England in 1845 and came to America in 1865. Like many other immigrant carpenters, he worked his way across the continent. He served as an apprentice carpenter in Ohio, moved to Chicago after the big fire in 1871, and finally to San Francisco for about four years where he worked as a carpenter on the construction of the famous Palace Hotel.

About 1878 he arrived in Woodland and established a general contracting business. Curson was married in Woodland to Harriette Jane Wyckoff, daughter of Nicholas Wyckoff, a pioneer farmer of Yolo County. Curson had strong leadership skills and rose to prominence. In addition to his contracting business, "Major" Curson, as he was respectfully known, was one of the organizers of the Woodland National Guard unit, Company F, which he commanded for several years. He was also very active in civic affairs and elected to the City Board of Trustees.

Over the course of a long building career, Curson completed several prominent buildings, several of which have been restored. They include: the landmark Spaulding-Boyer-Johnson home at 638 First Street (1892), the Woodland Public Library (1905), and the Odd Fellows Hall at Third and Main Street (1905), a gracious Spanish style building with an arched arcade affording protection from the elements *(fig. 40)*. He was also the builder of the original Opera House (1885), and the Oak Street Grammar School (1889, *fig. 41*), now the site of Dingle School. Curson's home stood at 650 First Street, but was demolished. Today it is a vacant lot used as a garden. William Henry Curson died in Woodland in 1922.

40. Odd Fellows Hall, 1905, William Henry Curson
courtesy Yolo County Archives

41. Oak Street Grammar School, 1889, William H. Curson, builder, Willam H. Carson, architect
courtesy Yolo County Archives

Elmer H. Fisher and Daniel McPhee

Designer/Builder Partners on a First Street Palace

Elmer H. Fisher
Special Collections Division, *University of Washington Libraries Negative No.: UW 12609*

The July 24, 1890 edition of the *Yolo Democrat* reported that a wealthy Woodland couple, Edmund and Lucy Lowe, were constructing a "beautiful palatial residence" at 458 First Street. This large picturesque home incorporated the late Shingle style and Queen Anne with its intricate array of exterior shingled textures, stained glass windows and three-story octagonal tower *(fig. 42)*. The newspaper noted the architect for the house was a "Mr. Fisher, of Seattle" and the contractor was Daniel McPhee of Woodland.

According to Jeffrey Ochsner at the Department of Architecture, University of Washington, and editor of the book, *Shaping Seattle Architecture,* Elmer H. Fisher (ca.1840-1905) was a prolific Seattle architect at this time. Prior to opening an office in Seattle in 1888, Fisher designed three existing buildings on Water Street in Port Townsend, Washington. Born in Edinburgh, Scotland, Fisher immigrated to the United States as a young man and worked his way across the country with jobs in mining and construction. In 1886 Fisher moved to Victoria, British Columbia where he began his architecture business. He later settled in Seattle, striking it big in 1889 after a fire wiped out a large section of the city. Fisher is credited with designing approximately 50 buildings in Seattle during the rebuilding period between 1889-91, including the Romanesque Revival style Pioneer Building, the centerpiece of historic Pioneer Square.

With his windfall income Fisher developed and

42. Lowe House, 1890, Elmer H. Fisher, architect, Daniel McPhee, builder
courtesy Yolo County Archives

operated a Seattle hotel and sold his architecture practice in 1891. Unfortunately the economy went sour, the Panic of 1893 struck, and his real estate investment failed. Elmer Fisher eventually moved to Los Angeles to work for the architecture firm of John Parkinson, designers of the Los Angeles Coliseum and City Hall. He died in 1905, never regaining the glory of his Seattle years.

Prior to moving to Woodland, Daniel McPhee lived in Port Townsend, Washington where he evidently was acquainted with Elmer Fisher or knew of his work and talents. It is likely that McPhee contacted Fisher on behalf of the Lowes for the set of house plans. At the time he built the house, McPhee may have been engaged to the Lowe's daughter, Anna, for they were wed within months of the completion of the house.

McPhee was an active builder in Woodland for a few years, completing several other prominent buildings, including the Romanesque style Farmers & Merchants Bank (1894) at Second and Main designed by Joseph Hall (demolished), the Armory Building (1895) on Bush Street (demolished), and the Yolo County Savings Bank (1903) at College and Main designed by William Henry Weeks.

George Barber

Providing Mail Order House Designs, Even Building Material

Beginning about 1888, George Barber, of Knoxville, Tennessee, began to publish architectural pattern books featuring his house designs and available by mail throughout the United States. Thumbing through the pattern books, clients could select a house design, make changes using supplied graph paper, and (for a fee) be sent a complete set of construction plans and specifications from the Barber firm.

Barber's house plan books were published periodically from 1888 to about 1908. Most of his designs were variations of the Queen Anne style — picturesque, asymmetrical, with exuberant use of textures and moldings. His late designs began to incorporate more subdued elements of the Colonial Revival style. Many of the designs had alternate southern and northern specifications to respond to the client's geographical area and weather.

Barber's mail order business blossomed and, by the late 1890s, shipped over 1,000 house plans a month. Barber plans were implemented in all states of the Union and even in foreign countries. If the client preferred, Barber was able to ship all or some of the crated building materials by boxcar along with the building specifications direct to the customer's town.

There are two Barber-designed houses in Woodland, both built by the Keehn Brothers. Keehn's clients selected these homes from Barber's pattern book, *Modern Dwellings,* published in 1901. In 1903 Edward and Cecilia Leake, owners of the Woodland *Daily Democrat*, selected the Barber house plan Design 54: *A Suburban Beauty,* to be built on their lot at 547 Second Street *(fig. 43)*. The cost for the house was estimated at $1,800 to $2,000, which is probably considerably less than the house cost to build in Woodland during that time. Comparing the catalogue design to the finished product, the Leakes requested alterations to the front porch of the house, opting for a simplified gabled stoop instead the more elaborate wrap-around sitting porch.

In 1906 local hardware dealer, Reuben B. Cranston, contracted with the Keehn Bros. to build a Queen Anne-Colonial Revival hybrid at 610 First Street *(fig. 44)*. Listed in *Modern Dwellings* as Design 36 with the caption *Hard to Beat*, it is easy to see why this house was one of Barber's most popular designs. In Barber's promotional pitch for the house he stated:

It is hard to imagine a home more beautiful than this one from every point of view. It has been built in every state in the Union, thus showing its adaptability to all climates.

The house exterior is identical to the Barber design although, as local folklore would have it, Mr. Cranston was emphatic about not wanting an "old-fashioned" fireplace!

43. Leake House, 1903, George Barber, architect, Keehn Brothers, builder
photo by Roger Klemm

44. Cranston House, 1906, George Barber, architect, Keehn Brothers, builder
photo by Roger Klemm

Keehn Brothers

Five Brothers Responsible for Major Residential Achievements

Benedict "Ben" Keehn

Frank Keehn

William Keehn

John Keehn

August Keehn

photos courtesy Joe T. Keehn

During a lengthy career spanning the late Victorian period through the modern Craftsman-Bungalow era, the Keehn Brothers' design-building firm erected many quality homes and buildings in Woodland. Comprised of five brothers, born of Vinzent and Monica Rastetter Keehn, natives of Germany, the Keehn Bros. firm was very active in Woodland and surrounding Yolo County from 1891 through 1928.

The oldest son, Benedict "Ben" Keehn (1862-1928) was born in Maulch, Germany shortly before the family immigrated to the United States. The next eldest son, William (1867-1945), was born in Newark, New Jersey. The other three sons, Frank (1868-1957), John (1869-1940) and August (1872-1952) were all born and raised in Waynesburg, Ohio. Though in 1881 the family settled in Missouri, in 1887 Ben Keehn moved to California where he worked as a carpenter in Los Angeles and Colusa. At Colusa he helped build the convent for the Sisters of the Holy Cross, where he met Father Michael Wallrath, who at the time was pastor of Holy Rosary Church in Woodland. Ben Keehn visited Woodland and liked what he saw. After returning to Missouri briefly in 1891, Ben and the entire Keehn family moved to Woodland, lured by the California dream of prosperity.

The five brothers and one sister lived for a period with their parents at the Keehn family home now located at 327 Sixth Street *(fig. 45)*. Constructed in 1897, this large Carpenter Gothic home was originally located on the corner of Sixth and Main streets, but due to commercial growth along Main Street was moved north one lot to its present location.

By the late 1890s the Keehn Brothers contracting firm was a going concern. Each of the five brothers had complementary roles within the company. Ben, the oldest brother, ran the business and was also the designer and draftsman; William was skilled as an expert furniture maker and wood carver; Frank and John were all-around carpenters; and the youngest brother, Gus, made cabinets and operated the planing mill.

The City Planing Mill, owned by the Keehn

45. Keehn Family House, 1897, Keehn Brothers
courtesy Yolo County Archives

Brothers, was located at 430 Fifth Street between Main and Lincoln. The mill is shown on Sanborn Maps of the 1880s as a "dwelling" (more likely a storage shed) situated behind Sam Caldwell's planing mill on the southwest corner of Main Street. Caldwell died in 1896 and the Keehn Brothers bought the dwelling from his widow, Tina Caldwell, shortly thereafter and converted the structure into a planing mill *(fig. 46)*.

Two of the earliest houses built by the Keehn Brothers, the Leake family home at 547 Second Street (1903) and the restrained Queen Anne residence at 610 First Street for Reuben B. Cranston (1906), were the catalogue houses designed by the talented mail order architect, George Barber.

In 1905, a stately Colonial Revival manor was built for Thomas B. and Virginia Gibson at 311 Gibson Road, as the centerpiece of the sprawling Roselawn Stock Farm *(fig. 47)*. Set back from the roadway with a large yard and swaying palm trees, at one time this gracious home was surrounded by acres of land. A similar style home of the period was built for lumberman J.J. Brown at 804 College Street (1904).

The Keehn Brothers were versatile, designing and building a variety of houses, including the first Crafts-

46. Gus Keehn at City Planing Mill
courtesy Joe T. Keehn

47. Gibson House "Roselawn", 1905, Keehn Brothers
photo by Roger Klemm

man style home in Woodland for prominent local physician, Dr. Fred Fairchild, at 754 College Street (1910, *fig. 48*). The design for this home closely resembles a house plan Gustav Stickley published in the *Craftsman* magazine in 1909. Other fine examples of Craftsman style homes completed by the Keehn Brothers include: the Alexander House (1910) at 152 First Street, which has a unique facade with paired Tuscan columns, the Alge House (1911) at 429 First Street *(fig. 49)*, and the Johnston House (1914) at 630 Elm Street.

In addition to many homes, the Keehn Brothers completed prestigious institutional structures. The Holy Rosary Academy contracted with the Keehn Brothers to construct a new three-story addition to the campus on Main Street to be used for administrative offices and an entertainment hall (1912). From plans drawn by architect William H. Weeks, the Keehn Brothers partnered with Woodland contractor William Henry Curson to construct the classic Mission Revival style Primary School at 175 N. Walnut Street (1915).

Keehn Brothers also constructed two downtown commercial buildings. The original Electric Garage Building (1910) at 801 Main Street, since enlarged and remodeled, and the French Laundry Building (1914) at 927 Main Street.

48. Dr. Fred Fairchild House, 1910, Keehn Brothers
from *Yolo in Word & Picture, Woodland Daily Democrat* 1920
courtesy Yolo County Archives

49. Alge House, 1911, Keehn Brothers
photo by Roger Klemm

When Ben Keehn died in 1928 at the age of 65, the Keehn Brothers firm was dissolved. Frank Keehn moved that year to San Francisco to manage an apartment complex and died in 1957. John Keehn died in 1940 and William Keehn in 1945. The youngest brother, Gus Keehn, continued to operate the family planing mill until it was sold in 1944 to William "Bill" Phillips. Gus lived at the old Keehn family home on Sixth Street until his death in 1952.

Evolution of a Planing Mill:

Making the Materials that Made the Structures

The City Planing Mill, started by the Keehn Brothers in the 1890s and operated by Gus Keehn until 1944, is the oldest surviving planing mill in Woodland, dating to the Victorian era when several local mills were in operation. Bill Phillips, who established himself in the local milling trade through stints at the Burnett & Sons planing mill in Sacramento (still in operation today) and association with Joseph Motroni in Woodland, purchased the mill on Fifth Street from the Keehn estate in 1944 after Gus Keehn retired *(fig. 50)*.

At the time he purchased the Keehn mill, Phillips was well known among builders in Woodland as a businessman, having run Motroni's mill on Beamer Street for a few years under a lease arrangement. After signing the lease agreement with Motroni, Phillips renamed the shop "Phillip's Planing Mill," much to the chagrin of Motroni. The lease arrangement with Motroni was not working smoothly, so Phillips purchased the Keehn mill, moved across town, and cut his ties with Motroni.

Through the 1940's and 1950s, Phillip's Planing Mill churned out window sash, stairs, doors, screens, casings and modest amounts of cabinetwork for builders in Woodland. Phillips made improvements to the building, adding a new stucco facade and an addition to the front of the old wooden structure. L. Scovel became the proprietor of the mill in the early 1950s, apparently leasing the facility from Phillips.

One of Phillips' employees during his tenure as a planing mill owner was a young man named Ray Colombara who started working for Phillips in 1944 as a boy at Motroni's mill. Born in Illinois in 1931, Ray Colombara moved with his family to Woodland in 1932 after Ray's father, John Colombara, read in a "help wanted" ad in an Italian newspaper circulated in Illinois that someone named Motroni in Woodland, California needed a carpenter. In 1955 Phillips sold the planing mill business to his former employee, Ray Colombara, by now a seasoned mill operator himself.

Seizing the opportunity afforded by the strong growth in post WWII home building in Woodland, Colombara purchased properties on Fourth Street behind the old mill to expand the business. By now, the focus of the milling operation had changed to cabinetwork, as home builders were now specifying more elaborate built-in cabinets for the contemporary homes of the 1960s.

Today, the old mill building functions as a storage facility, but remains a visible reminder of the long tradition of locally operated planing mills. The mills were crucial in the development of Woodland since they provided many of the wooden building materials needed for construction. They were local outlets for building products long before the advent of mass-

50. Planing Mill on Fifth Street (still standing)
courtesy Ray Colombara

produced and mass- marketed materials. They also enabled local builders to customize their houses through the production of differently designed brackets, friezes, doors, and moldings. And, significantly, they were symbolic of the ingenuity and all-around skill of local contractors who not only constructed the buildings, but also designed and manufactured the materials necessary for the task.

John Walter Dolliver
from *Commercial Encyclopedia of the Southwest* by E. Davis, ed., 1911
San Francisco Public Library

Dodge & Dolliver

Designers of a Classic Carnegie Library

The Woodland Public Library is among the few Carnegie-funded library buildings still in operation in California. Many have been replaced by larger, modern facilities in communities across the state. Woodland's Mission Revival style library was built in several phases. The original structure, with the entrance on First Street, was completed in 1905 *(fig. 51)*. Mission Revival architectural elements include the tile roof, a shaped parapet above the main entrance with star-shaped quatrefoil and arched windows. There is a rotunda in the front lobby. In 1915 the Yolo County Library added a west wing with an entrance on Court Street. In 1927-29 there was another expansion and in 1985 voters approved a $2.5 million expansion, including the Leake Room and an interior courtyard.

The architect for the first phase of the library was the San Francisco firm of Dodge & Dolliver. The short-lived partnership of John Walter Dolliver (b. 1868) and George Allen Dodge lasted from 1903 to 1905. During this period the firm completed two Bay Area landmarks: the Romanesque-style San Mateo

51. Woodland Public Library, 1905, Dodge & Dolliver, architect, William Henry Curson, builder
courtesy Yolo County Archives

County Courthouse in Redwood City (1904) and the rustic St. John's Presbyterian Church at the corner of Sacramento and Arguello in San Francisco (1905). Little is known about George Dodge. A short biography of John Dolliver appeared in the *Commercial Encyclopedia of the Southwest* in 1911. Born in San Francisco, Dolliver studied architecture in Europe, graduating from the Polytechnic Institute of Munich in 1890. After practicing architecture in Boston and Milwaukee, he returned to San Francisco in 1900. After splitting up with partner Dodge, he practiced architecture independently.

Meyer & O'Brien

Accomplished Designers of a Timeless Georgian Revival Home

Frederick H. Meyer
from *The Architect and Engineer of California,* October 1909, *California History Section, California State Library*

Smith O'Brien
from *Commercial Encyclopedia of the Southwest* by E. Davis, ed., 1911 *California History Section, California State Library*

America's interest in the Colonial style of architecture revived around the time of the Centennial of 1876 held in Philadelphia. In anticipation of the milestone, articles began appearing in national magazines in the 1870s with illustrations of Colonial architecture. Although the Colonial Revival movement was partly born of nostalgia, it also tapped a deeper need in the American psyche, shaped by decades of urbanism and industrialization, for a return to a simpler and more natural lifestyle. The wide halls, masonry hearths, and low-beamed ceilings of the colonial style appealed with their sense of coziness and rusticity. The Georgian version of the colonial style was popular in American for most of the 18th century. The style emphasized classical details of the Italian Renaissance.

The Georgian Revival style reached Woodland in 1905 when the San Francisco firm of Meyer and O'Brien designed the elegant three-story house at 618 First Street for prosperous farmer Thomas R. Lowe *(fig. 52)*. Classical detailing is seen in the grand entrance with the balustrade and double columns and the dentil course beneath the cornice. The design is very ordered, with tight symmetrical spacing between the pedimented dormer attic windows and shuttered windows on the front of the house. A centered, second story Palladian window and doorway lead out to a balcony above the front entrance.

Frederick H. Meyer (1876-1961) and Smith O'Brien (b. 1858) were in partnership between 1902 and 1908. During this period the firm completed many large office buildings in downtown San Francisco, including the Monadnock Building at 685 Market Street and the Humboldt Bank Building at 783-85 Market Street.

Frederick H. Meyer was an accomplished San Francisco architect and planner of his era. He collaborated with John Galen Howard and John Reid, Jr. on the overall 1912 master plan for the San Francisco Civic Center. The Civic Center stands as an outstanding example of the "City Beautiful Movement," the offspring of a program developed at the influential Ecole des Beaux Arts in Paris. This modern urban planning program emphasized groupings of government buildings designed in the European Classical Revival style with public squares, fountains, landscaping, and broad avenues.

In addition to his involvement on the Civic Cen-

52. Thomas R. Lowe House, 1905, Meyer & O'Brien
photo by Roger Klemm

ter master plan, Meyer also collaborated on the design of one of the early Civic Center Beaux Arts buildings, the Civic Auditorium in 1913 (remodeled in 1964). A noted building that Meyer designed for a small town is the Beaux Arts style, terra cotta-clad Bank of America building in Red Bluff.

Smith O'Brien was born in Ireland in 1858, but immigrated to the United States where he attended college. Arriving in San Francisco in 1887, he went to work for prominent architect Clinton Day. In 1902 he formed the partnership with Frederick Meyer, and after the partnership dissolved in 1908, O'Brien worked independently.

William S. White

A Long Distinguished Career as a Designer, Builder, and Civic Leader

A native of New Brunswick, Canada, William S. White (1848-1936) apprenticed as a carpenter in Boston before moving to California in 1875. After stops in Napa and Solano counties he arrived in Woodland in 1878 and was hired by Sam Caldwell as a construction foreman. His brother, Charles, also lived in Woodland where he operated a planing mill and ran a contracting business, Glenn & White.

William S. White from *Grand Court Foresters of America,* May 1909, *courtesy Yolo County Archives*

William White worked for Caldwell for six years, building an array of houses and buildings in Woodland. He also built his first personal residence in 1882, a two-story Victorian in the Second Empire or Mansard style at 609 Third Street *(fig. 53)*. This style is characterized by a short second story with a curved exterior and dormer windows, as popularized by French architects. The first story has a small porch and front bay window. While several houses in the Second Empire style were built in Woodland in the 1870s, including Sam Caldwell's personal residence, White's is the lone survivor of the style.

After leaving Caldwell about 1884, White worked for a short stint for his brother's contracting company, Glenn & White, before he and his wife, Imogene, moved to Tehama County and farmed for about ten years. Returning to Woodland about 1896, he purchased the Ever Ready Planing Mill established by Glenn & White. Eventually, White converted the machine shop into more of a retail establishment, called the Cash Lumber Yard at 422 Elm Street.

White was a man of many interests and abilities. A dedicated designer, he kept up with the latest fashions in architecture. In addition to his building and lumber businesses, he was active in civic affairs and was elected to the Woodland Board of Trustees, serving from 1907 to 1911.

Of greatest importance to his career, White designed and constructed several houses in Woodland in the Shingle style, a progressive style of residential architecture popularized on the East Coast in the 1880s. Illustrations of Shingle style houses by trend setting architects were published in architectural periodicals of the era that White probably read. White's second personal residence at 437 Walnut Street (1905) featured a large front gable, characteristic of the style, and an exterior clad in wooden shingles with very little adornment or surface textures *(fig. 54)*. Unfortunately, today White's house is virtually unrecognizable: its shingles are covered with synthetic siding.

In 1908, compared to his personal residence, White constructed a more upscale variation of the Shingle

53. White House, 1882, William S. White
courtesy Yolo County Archives

54. White House, 1905, William S. White
courtesy Yolo County Archives

55. Hyman House, 1908, William S. White
photo by Roger Klemm

style for William and Gertrude Hyman at 639 First Street *(fig. 55)*. A long-time principal at Woodland High School, Hyman's intellectual bent likely drew him to the latest architectural fashions promoted by his designer-builder, White. A large, shingled gable dominates the massing of the Hyman house. Further, White included diamond-shaped windows on the gable to complement a shallow bay window; this playful use of glass is carried to the half-wide sitting porch where small rectangular windows adorn each side of the front door.

Another notable house constructed by White in the Shingle style is the Dungan house located at 637 Second Street. This house has the archetypal large gable spanning the front of the shingle-clad house, with centered double-hung windows flanked by tiny ornamental rectangular windows. The sides of the roof have large recessed gabled dormers that mimic the front gable and shed dormers. The lower story, finished in shiplap siding, has a half-width porch with one simple column and an assortment of window shapes.

In 1910 White constructed a Craftsman style Unitarian Church on Lincoln Street, with plans provided by Napa architect Luther Turton. William and wife Imogene were both members of the Unitarian Church.

White retired from the building business in 1923 and died at home in 1936, three days shy of his 88th birthday. He and Imogene had been married for 64 years.

Luther M. Turton

Accomplished Napa Architect
Recruited For Woodland Sanitarium

Luther M. Turton
courtesy Napa Historical Society

Luther Mark Turton (1862-1925) was Napa's foremost architect of the late 19th and early 20th century. Opening his office in the city of Napa in 1887, he is credited with designing several early commercial and school buildings. Several of his buildings have been preserved, contributing significantly to Napa's historic core area. Born in Nebraska, Turton's family settled in Napa

56. Unitarian Church, 1910, Luther M. Turton, architect, William S. White, builder
courtesy Yolo County Archives

in 1876 where he attended Napa College and then completed a two-year architect apprenticeship at the offices of B. McDougall & Sons in San Francisco.

In 1910 the Woodland Unitarian Church commissioned Turton to design a new church to be located at 417 Lincoln Street *(fig. 56)*. The church was designed in the Craftsman style, with heavy exposed wooden beams, low slanted gables and clad in wooden shingles. The church had a gabled front entrance complementing the sweeping gabled roofline, with a generous use of elbow brackets supporting the many gables on the building. The dormer windows that barely projected from the roof accentuated the flatness of the building. The facade of the building featured large round rosette windows in addition to the gabled vertical windows. Simple unadorned steps flowed out from the front entrance.

The Town & Country Club substantially remodeled the former Unitarian Church in 1941. The large round windows were removed and the front facade was extended. As the building aged, the exterior wooden shingles were covered with synthetic siding and painted contemporary colors. The interior of the building, however, retains its warm, natural wood appearance.

In 1911 Turton was selected to design the new Woodland Sanitarium. The project was the vision of four Woodland physicians, Fred Fairchild, his brother Chester Fairchild, Hiram Lawhead, and William Blevins, Sr., who merged practices to form the Woodland Clinic Medical Group. Before constructing the modern 1911 building, the physicians practiced at a converted house located at 110 College Street. This location marks where the Woodland Sanitarium began

57. Woodland Sanitarium, 1911, Luther M. Turton
Courtesy David Herbst

in 1907 when registered nurse Kathleen McConnell started the hospital.

Built on the northwest corner of Third and Cross streets, Turton's Mission Revival style design for the Woodland Sanitarium had an informal, non-institutional appearance *(fig. 57)*. The building, costing about $15,000 and looking more like a large house than a hospital, conveyed an inviting and relaxed ambience and yet was designed to allow for future expansion. The first floor housed the operating tables and rooms for up to 20 patients while the second story provided private rooms for nurses and attendants, plus a kitchen serving the first floor via a dumb waiter. Turton used wooden pergolas to shade the front entrance of the building and the roof garden where patients could get fresh air.

In 1928 this structure was replaced by a larger hospital. A three story concrete structure was designed by the William Weeks firm and used as the community's main hospital until a new facility was built in 1967 on Gibson Road.

William Henry Weeks

Big City Sophistication on a Small Town Budget

William Henry Weeks
from Betty Lewis, *W. H. Weeks, Architect (Fresno, 1985)*

Between 1890 and 1930 the prolific architectural firm of William Henry Weeks (1862-1936) designed hundreds of remarkably pleasing and enduring buildings primarily in small towns throughout northern and central California, including several landmark Woodland buildings. Weeks was born in Prince Edward Island, Canada. He graduated from Brinker Institute in Denver, Colorado and in 1885 started his professional career with his father in Wichita, Kansas. He subsequently practiced architecture in Seattle, Watsonville, Palo Alto, and Oakland before permanently locating his office in San

Francisco in 1905. He practiced architecture there until his death in 1936.

In 1915 the trade journal, *The Architect and Engineer,* praised Weeks' unique ability to design buildings of high quality and taste for the small town market:

> *Mr. Weeks is essentially the architect of the plain citizen — the average owner, whether he has individual or collective corporate existence. For such owners architectural problems are direct and simple. Plans must serve very plain and practical ends and in all cases design must be well within the scope of local craftsmanship. Above all, cost must not exceed appropriation. An architect who has the experience to command confidence can, if he chooses, practically dictate the style of design. And hence it is that with his enormous experience Mr. Weeks has been able to overcome the questionable standards of much small-town work and achieve the surprising successes . . . Indeed, we can have no hesitation in saying that such a leaven of excellently planned and cleanly designed buildings throughout the state must have exerted a wonderful influence for good and helped other architects noticeably to attain higher standards by far than usually prevail in smaller cities (p. 49).*

Indeed, the first building designed by Weeks in Woodland, the Yolo County Savings Bank (1903), added a touch of class to the prominent northwest corner of Main and College streets *(fig. 58).* A banking group headed by wealthy businessman, Adelbert D. Porter, developed this sandstone Romanesque style building. The upper story, used for offices, had many arched Tiffany-type glass windows and the roofline was capped by a cornice and balustrade. Tuscan marble columns flanked ornate copper doors at the corner entrance of the bank. In 1914 the building was extensively remodeled with the corner entrance shifted to the present Main Street side.

In 1913 Weeks designed the elegant three-story Porter Office building located across the street from the Yolo County Savings Bank at 511 Main Street. The building was developed by the Porter family and named in honor of A.D. Porter, who died before the

58. Yolo County Savings Bank, 1903, William H. Weeks, architect, Daniel McPhee, builder
courtesy Yolo County Archives

building was completed. The exterior of this Renaissance Revival style landmark is crafted of buff-colored thin Roman brick with matte glaze terra cotta architectural details and prismatic glass transom windows. Pilasters divide the window bays, while the cornice is particularly decorative, layered with a dentil course, brackets, and garlands. An elaborate arched entrance leads to the front lobby *(fig. 59).* The building was innovative for its era, boasting several "technological firsts" for Woodland, such as an electric elevator, steam heating system, and telephone service to each office.

Weeks was a noted designer of an impressive number of school buildings scattered throughout northern California. His schools were recognized for their beauty and innovative features. Weeks' designs for several Woodland schools, financed largely with local bond measures, established Woodland as a community with modern school facilities unsurpassed by any town its size in California.

Weeks' Renaissance Revival style Woodland High School building (1913) replaced the old Hesperian College that had been converted to Woodland's first

59. Entrance to Porter Building, 1913, William H. Weeks
photo by Roger Klemm

public high school *(fig. 60)*. The striking Mission Revival style Woodland Primary School (1915), located at 175 N. Walnut Street, features twin bell towers and a courtyard *(fig. 61)*. Weeks' handsome brick and terra cotta Woodland Grammar School (1924) on Elm Street was the first in the United States to feature inclines in place of stairs *(fig. 62)*. The High School and Grammar School (later re-named Dingle School) were both demolished in the early 1970s due to earthquake safety deficiencies. The Primary School building survived and has been used by both the Woodland School District and Yolo County Superintendent of Schools for offices.

The Woodland crown jewel of the Weeks firm, the Yolo County Courthouse, was built in 1917 to replace the original 1864 Courthouse *(fig. 63)*. A county-wide bond measure raised $200,000, although the project ended up costing about $300,000. The Renaissance Revival design, constructed by contractor Robert Trost of San Francisco, is a masterwork of architectural terra cotta.

Between February and October of 1917, the Gladding, McBean terra cotta plant in Lincoln, California shipped 14,860 pieces of terra cotta to Woodland where tile setters attached and grouted the pieces onto the shell of the building creating a sculpted image of Romanesque inspired architecture. Between the granite base of the building and the second story parapet, tile setters fitted the intricate tile pieces into columns with elaborate capitals, pilasters, and cornices. The columned entrance to the building has a cornice with figures of two Roman soldiers and two robed women who symbolize the classical virtues of law and justice.

In 1918 five hundred additional pieces of Gladding, McBean terra cotta were shipped to Woodland to build the balustrade and seats in front of the Yolo County Courthouse.

Upon completion, this beautiful building attracted the attention of many architects and builders throughout California and the nation, becoming a showcase project for Gladding, McBean. The courthouse was refurbished in the 1990s and is now listed on the National Register of Historic Places.

By 1920 the Woodland Sanitarium had outgrown its facility built in 1911 at the northwest corner of Third and Cross Streets. Woodland's steady population growth, the need for long-term care beds, and the regional draw of the hospital, the result of its outstanding reputation, necessitated enlarging the Sanitarium to triple its initial capacity.

60. Woodland High School, 1913, William H. Weeks
courtesy Yolo County Archives

Weeks' design for the enlarged Sanitarium incorporated Luther Turton's original 1911 Spanish-style building into the overall plan. Weeks' new plan was Spanish Colonial Revival in appearance. The main entrance was in the two-story administration building fronting Third Street, possibly finished in stucco, with either a concrete or terra cotta classical entrance of arches and pilasters; the classical detailing extended to the second story adorned with a cartouche. North and south patient wings flanked the administration building, while the south wing overlaid the remodeled 1911 building. Extending along the entire east frontage of these wings was a glassed-in sun porch, with each one of the 14 rooms on the east side having access to this space by French doors. This format enabled every patient to enjoy sun and outside air or gain the privacy of a shaded room without being removed from bed or disturbing others.

A trellised sun deck was retained on the south wing as a holdover from the 1911 building. A courtyard was placed in the center of the Sanitarium for the same enjoyment as those patients on the central wing. Weeks himself, whose firm was responsible for designing hundreds of buildings throughout northern California, considered this 1920 medical facility outstanding, the best-appointed private hospital in California at the time.

Of significance historically, the Woodland Clinic represented the vanguard of the national "group practice" movement originated by the Mayo Clinic in Minnesota. According to Eleanor Fait, daughter of William Fait, who constructed the facility, Dr. Charles

61. Woodland Primary School, 1915, William H. Weeks, architect, William H. Curson & Keehn Brothers, builders
photo by Roger Klemm

62. Woodland Grammar School, 1924, William H. Weeks
courtesy Yolo County Archives

63. Yolo County Courthouse, 1917, William H. Weeks
courtesy Yolo County Archives

Mayo visited Woodland several times to consult with Clinic doctors and contractor Fait during construction of the Woodland Sanitarium.

In 1922 an office building for the Woodland Clinic was erected at the north end of the Sanitarium on Third Street. In 1928 another major expansion occurred when a three-story hospital wing was built on the corner of Third and Cross partially replacing the 1911 building. The Weeks firm also designed this simplified Classical Revival structure *(fig. 64)*.

During the 1930s the name of the Woodland Sanitarium was changed to the Woodland Clinic Hospital and again in the 1960s to the Woodland Memorial Hospital, by now a non-profit facility. With the exception of the 1928 three-story building, today functioning as a skilled nursing facility, all other portions of the Sanitarium have been demolished. A larger, modern hospital was completed on Gibson Road in 1967.

In 1920 a keen interest developed among a group of Woodland business people to build a new upscale hotel. An investment group was formed to offer subscriptions for stock ownership in the new venture. When substantial funds began to accumulate, approaching the threshold necessary to construct the hotel, Weeks was brought in to develop preliminary plans. Although this hotel never materialized, the idea would resurface in a few years with Weeks as the key figure.

The Woodland Elks Club commissioned Weeks to design a new facility at 500 Bush Street in 1926. Designed in a subtle, restrained Mediterranean Revival style with Moorish features, the elegant building has

64. Woodland Clinic Hospital (left) and Clinic Facilities, 1920-22-28, William H. Weeks
courtesy Yolo County Archives

a grand, segmented arched entrance repeated on the upper windows with decorative grills evoking Moorish imagery. The building is finished with a rustic stucco in a soft earth tone and a tile roof.

By 1928, with its reputation as an idyllic rural community rippling throughout the state, Woodland thrived as a stopping point for tourists and hunters. This prosperity again inspired plans for a new upscale hotel, like that envisioned in 1920 but never built. The consequence would be the Hotel Woodland, representing William Weeks' last, major project in the small town that over a 25-year relationship had benefited greatly from his talents *(fig. 65)*.

The Hotel was developed by the Weeks Securities Corporation, organized by Weeks in 1928 and capitalized by private stock offerings. The Weeks Securities Company developed several hotels in northern California during this period, including the Durant in Berkeley, the DeAnza in San Jose, the Resetar in Watsonville, and the Palomar in Santa Cruz. About 50 Woodland businesses and individuals invested in the Hotel Woodland, raising 10% of the total $500,000 estimated to construct the building.

The Hotel Woodland was designed in the popular Spanish Colonial Revival style, sometimes referred to as the *Churrigueresque* style. A derivative of Mex-

65. Hotel Woodland, 1928, William H. Weeks
courtesy Yolo County Archives

ican ecclesiastical architecture, the Spanish Colonial style was popularized in North America beginning with architect Nathaniel Goodhue's California State Building for the Panama-California Exposition held in 1915-16 in Balboa Park in San Diego.

Although offering a simplified commercial form in the Spanish Colonial Revival style, the Hotel Woodland exhibits *Churrigueresque* detailing with the festively painted cut-stone moldings bunched together around the upper arched window of the central tower of the building. The scrolled moldings adorning the scalloped-shaped roofline of the hotel and the oval wrought-iron balconies evoke a gracious Hispanic ambience. The clay tile roof and decorative spiral columns adorning the entryway of the hotel and the light-colored smooth exterior complete the Mexican imagery. The 2,000 square-foot lobby featured beamed, stenciled ceilings, wrought-iron chandeliers, a large fireplace, and cement floor resembling Mexican tile.

The Hotel became the quality destination spot for visitors and gathering place for important community functions and celebrations; its grandeur and prominent location on Main Street — as well as its expense, size, and beauty — created a major focal point, transforming the character of downtown.

There are hundreds of Weeks buildings scattered throughout northern and central California in small towns, with a large concentration in Watsonville where William Weeks lived and worked during the early part of his career. Weeks' impact on Woodland's physical character was immense in terms of the quality and quantity of public and commercial buildings he designed. The Weeks story demonstrates how the physical character of Woodland was significantly upgraded when local vision, inspiration, and capital were combined with the talents of a superior architect. Weeks' career was remarkable, considering he started out in a small town (Watsonville) and, by the time of his death in 1936, his firm was one of the oldest and largest in California, with sizeable offices in Oakland and San Francisco.

Ira Wilson Hoover

Partner of Julia Morgan Designs Stylish Woodland Bank

The rumor on Woodland's Main Street is that Julia Morgan, the famous Berkeley architect of Hearst Castle fame, designed the old Bank of Yolo in Woodland, since remodeled into 1960s blandness. Fact or fiction? While there is truth of an indirect connection between this venerable bank and Morgan, the architect who stepped off the Southern Pacific train in Woodland in 1907 with a set of blueprints under his arm was a more obscure architect: Ira Wilson Hoover (1871-1941).

Hoover knew Morgan well, and in fact the two young architects were partners from 1904 to 1910 before Hoover moved to Pittsburg. Morgan then pursued a brilliant solo career, famous for her design of the noted California landmarks, Hearst Castle and Asilomar Conference Center, and many beautiful houses and buildings in the Bay Area. In 1907, when Hoover was summoned by Bank of Yolo principals to design a new financial temple at 500 Main Street in Woodland, Hoover and Morgan were young, idealistic, and just a few years removed from apprenticeships with John Galen Howard, the founder of the influential School of Architecture at the University of California, Berkeley.

It is unclear whether Morgan and Hoover were acting as partners on the Bank of Yolo project. Woodland press reports during the time do not mention the firm of Morgan & Hoover and only refer to Hoover as the architect. He is praised as an architect "with a national reputation," a bit of hyperbole, but indicative of the prestige associated with the selection of a reputable Bay Area firm. Neither Hoover, nor Morgan boasted much of national reputation at this early stage of their careers; that belonged to their mentor, John Galen Howard.

Hoover was a draftsman for John Galen Howard

66. Bank of Yolo, 1907, Main Street view, Ira W. Hoover

67. Bank of Yolo, College Street view

in Philadelphia before moving to Berkeley in 1903 to rejoin the man who had settled in as the chief architect at the University of California. Howard was a superbly trained architect who attracted the first wave of talented young artists, who converged on Berkeley to study and train with him before opening their own architectural firms. A graduate of the Massachusetts Institute of Technology, Howard also studied at the prestigious Ecole des Beaux-Arts in Paris. Before his move to Berkeley, he worked for famous firms on the East Coast, including the offices of Henry Hobson Richardson and McKim Mead and White. Founding the School of Architecture at U.C. Berkeley in 1903, Howard was the chief architect for the Berkeley campus from 1902 to 1924.

Born in Oberlin, Ohio, Hoover distinguished himself at the School of Architecture, University of Pennsylvania, where he graduated in 1900. In 1901 he studied at the American Academy in Rome, funded by a John Sewardson Memorial Traveling Scholarship in Architecture. Upon returning to America, he worked briefly for firms in New York and Chicago before moving to Berkeley to work for Howard's firm, then became busy designing new buildings for the University of California campus. Julia Morgan was also an assistant of Howard during this time. In 1904 Morgan and Hoover left Howard to start their own firm known as Morgan & Hoover.

68. Bank of Yolo,
Interior
All photos from
The Brickbuilder and Architectural Monthly,
December 1911
courtesy Bill McCandless

So, Hoover arrived on the scene in rural Woodland in 1907 with solid credentials and worldly experience. Not surprisingly, his design for the Bank of Yolo was very progressive for its day *(fig. 66-68)*. Hoover's inspiration for the bank was heavily influenced by the style of the nationally prominent Chicago architect, Louis Sullivan, whose designs of bank buildings in small mid-western towns qualify as classics of American architecture. Having worked in Chicago, Hoover had first-hand knowledge of Sullivan's work.

The cubic massing and thick walls employed by Hoover on the Bank of Yolo evoked an image of strength and security, yet the building's turnstile entrance under a large Roman arch was inviting from Main Street. Marble steps led up to the front entrance, flanked by marble columns and the single story building had thirty-foot ceilings. Building materials specified by Hoover were imaginative and artistic, as the base was granite with terra cotta bricks extending to the windows. The woodwork of the cornice was stained a golden brown, with green-colored terra cotta blocks beneath and a Mexican tile covering. The terra cotta architectural moldings surrounding the large arched windows were manufactured by Gladding, McBean in Lincoln, California. The Gladding, McBean purchase order specified that the terra cotta was "gray speckled" to match the brick furnished by Steiger Pottery and Terra Cotta Works.

Photos and architectural drawings of the Yolo Bank were published in the December 1911 edition of *The Brickbuilder and Architectural Monthly*, a building trade periodical published in Boston.

When the terra cotta-clad Classical Porter Building (1913) and the Spanish Colonial Revival Hotel Woodland (1928) joined the Romanesque Yolo County Savings Bank (1905) and elegant Bank of Yolo at the intersection of College and Main, Woodlanders could revel in the beauty and charm of top-notch small-town architecture. These four works of art remained intact for a couple of generations.

The Bank of Yolo was dissolved during the Great Depression, but other banks used the building for many years, including Bank of America. In 1961 Hoover's design was lost forever when the building was completely modernized into its current configuration. Fortunately, the other three local landmarks have survived fickle public taste and the economic vicissitudes of the last century, although the Porter Building awaits a new facelift on the order of the Hotel Woodland.

And what became of Ira Hoover? After moving to Pittsburgh, Pennsylvania in 1910 for a short period, he returned to Chicago and worked with the accomplished architect, Charles S. Frost, for five years. After World War I, Hoover moved back to California, designing buildings in Fresno and Merced. In 1924 he moved to Los Angeles where he practiced until his death in 1941.

Although Hoover never designed another building in Yolo County, Julia Morgan designed at least one house in Yolo County: a small shingled cottage at 215 Rice Lane near the U.C. Davis campus is attributed to her firm.

William C. Hays

The Creator of St. Luke's: A Woodland Crown Jewel with a Gothic Lineage

William C. Hays
courtesy St. Luke's Episcopal Church

The rustic, Gothic-revival style St. Luke's Episcopal Church has graced 515 Second Street in Woodland since 1912. Designed by prominent Berkeley architect, William Charles Hays (1874-1963), the church is a fine example of the medieval tradition of melding woodcarving, stained glass, and natural materials into an organic and inspired whole. Berkeley contractor, P.N. Schmidt, built the church.

Nineteenth century English art and social critic John Ruskin and artist William Morris were influential in reviving interest in the arts and crafts techniques and in Gothic imagery. Hays had first hand knowledge of medieval architecture, having studied in Europe and he employed Gothic design and arts and crafts details in designing this beautiful small church, modeled after the original Anglican Church in Amer-

69. Artist's sketch of St. Luke's Episcopal Church from the *Yolo Semi-Weekly Mail,* April 19, 1912, pg.1

ica built in Smithfield, Virginia in 1632 *(fig. 69-70).*

The exterior is constructed of brick with pilasters between the exterior windows. A rectangular-shaped bell tower, positioned at the edge of the Second Street frontage, has an arched main entrance with double doors. Woodcarvings in the Gothic tradition decorate the rear gable and the interior exhibits a rich display of wood craftsmanship with intricate ceiling and pews. In 1922 three stained glass windows, created by the world-famous Louis Tiffany Studios, were installed above the altar to replace the original windows. Rose Nelson purchased these beautiful windows in memory of her husband, Charles Q. Nelson. Another stained glass window, made by Cummings Studio, was added to the church in 1952, followed by four more in 1966, all from the Geo. Payne Studios. Finally in 1974, the remaining six windows were replaced by stained glass from the Exeter Studios. St. Luke's parish had the Tiffany windows restored in the 1990s, and the church and grounds as a whole are beautifully maintained.

The Guild Hall, following the Tudor Revival style of design, was added to the main part of the church in 1928. Its designer was Woodland resident C. Carleton Pierson and the builder was Joseph Motroni. In 1929 Woodland contractor Brown & Woodhouse built the Rectory in the Tudor Revival style with half-timbering wood decoration. The latest addition to St. Luke's was the Great Hall and Education complex built in 1955. The architect was Constable & Constable of Sausalito.

In recognition of the outstanding architecture and the history of the church in the community, St. Luke's Episcopal Church was designated a City of Woodland Historical Landmark in 1993.

Born in Philadelphia, Hays graduated from the University of Pennsylvania and did post-graduate study in Rome and Paris. Like several other leading young architects who contributed to Berkeley's noted regional architecture, Hays came to Berkeley in 1904 to work under the noted architect, John Galen Howard.

In 1908 Hays opened his own business and began a distinguished career. In addition to his private practice, he also taught architecture at U.C. Berkeley for many years. From 1918-1923 he was the Supervising Architect for the City of Berkeley School District and designed Thousand Oaks Elementary School in 1919.

As the Supervising Architect for the University of California, Davis from about 1927 to 1940, Hays designed several other Yolo County buildings. His

70. St. Luke's Episcopal Church, 1912, William C. Hays
courtesy St. Luke's Episcopal Church

contributions to this campus include the Moderne/Spanish Revival style George Hart Hall (1928), a picturesque building on the Quad. Hart Hall had a narrow escape from destruction in the 1980s, but was saved by a concerned group of people and eventually rehabilitated by the University. Other U.C. Davis buildings designed by Hays are Walker Hall (1927), Hickey Gymnasium (1938) and several utilitarian structures.

There are several good examples of Hays' work in the Bay Area, including Giannini Hall at U.C. Berkeley, the Old First Church in San Francisco on the corner of Van Ness and Sacramento, and the First Presbyterian Church in Oakland at 27th & Broadway. William Hays died in Berkeley in 1963.

Arthur D. Nicholson

The Two Lives of the Train Depot: Once Created, Then Recreated

Arthur D. Nicholson from *Commercial Encyclopedia of the Southwest* by E. Davis, ed., 1911 *California History Section, California State Library*

On July 4, 1912 Woodlanders had more to celebrate than just Independence Day. On this day the first electric train connecting Woodland with Sacramento rolled into the new "Vallejo & Northern Railroad Co." depot on the southwest corner of Main and Second streets *(fig. 71)*. The Sacramento and Woodland Railroad, a subsidiary of the Northern Electric Railroad Company, built the line connecting Woodland with Sacramento. The train entered the depot on the diagonal through a large arched opening and the tracks extended through the building for a short distance on Second Street. The passenger terminal was on the Main Street side and the railway express office was on the Second Street side of the depot.

The facade of the depot is an assortment of California Mission imagery imaginatively composed by architect Arthur D. Nicholson (b. 1882). Born in Glasgow, Scotland, Nicholson studied architecture at the Glasgow School of Art. After traveling to Italy and practicing architecture in Scotland for one year, he came to San Francisco in 1906, lured like many others by the opportunity and adventure of rebuilding the city after the massive earthquake and fire. He became active with the San Francisco chapter of the American Institute of Architects and developed a solid practice in a short period of time.

Six years after his arrival in the Golden State, he designed the Woodland depot in a contemporary California style rooted romantically to its Spanish past. A Mission style quatrefoil and rounded roof parapet shaped the arched train entrance. A tall rounded tower with Mexican tile roof extended above this central parapet to anchor the Main Street side. A shorter, decorative, Mission style bell tower was placed on the Second street elevation. Each side of the depot offered a series of arched openings recalling the arcades of the California Missions and complementing the neighboring arcaded Odd Fellows building at Third and Main (1905).

Nicholson was active in San Francisco, designing apartments and office building until about 1915 when he moved elsewhere. He designed the Oroville Northern Electric depot in 1911 and a large house at 2120 V Street in Sacramento in 1913. This house was sold in 1914 to Dr. George H. Jackson who lived here until 1919. In his younger years, Dr. Jackson practiced medicine in Woodland and developed the Jackson Apartment Building, now restored and housing Morrison's Restaurant, and the Julian Hotel.

The Woodland depot was used until the early 1940s when electric train service declined in favor of the automobile. The building was partially destroyed by fire before being razed and the site was used for a parking lot until the 1980s.

In 1986, inspired by blueprints of the depot he

71. Vallejo & Northern Train Station, 1912, Arthur D. Nicholson
courtesy Yolo County Archives

72. Recreated Vallejo & Northern Train Station Commercial Building, 1986, Duane Thomson
photo by Roger Klemm

discovered at the California State Archives, Woodlander Tom Stallard redeveloped the depot for modern-day use as a commercial building *(fig. 72).* Woodland architect, Duane Thomson, faithfully recreated the exterior of the building that delights a new generation of locals who can only read and dream about the convenience and economy of electric mass transit of yesterday.

Cuff & Diggs

Early Modernism Moves into Woodland's Front Yard

In 1912 Claire and Mattie Rasor commissioned the Sacramento architectural firm of Cuff & Diggs to design a modern house at 555 College Street *(fig. 73).* Claire Rasor was a prominent and progressive physician involved in the formation of the Woodland Sanitarium in 1911. For its day and particularly in Woodland, the Rasor house was cutting-edge modern. The horizontal massing of the house and flat roof were major departures for Woodland and its grounded positioning level to the yard defined another modern innovation. Overhanging rooflines afforded protection from the elements; limited glazing followed windows that wrapped around corners of the house. Unlike the woodsy, organic Craftsman homes of the era, this house had a light-colored stucco finish. Massive porch columns and a pergola united the house with the large yard and its many palm trees. The columns were originally clad with lattice and vines, inviting use as an outdoor room.

Cuff & Diggs was comprised of Clarence C. Cuff and Woodland native Maury I. Diggs. The partnership was formed in 1911 and designed several noted downtown Sacramento buildings during the early part of the century, including the Travelers Hotel at J & 5th Streets (on the National Register), the Thomson-Diggs Company Warehouse at Third and R Streets (Maury Diggs' uncle, Marshall Diggs, was a partner in this company), and the Diepenbrock Theater (demolished). Other prominent works designed by this firm include the old Charles L. Nelson residence north of Woodland, destroyed by fire in 1949, Marshall Diggs' large house in North Sacramento, and the El Dorado County Courthouse in Placerville. The Cuff & Diggs partnership was dissolved in 1913, and both architects went on to long and successful careers.

Maury I. Diggs (1887-1953) was the grandson of Yolo County pioneer, David P. Diggs, son of Irvin P. Diggs and the nephew of Marshall M. Diggs of Woodland. Although Maury Diggs was the first native Woodlander to become a licensed architect, he did not have an office in Woodland. The early part of Diggs' career was spent in Sacramento, where both he and Clarence Cuff trained under State Architect, George Sellon, a partner in the firm that designed the Hotel Sacramento (owned, incidentally, by a corpo-

73. Rasor House, 1912, Cuff & Diggs
photo by Roger Klemm

ration whose Board of Directors included Marshall Diggs). Sellon helped Maury Diggs become Acting State Architect and, during his tenure working for the state, Diggs assisted with the design and construction of San Quentin prison and buildings at San Jose State Teachers College.

In 1915 Diggs became the defendant in a sensational trial whose appeals went all the way to the Supreme Court. He and a friend, P. Drew Caminetti (both 27 years old and married with children), transported two 19 year-old women from Sacramento to Reno where they intended to reside for six months to secure divorces from their wives. Caminetti was the son of United States Congressman, Anthony Caminetti. The fathers of the young women who had eloped with Diggs and Caminetti charged the men with contributing to the dependency of minors (the Diggs and Caminetti children) and United States Attorney John L. McNab tried the men in federal court.

As a result, Diggs and Caminetti were convicted of violating the Mann Act (White Slave Trade Act of 1910). While the case was on appeal, Diggs was divorced by his first wife and in December 1915 he married Marsha Worrington, with whom he had tried to elope. The Supreme Court upheld the conviction and President Wilson denied the application for pardons. Diggs paid a $2,000 fine and served eight months of the two-year prison term before being paroled in 1917.

His legal problems resolved, Diggs moved to Oakland about 1920 and set up his own successful firm. In downtown Oakland he designed several landmarks, including the terra cotta Beaux Arts style Oakland Title Insurance and Guarantee Building (1921), the Lakeshore Drive Apartments, the Latham Square Building, and the Fox Oakland Theater Building (1928), patterned after a Brahmin Temple in India. In 1921 Diggs and Dr. Claire Rasor again collaborated on a house at 2832 Lakeshore in Oakland. Rasor moved his medical practice from Woodland to Oakland about 1917.

Further, Diggs made a name for himself as an innovative designer of California horse racing tracks. His credits include the remodeled Bay Meadows track, Golden Gate Fields in Albany, and Hollywood Park.

After retiring as an architect, Diggs invented a commercially successful insecticide and, during World War II, invented a thermo paint used on landing barges. The multi-talented Maury Diggs died in Napa County in 1953.

Clarence Cuff (1871-1965) practiced architecture in Sacramento until his retirement at age 90 in 1960. Born in Toronto, Canada, Cuff immigrated to the U.S. in the 1890s where he found work as a contractor, constructing some of the buildings at the West Point Military Academy. Arriving to work on the old Sacramento Hotel, his apprenticeship with architect George Sellon initiated a Sacramento architectural career that spanned 50 years. Reflecting on his varied career, Cuff quipped: "I've done everything from bordellos to shrines."

Earle L. Younger

Construction of the Porter Building Draws a Prominent Contractor to Town

Earle L.Younger
courtesy Sue R. Younger

In 1913 construction bids were advertised for an elegant, three-story Renaissance Revival office building for the northeast corner of College and Main Streets. Designed by the prominent Bay Area architectural firm of William H. Weeks, the building was named in honor of local businessman and city benefactor, A.D. Porter, who died before the project was completed. The low bidder for the project was a general contractor from San Jose, Earle L. Younger (c.1877-1955), who subsequently relocated to Woodland. According to family members, Younger was acquainted with architect Weeks and their paths probably crossed in the Bay Area where Weeks was headquartered.

The Porter Building was a major construction project of sophisticated design and modern technology and required the skills of an advanced and experienced general contractor *(fig. 74)*. The successful completion of this landmark building established Younger as one of the premier commercial builders in Woodland from 1913 through the 1940s.

Though a native of Iowa, Earle Leslie Younger as a boy moved with his family to Hollister, California where his father established himself as a builder. He presumably learned his trade from his father before starting his own contracting business and moving to San Jose.

In addition to the Porter Building, Younger completed several other major commercial projects in Woodland, including the Webster-Granada Theater (1922) for businessman W. Stuart Webster. The Webster-Granada became Woodland's premier motion picture theater of the era, eclipsing the Strand Theater also developed by the Younger-Webster team in a remodeled building vacated by Cranston's Hardware in 1914 on the northwest corner of First and Main. The Webster-Granada, located on the southeast corner of Elm and Main, was also a remodeled building, originally constructed in 1886 by Glenn & White for hardware dealer, Thomas B. Gibson. George Atkins, the current occupant, moved his hardware business out of this building to the other side of Main Street to make room for the movie theater.

Younger's contract to build the Granada was substantial — the project cost $105,000. By all accounts the theater turned out splendidly, as reported in the *Daily Democrat* on March 30, 1922:

> *E.L. Younger, the general contractor on the job, has completed his work so satisfactorily that prospective theater owners from other sections of the state have already started wending their way to Woodland to view the new home of make-believe.*

The Granada had balcony seating and a house organ. The projection room was lined with metal (because early film celluloid was highly flammable) and all the machinery was electrically operated, the

74. Porter Building, 1913, William H. Weeks, architect, Earle L. Younger, builder
courtesy Yolo County Archives

75. Gregg House, 1919, Earle L. Younger
photo by Roger Klemm

object being to make the building fireproof. The movie screen, devised from the latest technology, claimed to "eliminate eye strain and flicker," according to the local press. The Granada Theater was the premier motion picture theater in Woodland until the opening of the State Theatre in 1937. The Granada was later renamed the National Theater and then became the Yolo Theater with a fancy neon marquee. Fireproofing precautions notwithstanding, the building burned down in 1964.

Ross Wilson commissioned Younger to design and build a Mexican Hacienda style funeral home at 458 College Street in 1924. The building was designed to convey a warm, relaxed, non-institutional ambience, and the exterior was finished in smooth plaster with a red tile roof. The Wilson family lived upstairs in an apartment.

Further contributing to town development, Younger constructed a new building along the alley behind the Porter Building at 327 College Street in 1924 for use as a post office. About 1936 this building was remodeled into the Porter Movie Theater after the post office moved to its new (and present) location on Court Street.

In 1925 the prominent Sacramento architectural firm of Dean and Dean designed a Spanish Revival style *Daily Democrat* newspaper building to be built on the southeast corner of Court and Second Streets. Ed Leake, owner of the *Daily Democrat*, committed himself to hiring a "local" contractor and Younger won the prestigious contract. Leake praised Younger for completing the project within a short time frame. In 1999 this building was rehabilitated and incorporated into a larger addition now used for the Yolo County District Attorney's offices.

Another significant commercial building built by Younger was the Sanitary Dairy at 1021 Lincoln Avenue (1940). The Morris family operated this well-known commercial enterprise for many years.

Younger was also a fine house builder, whose credits include the artistic house built for Charles F. Thomas at 515 First Street (1920) designed by John Hudson Thomas. Other houses built by Younger include the large bungalow in Beamer Park for Ida Gregg at 15 Palm Avenue (1919-*fig. 75*), the J. I. McConnell home designed by William H. Weeks at 705 First Street (1922), and the Russell Lowe house designed by Dean & Dean north of Woodland on Road 98 (1922).

The Younger Dehydrator Company, run by members of the Younger clan, was significant as one of the first fruit dehydrators on the west coast. Earle Younger also owned a Woodland drive-in restaurant called the "Roundhouse," located on the north side of Main

76. Roundhouse Restaurant (date unknown),
Earle L. Younger
courtesy Yolo County Archives

Street east of West Street *(fig. 76)*. In the early 1940s this was a local "hangout" for high school kids.

Earle Younger and his wife, Anna Belle, lived for many years in a Craftsman Bungalow at 736 Second Street (although this house was not built by Younger). Younger died in Woodland in 1955 at the age of 78.

Olin S. Grove

He Could Design Fashionable Houses — and Sell You a Phonograph

A new style born of the new century, the Craftsman style house was conceptualized, romanticized and promoted by Gustav Stickley beginning in 1901 in his magazine, *The Craftsman*. For two decades, Stickley published elevations and floor plans in his magazine and by 1910 in books. The Craftsman house follows the principles of simplicity, economy, comfort, and use of natural building materials. Ornamental exterior decoration, central to the Victorian aesthetic, disappeared from Craftsman houses in favor of an organic and natural appearance, using wood shingles, cobblestones, and clinker bricks. Its stylistic presence extended across the country and throughout every region. Its core aesthetic, encouraging greater comfort and coziness, with inglenooks, built-in cabinetry and more interior open planning (especially avoiding earlier boxiness) coincided with more informal lifestyles and more middle-class budgets.

The Craftsman philosophy and design appealed to Chester and Fred Fairchild who, besides being brothers, were both physicians and co-founders of the Woodland Clinic. Fred's house was built in 1910 at 754 College Street by the Keehn Brothers and that same year Chester had a small Craftsman house built at 744 Second Street. Chester and his mother, Susan, lived here until 1913, when Chester moved into his own Craftsman house at 914 First Street. Olin S. Grove (1881-1953), a house designer from Oakland, drew the plans for Chester's house *(fig. 77)*. Oakland City Directories indicate that Grove was active as a designer in the East Bay during the boom period from about 1909 to 1918, with several houses documented in Berkeley and Oakland. After his short career as a house designer, he operated phonograph and radio shops in Oakland.

The impressive Craftsman house that Grove cre-

77. Chester Fairchild House, 1913, Olin S. Grove
photo by Roger Klemm

ated for Chester Fairchild is very similar in shape to Fred's, highly influenced by Stickley's prototype design published in the *Craftsman* in 1909. The house has a sweeping overhanging roofline with a wide shed dormer and a pair of triplicate windows that light the second story. The upper story is clad in wooden shingles and the lower story, chimney and pergola are built of concrete blocks that imitate stones. The house is built level to the ground, with a recessed front entrance that affords protection from the elements. The natural look of the house fits well with the double-lot yard and surrounding vegetation.

78. Beamer's Woodland Park, c1913, before development
courtesy Steve Sabadini

Beamer's Woodland Park

Enter an Upscale Residential Enclave — A Surge of Stylistic Variety plus Motroni Gems

The charming neighborhood on the north side of Woodland with a main entrance at Third and Beamer Streets was originally a pioneer homestead and farm belonging to Richard L. and Rebecca Beamer *(fig. 78)*. Their farmhouse, which was enlarged several times from its humble brick beginnings about 1860 to its current Monterey Colonial Revival style, stands just inside the entrance to the Park at 9 Palm Avenue. Prior to constructing the brick house, Beamer built a wooden house near Beamer and Third streets when he and his family first settled in Woodland in 1853. Painted red, this house was reportedly one of the first frame residences built in Woodland. It was torn down about 1914 during the construction of the new subdivision.

After Rebecca Beamer passed away, family heirs sold 130 acres of the Beamer homestead for $100,000 to Hewitt Davenport (1880-1965), principal of Keystone Development Company of Oakland. A native of Massachusetts, Davenport graduated from the University of California, Berkeley in 1902. He was a young man of thirty-three in 1913 when his investment group began to develop the new Beamer subdivision.

Davenport had a strong vision for his housing tract. He sought to develop a suburban style enclave on the outskirts of Woodland proper that would set it apart from the grid layouts of traditional Woodland neighborhoods and appeal to affluent home seekers.

79. Mark R. Daniels
from *Commercial Encyclopedia of the Southwest* by E. Davis, ed., 1911, California State Library

To realize this vision, Davenport hired prominent landscape engineer, Mark R. Daniels *(fig. 79)*. Born in Michigan in 1881, Daniels also attended U.C. Berkeley, graduating with a degree in engineering in 1905. In 1914, the year that Daniels laid out Beamer Park, he was appointed General Superintendent and Landscape Engineer for the National Park System. Daniels advocated improved public accessibility to national parks and the development of facilities for tourism. Daniels designed a master plan for Yosemite Valley with roads, tourist accommodations, stores, and utilities. His plan for Yosemite was based upon his philosophy that "economics and esthetics really go hand in hand." Daniels

80. Gateway to Beamer's Woodland Park, 1914,
Mark R. Daniels
courtesy Steve Sabadini

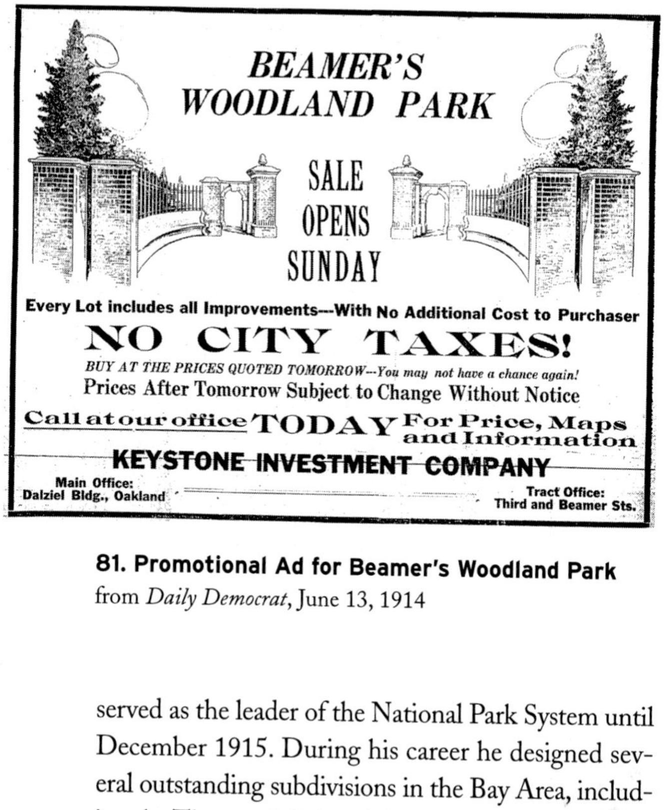

81. Promotional Ad for Beamer's Woodland Park
from *Daily Democrat,* June 13, 1914

served as the leader of the National Park System until December 1915. During his career he designed several outstanding subdivisions in the Bay Area, including the Thousand Oaks subdivision in Berkeley (1910) and Forest Hills (1915) and Sea Cliff (1912-15) in San Francisco.

Beamer Park was designed to feel suburban and different from older parts of town. Daniels designed a grand entrance to *Beamer's Woodland Park,* as the tract was officially named. A brick and wrought iron gateway to the Park was constructed in 1914 on both sides of Palm Avenue *(fig. 80).* The gateway evoked an image of exclusivity and prestige that targeted the upper middle class homeowner. The *Beamer Arches,* as they came to be called, indeed have arches over the sidewalks beckoning pedestrians into the Park. The gateways have brick pillars at each end capped with concrete moldings, including an acorn-shaped finial on the Palm Avenue side.

A short distance through the gateway to Beamer Park, Daniels placed an elevated roundabout on Palm Avenue with terraced steps and a fountain. Keystone Avenue, the namesake of Davenport's development company, and Hollister Drive form an elliptical pattern through the subdivision, a major departure from Woodland's traditional grid street pattern.

Beamer Park was divided into 19 blocks that extended from Beamer Street north to Woodland Avenue and from Pershing Avenue on the west to Sutter Street on the east. Davenport donated land within the subdivision to the City of Woodland to be developed into a public park for the enjoyment of Beamer Park residents. This site had historically been a school for pioneer children.

Plenty of advance advertising and hoopla led to Davenport's grand opening of Beamer Park on June 14, 1914 *(fig. 81).* Leaving nothing to chance, Davenport even arranged for a special excursion train of six coaches to be chartered from Sacramento to transport invited guests, as announced in the June 11, 1914 edition of the *Daily Democrat:*

> *Next Sunday morning Woodland will be invaded by the largest body of visitors that ever came to the city on one train. The occasion will be the opening of the new Beamer Park subdivision. It became known today that almost a thousand Sacramentans will take advantage of the free excursion to Woodland. Special invitations have been issued to the officials, bankers, professional and business men of the capital city to be the guest of the Keystone Investment Company . . .*

Hewitt Davenport, under whose direction the work of the subdivision has gone ahead, is providing for the inner wants of the visitors as well as for the business end of their company. He has ordered 3,000 sandwiches and 50 gallons of lemonade. Water wagons laden with ice water will circulate about the park to see that no one feels the need of liquid refreshment.

Davenport's payoff for the grand celebration was the sale of 21 lots totaling about $20,000 on opening day. During the next three years before World War I, Woodland contractors, notably William Fait, constructed a few homes for well-to-do clients along Palm Avenue. But Beamer Park never became the grand success that Davenport had envisioned. The overall build-out of the Park was very gradual, disrupted by World War I, the slow growth of the town, and competition from other subdivisions on the south side.

In 1919, after the War ended and soldiers were returning home, the housing industry picked up and there was a concerted patriotic push among banks, thrifts, and the federal government to promote home ownership. The prospects for renewed building in Beamer Park suddenly brightened. By May of 1919, four new homes were under construction in Beamer Park, including two by Fait: a $10,000 house for Fred Willis on the circle at 41 Palm Avenue *(fig. 82)* and a Bay Area style shingled house for W.H. Arata at 55 Pershing Avenue. On May 18, 1919 the *Daily Democrat*, in a special supplement devoted to house building, portrayed Davenport as a spinner of dreams in the fairy land of Beamer Park:

Beamer Park is a dream come true. Hewitt Davenport, who is the good fairy of Beamer Park, first beheld the green and spreading acres of the Beamer tract with their wonderful old oak trees not so many years ago. From the moment that the sight first broke on his vision Davenport like Clarence, henchman of Richard III "dreamed a dream," but unlike the wicked Clarence, Davenport's was not a "strange wild dream." It was a lovely dream wherein the sweeping acres of grain and

82. Willis House, 1919, William R. Fait
photo by Roger Klemm

83. Barth House, 1929, Joseph Motroni
photo by Roger Klemm

spreading oak trees and verdant grass were transformed by the magic touch of a fairy wand to lovely home sites laid out in rounded curves, and where the great oaks spread their shade over sweeping driveways; where the prattle of little children playing on the terraced lawns could be heard on the cool of the evening while the tired business man and his wife sat on the veranda of a lovely home and feasted the eye on the far stretch of beautiful country.

In 1920 Keystone Development made a renewed commitment to Beamer Park when Charles M. Binford relocated from Davenport's San Francisco office to take up residence at the old Beamer house inside the entrance to the Park. Binford purchased the Beamer house, remodeled it for his family and, as sales manager, presided over the sale of lots and the building of speculative houses for his boss in Oakland. Binford was no stranger to Woodland. Before his job in the Bay Area, he worked as the auditor for the Yolo Water and Power Company.

Binford's first order of business was to petition the City Council for drainage improvements to the interior of Beamer Park. In return for the public improvements to the property, Binford assured the Council that upwards of $250,000 would be invested in Beamer Park in the foreseeable future by Keystone and other local house builders. The Council granted Binford his request in September 1920 and also began discussions to annex the property to the city. (City maps indicate that Beamer Park was not actually annexed into the city until 1928.)

Within days of this decision by the City Council, Woodland contractor William E. Underwood, former sales manager for the Beamer tract, purchased two acres of Beamer Park land from his former company and began to build houses. He and his wife, Ethel, moved into their personal residence, a Prairie style bungalow at 26 Palm Avenue, in 1920. In March 1922 Charles Binford resigned as sales manager to pursue his accounting career and was replaced by Alva

84. Traynham (left) and Schoen Houses, Beamer's Woodland Park, Joseph Motroni
courtesy Josephine Motroni Gillette

McBrown. That same year Davenport paved a few more streets in Beamer Park, including Keystone Avenue. In 1924 Davenport was back in Woodland to announce that Wraith & Farish, local realtors with offices on Main Street, were the new sales agents for Beamer Park lots.

The 1920s saw more sustained construction activity in Beamer Park. In 1922 Underwood built a large home at 803 Woodland Avenue on the northern boundary of the subdivision for R.H. Cost. In 1924 Harry and May Crego contracted with Underwood to build a picturesque Tudor Revival home at 45 Palm Avenue, as the lots on the main thoroughfare inside the subdivision began to fill.

By 1929 Woodland contractor Joseph Motroni became active in Beamer Park. He built a handsome brick Tudor Revival house for Emil and Noreen Niclas at 47 Palm Avenue and a beautifully crafted brick Bungalow for J. Barth at 51 Pershing Avenue *(fig. 83)* as Beamer Park homebuilders began to push outward from the core area.

Though slowed by the Great Depression, this expansion carried into the 1940s. Motroni, working in the outer reaches of Beamer Park from the mid 1930s up to World War II, designed and built many fine homes, with a high concentration along West Keystone Avenue. Motroni's masonry skills are exemplified by the Traynham house at 527 W. Keystone (1933) and the home at 511 W. Keystone constructed of volcanic rock (1937). Motroni designed several homes in the Mediterranean Revival style, including the Wilson house on a corner lot at 605 W. Keystone (1937) and Motroni's own house at 524 W. Keystone (1938). Perhaps more than any single house builder, Joseph Motroni shaped the look of today's Beamer Park *(fig 84)*.

In 1996 the aging Beamer Arches were restored through the efforts of a local homeowners committee and volunteers, sparked by a grant from the Woodland Stroll Through History committee.

William R. Fait

Self-Made Entrepreneur Comes of Age in Woodland

William R. Fait
from *Yolo in Word & Picture, Woodland Daily Democrat* 1920 *courtesy Yolo County Archives*

William Rutherford Fait (1879-1930) was involved in the construction industry in the great Northwest before establishing himself in Woodland. Born in Indiana, Fait moved with his family to Washington when he was a boy. When the Spanish-American War broke out, he volunteered for service. He survived the war but suffered partial loss of hearing and an arm wound.

After the war, he and his wife, Katherine E. Brasfield, formerly of Colusa, moved from Spokane to San Francisco where Fait struggled financially for several years while learning the carpentry trade. During periods of hard luck he was forced to leave San Francisco to work in rural lumber mills or mines. In 1905 the Faits managed to build a small house at 158 Lisbon Street in San Francisco.

Fait eventually began a small contracting business in San Francisco, but shortly thereafter the earthquake and great fire of 1906 disrupted his dreams. He moved back to Spokane where he started a contracting business with a partner named Strain. Between 1906 and 1911 Fait & Strain built several noteworthy houses in Spokane, including a southern style mansion for George W. Odell, designed by the noted Spokane architect, W.W. Hyslop.

In 1911 William Fait visited Woodland where his wife's cousin Geneva Cobb lived with her husband George at 803 College Street. Aside from the family connection, other aspects of Woodland intrigued Fait: a drier climate and the wealth of the community, both

85. Bullard House, 1913, William R. Fait
courtesy Yolo County Archives

of which created the potential for year-round building. He stayed in Woodland briefly and completed a job for Asa Morris before returning to Spokane. In 1912 Fait and his family left Spokane permanently for Woodland. The timing of his decision to take a chance on Woodland was fortuitous because there was a growth spurt in Woodland with many homes being built and general contractors in high demand. As reported in the *Daily Democrat* on July 30, 1912:

> *Boom! Boom! Boom! That's Woodland just now. Woodland is booming herself beyond recognition and realization. With one hundred buildings, newly erected or still in the course of construction, Woodland has set an entirely new record for itself, and in a few months has surpassed the work of the last decade.*

Once in Woodland, the Faits purchased a lot at 448 Pendegast Street. After completing a temporary dwelling on the front of the lot, Fait built a large two story home with Old English half-timbered design elements, completed in 1913. The house has similarities to a fancier version that Fait had built in Spokane. In 1915 the Faits sold this home to Perry Hiatt probably to raise capital for his fledgling contracting business. After the sale of the large house, the Faits moved a short distance to 765 Third Street into a much smaller shingled bungalow that he built.

Due to the steady pace of building in Woodland during this period and Fait's skill as a design-build contractor, he rapidly established his business in the community. Shortly after his arrival in Woodland, Fait secured a major contract with E.A Bullard to remodel a ranch house on Roads 99 and 27 into a southern style plantation house with a manorial Greek Revival pediment and Ionic columns (1913-*fig. 85*).

During the course of his career in Woodland, Fait designed and built many outstanding homes, including several interesting versions of the California Bungalow. His flair for design is exhibited in such contrasting bungalows as the following: Bailey House at 421 Pendegast (1912-*fig. 86*), the Brink House at 411 Pendegast (1914), which appears to have been built (or at least inspired) from a *Sears Catalogue* plan

86. Bailey House, 1912, William R. Fait
photo by Roger Klemm

87. Boyce House, 1916, William R. Fait
photo by Roger Klemm

88. Fait House, 1918, William R. Fait
photo by Roger Klemm

called the "Hollywood," the Hays Gable House at 650 Second Street (1914), and the Boyce House at 907 First Street (1916-*fig. 87*).

When Beamer Park opened in 1914, Fait was one of the first contractors to build there, and through the 1920s he was the most prolific house builder in this prestigious subdivision. Fait moved his family to a bungalow he built at 19 Palm Avenue in (1917) in Beamer Park shortly after its opening. The peripatetic builder stayed in this house only one year before moving the family next door to another bungalow he built at 25 Palm Avenue (1918-*fig. 88*). In 1919 Fait constructed a fine version of the Bay Area shingled style house for W. H. Arata at 55 Pershing Avenue *(fig. 89)* and a stately Colonial Revival home on the Beamer circle at 41 Palm Avenue for Fred Willis. Late in his career, Fait built a charming English-style cottage for Julian Williams at 39 Pershing Avenue (1929).

In a 1919 supplement in the *Daily Democrat* to promote home ownership and economic development in Yolo County just after World War I, Fait published an article in which he waxed metaphorical about his home design philosophy:

89. Arata House, 1919, William R. Fait
photo by Roger Klemm

90. Cranston's Hardware Building, 1914, William R. Fait
courtesy Yolo County Museum

Individuality is possible in the home as in individuals, because there are a thousand ways of being beautiful. The beauty of a violet is different, though perhaps not less than the beauty of a rose and by the same token a cottage may be made as beautiful in its way as a palace — more beautiful in fact. As I see the matter, dignity is expressed largely by the roof, comfort by lowness and breadth, hospitality by the entrance. I am very particular about the roof. It determines the quality of self-respect. Objectively stated, it must be adequately large and broad and unashamed. Scant measure suggests nothing more impressive than the lid of a pot.

In addition to home building, Fait constructed several large institutions, including the second phase of the Woodland Sanitarium near Third and Main in 1920, designed by William Henry Weeks.

Fait also completed the elegant Classical Revival First National Bank building in Knights Landing (1920). Designed by Weeks, the bank building resembled a small financial temple. Its ornamental exterior of columns and classical detailing were constructed of terra cotta tile, like that used on the Yolo County Courthouse. Although the shell of the building survives to this day, the building has been gutted and has fallen into serious disrepair.

School buildings also attracted the interest of Fait. He built parts of the Woodland High School, including the Gymnasium and Industrial Arts Building in 1914 (demolished) as well as the Agricultural Mechanics Building (1924) located at 910 College Street and still in use today as a shop for the Woodland Unified School District. This Mission style building was one of the first constructed with reinforced concrete walls.

In the downtown area, Fait designed and built the Mission Revival style Cranston's Hardware Store (1914-*fig 90*) and the Fred Meier Ford Agency on the corner of Bush and College (1921). He rebuilt the Julian Hotel on Main Street (1922) after a fire destroyed the top story of the building. Fait was also the contractor for the Mission Revival style Methodist Church (1925) designed by Rollin S. Tuttle.

William Fait was one of the original promoters of the Yolo Fliers Club, headed by O.W.H. Pratt. This was one of the first clubs in the region that combined aviation, golf, swimming and country club activities in one location. Fait worked closely with architect William H. Weeks on the design and construction of the clubhouse and pool and participated in designing the airfield and golf course. Most of this work was completed in 1921-22.

An entrepreneur and speculator throughout his career, Fait invested in farmland, oil wells, and a truck dealership — all with limited success. In 1915 he purchased 160 acres in Mexico with the dream of developing it into a productive farm. By 1916, however, all foreigners were ordered out of the country due to the escalating revolution and the land was eventually sold. In 1918 he became a dealer for Grant Six trucks, but the business lasted less than one year. In 1922 and 1923 Fait developed two vineyards and for a short period grew premium quality Zinfandel grapes that were shipped east by the Earl Fruit Company. These two ranches, comprising 70 acres, were located along Cache Creek in the Willow Oak Park area (now the site of Teichert Aggregates).

In 1927 Fait bought 160 acres four miles south of Woodland along the old Davis Highway where he planted prune trees and farmed lettuce. For a short period he operated a gas station on this site. Neither venture paid off and the property was foreclosed.

Katherine E. Fait served two terms on the Woodland Board of Education from 1923 to 1931. She and others were elected at this time as "reform" candidates to combat the prevalent practice of kickbacks given by vendors and contractors to certain Board members. She also was an annual organizer of the Chautauqua that came to Woodland each year for a one-week engagement. The Chautauqua was a traveling show held under a large tent featuring lectures, music, plays, and scientific demonstrations before the advent of radio home entertainment.

Tragically, William Fait was injured in a 1929 building accident that may have led to his death. While building a house in Beamer Park, he sustained a head injury from a falling board. Shortly after, he experienced headaches and was diagnosed with a brain tumor. Brain surgery at the Presidio army hospital in San Francisco was unsuccessful. William R. Fait, the Spanish American War veteran, was laid to rest at the age of 51 in the Presidio cemetery in 1930.

John Hudson Thomas

A Bay Area Master —
and Three Artistic Woodland Homes

John Hudson Thomas, Self-Portrait
courtesy Dick & Renie Riemann

Many Woodlanders refer to the eccentric house at First and Pendegast Streets as the "Frank Lloyd Wright" house. No, this American icon did not design any houses in Woodland. However, a brilliant architect in Berkeley, who admired Wright and other pioneering innovators, vigorously integrated modern breakthroughs into his original designs. His remarkable local output gives Woodland architecture buffs something to cheer about. His name was John Hudson Thomas (1878-1945) who, like Wright, used all three of his names.

Thomas was born in Ward, Nevada where his father worked for a time as a mining engineer. The family's home base, however, was Berkeley where Thomas grew up on Dwight Street, near the university. After graduating from Yale University in 1902, Thomas entered the Department of Architecture at U.C. Berkeley to study with John Galen Howard and Bernard Maybeck. After receiving his degree in architecture, like Julia Morgan, Ira Hoover, and William Hays, he worked for Howard for a short period before forming a partnership with George T. Plowman in

1906. In 1910 Thomas established an independent practice. Thomas married Ida Wickson, whose father was Edward James Wickson, who was involved in the formation of U.C. Davis and for whom Wickson Hall is named.

Known as brilliantly eclectic and a daring designer of houses, Thomas' stature as one of the creators of the "Bay Area" style of architecture is now well established by architectural historians. Particularly in his early work between 1910 and 1920, Thomas' houses synthesized a wide variety of imagery and historical references in odd juxtapositions to create eccentric but alluring designs.

John Hudson Thomas was a prolific designer of houses. Between 1910 and 1920, during the post-1906 earthquake building boom in Berkeley, he completed 145 documented projects — mostly houses. Although the great fires in the Berkeley hills in 1923 and again in 1992 destroyed several of his creations, fortunately Thomas' houses are scattered throughout Berkeley and surrounding East Bay communities; many that survived the fires are catalogued in several architectural guidebooks.

Thomas designed only three Woodland houses, all located on First Street, but left a permanent mark on Woodland and a heritage of truly creative designs. These houses reflect Thomas' eclecticism and showcase the wealth of his ideas. Constructed in 1916 at the height of the Arts and Crafts period in California, the house at 756 First Street (at Pendegast) fuses horizontal elements of the then-modern Prairie Style of architecture, created by Wright, with vertical "half timbering" wood trim from the Tudor period *(fig. 91)*. This medieval touch may have been influenced by Thomas' mentor, the great architect-visionary Bernard Maybeck, who was attracted to older European forms.

91. Stephens House, 1916, John Hudson Thomas
photo by Robert Campbell

The radical design of this highly stylized house created a stir in Woodland in 1916 in a neighborhood of mostly Victorians — and stands today as one of Woodland's brilliant successes, combining traditional with modern techniques into a highly functional family home.

Actually, its design makes eminent sense for the flatlands of Woodland baked by sweltering summer heat. Its horizontal massing and wide overhanging eaves conform to the climate and geography by providing shade and shelter, encouraging an abundance of windows to flood the interior with light, provide ample fresh air, and create a strong connection to the outside world. A central dining room on the front of the house, enclosed almost entirely by glass, creates transparency between interior shelter and the natural world of the towering ancient Valley Oak. A cantilevered roof, reinforced by chains, protects the dining room and front entrance. A small concrete terrace with a seating bench is integrated with the front yard by three short steps.

The house is innovative and modern in other practical ways: it boasts an attached garage, representing a new concept for Woodland homeowners. Like all of Thomas' Woodland houses, this home is finished in stucco, providing a durable finish. Built for William and Florence Stephens, the house was restored by owners Ann and Frank Joule, who deserve credit for perfectly matching a new garden wall in 1993 with the stucco relief work and vertical wood pattern that distinguishes the house.

Why did the Stephens choose someone as sophisticated and experimental as Thomas as their architect? The answer remains a mystery. When asked this question, the Stephens' sons did not recollect their parents having any connection to Berkeley or any prior relationship with Thomas.

However, there *is* a connection between the Stephens house and the Thomas-designed home at 515 First Street, constructed in 1920 by Woodland contractor, Earle L. Younger *(fig. 92)*. This splendid house was built for Charles F. Thomas (no relation to the architect), a wealthy Woodland grain broker and partner to his neighbor down the street, William

92. Thomas House, 1920, John Hudson Thomas, architect, Earle L. Younger, builder
photo by Roger Klemm

93. Blevins House, 1927, John Hudson Thomas, architect, Joseph Motroni, builder
photo by Roger Klemm

Stephens. Judging from the free-form styles of both houses, neither man was interested in restraining Thomas' originality or boldness as they both evidently sought something modern and different for their showcase homes.

In contrast with the horizontal look of the Stephens house, John Hudson Thomas featured vertical massing for the C. F. Thomas house. Here is a good example of the architect's inclination to experiment with odd but interesting clashes in scale and unorthodox juxtapositions of details from different historical styles. An exposed brick chimney on the massive front facade of the house cuts abruptly through the Dutch Colonial roofline. The scale of the gambrel facade dwarfs a short column adjacent to the front door.

The north-facing gambrel has an attached rectangular lower story with upstairs balcony. There is another small balcony inset between the gambrels. Attached to the rear of the house is the original brick icehouse built in 1861 as part of the large Victorian that occupied the site. The matching carriage house was re-built in 1979 and this house has been beautifully restored and the grounds upgraded by owner Fred Harvey.

Rounding out Thomas' endowment to Woodland is the rustic and romantic Tudor Revival home at 742 First Street, constructed in 1927 by Woodland master builder, Joseph Motroni, for Dr. William J. Blevins, Sr., one of the founders of the Woodland Clinic *(fig. 93)*. This work reflects Thomas' shift in the 1920s away from grand synthesis of different styles and highly varied design elements to almost exclusively medieval imagery. The exterior is made of rusticated stucco with a light brown tint. The extra tall, angled bay window on the front of the house teems with windows opening the house to the street. A dormer window built perpendicular to the double gabled rooflines adds visual interest and extra light to an upstairs room. Owners James and Lois Lawson have beautifully maintained this lovely home and large yard.

John Hudson Thomas' artistry endowed Woodland with cutting-edge architecture that continues to fascinate with its wholly original look and appeal. His three First Street houses represent high points in the town's architectural heritage. He died in 1945, leaving behind an exuberant and exciting collection of houses reflecting his broad and passionate interest in art and the progressive period in which he worked.

Dean & Dean

Quality Designers of Revival Style Homes and Buildings

James S. Dean **Charles F. Dean**

photos courtesy Nicholas Tomich

In 1922 the Dean & Dean architecture firm of Sacramento was formed by two brothers, Charles F. Dean (1884-1956) and James S. Dean (1886-1963). Natives of Texas, the Dean brothers received outstanding academic training and worked for several years in the public sector before organizing their own firm. Both of the Dean brothers received architecture degrees from Texas A&M University. James Dean also did graduate study at M.I.T. Charles arrived in California in 1908 and James in 1912 to work at the State Architect's office. Charles worked as a designer for the state building program for 13 years and James was the Assistant State Architect from 1916 to 1920 under George B. McDougall.

Dean & Dean combined the formidable talents of Charles as the lead designer and James as the business executive. Earl R. Barnett joined the firm in 1925. He was a well-known northern California artist and a former student of Maynard Dixon, the Fresno-born artist who painted the murals at the old State Library building in Sacramento — enduring canvases that capture the spirituality of Native Americans and the deserts of the Southwest. Barnett's specialty was interior design, which he put to good use for the firm's many church and school projects. European art and architecture were an inspiration for both Charles Dean and Earl Barnett. Whereas Barnett was a world traveler, experiencing timeless works of art first hand, Dean's knowledge of European design was gleaned largely from books.

James Dean only stayed with the firm for about eight years, leaving in 1930 to become City Manager of Sacramento, a position he held until 1942 when Governor Earl Warren appointed him State Finance Director. He retired from that post in 1954 and later was named a Director of the California State Fair.

Many notable and picturesque buildings in Sacramento and throughout northern California were designed by Dean & Dean, often with the Mediterranean and Mexican influence so admired by Charles Dean and reflective of the public romance with California's Hispanic legacy. The firm's many extant landmark buildings in Sacramento form an impressive list that includes: the Byzantine-style Westminster Church on N and 13th Streets across from Capitol Park, Trinity Cathedral at 27th and Capitol, the Sutter Club at 9th & M, Sacramento Memorial Auditorium at J and 16th , the YWCA Building on 17th Street, and the original buildings on the Sacramento City College campus. Dean & Dean was also responsible for many beautiful homes gracing the streets in the Fabulous 40s neighborhoods of Sacramento.

Dean & Dean's extensive work in Woodland includes commercial, residential, and public buildings.

94. Daily Democrat Building, 1925, Dean & Dean, architects, Earle L. Younger, builder
courtesy Yolo County Archives

Their first known commercial project in Woodland was Fitch's Variety Store at 508 Main Street (1924) built by Joseph Motroni. This was the first of several Woodland Hispanic style buildings designed by Dean & Dean, eventual masters of this gracious style. The front facade of Fitch's building was designed to be elegant and inviting. The large show windows were placed in copper frames resting on a base of marble. A marquee hung with chains extended over the sidewalk, providing shelter from sun and rain. Above the marquee a large plate glass window, ten feet in width, flooded the interior with natural light. The roof surface on the front of the building was of Cordova tile of variegated colors. Most of these elegant design elements on the front of the building have since been removed, although the building is still in use today as a shoe store.

The following year, newspaper publisher Ed Leake retained Dean & Dean to design a new building for the *Daily Democrat* newspaper offices at 702 Court Street (1925-*fig. 94*). Spanish in inspiration, there is a restrained elegance in Dean's styling of the building. He used a simple geometric box with a flat roof, brick banding, wrought iron window decoration, and attic air vents grouped in a grid pattern. An arched opening on the corner of the building leads to the front entrance and may have been inspired by a similar arched entrance to the Julian Hotel one block away at Second and Main (demolished in 1967). The *Daily Democrat* was based at this location until 1987 when it moved to its present facility on Main Street.

In 1999 the old *Daily Democrat* building was rehabilitated and incorporated into a large new addition, sympathetic and compatible with the original design of Dean & Dean. Architect Jim Plumb used similar geometric massing and design trim as did Dean and added a picturesque tower with copper finial to the Second Street facade and two-tone exterior colors. The building is now used for the Yolo County District Attorney's offices.

By 1927 the Kraft Brothers Mortuary had outgrown their old location at Third and Main, where a furniture maker-turned undertaker named Peter Krellenberg established the company in 1869. Krellenberg's nephews, Emil and Julius Kraft, sought out Dean & Dean to create a contemporary design for a new chapel and mortuary. In typical fashion, the architects crafted a lovely Mission Revival style chapel at 175 Second Street *(fig 95)*. When master builder Joseph Motroni completed this building, the chapel drew raves from the newspaper and general public. The simplicity, rus-

95. Artist's Rendering of Kraft Bros. Chapel, 1927
Dean & Dean, architects, Joseph Motroni, builder
from *Daily Democrat*, September 8, 1927

tic features, and attention to detail, so characteristic of this outstanding design team, evoked a strong image of the historic Spanish missions. Before drawing plans for the building, the architects inspected many of the most modern mortuaries in California. Their goal was to see that the Woodland building "compared more than favorably with any that we have seen in the state," according to James Dean.

Dean noted that some items, such as the light fixtures for the front of the building had to be specially designed because the architects were not satisfied that available lighting would harmonize appropriately with the Spanish motif of the building. Said Dean:

> *The same idea is manifest throughout, every detail blending into a whole that is as perfect and as faithful to the conception that we were carrying out as we could make it.*

The perfectionism embodied in Dean & Dean's work on the Kraft Bros. Chapel greatly impressed visitors at the grand opening of the building in September 1927, as reported in the *Daily Democrat*:

> *It takes one's breath away to enter for the first time… A surge of veneration sweeps over him and then, as the details are taken in by the eye, the faithfulness in which it follows the Missions grows on one. Most impressive of the chapel's features is the apse or semicircular depression where the body of the departed will lie during services. Architectural treatment of the windows gives an impression of thick walls. The beautiful simplicity of the chapel is enhanced by the heavy dark beam ceiling. And gem of the crown are the three great rusty-iron chandeliers, each bearing twelve candle-lamps.*

Other Mission style features included the red roof tiles, installed in the irregular pattern customary to mission work by Indians of early California. The doors were tinted in Mediterranean blue, carved and studded to lend a rustic appearance.

Dean & Dean's design for the Woodland Fire Station and Jail (1932) at 300 First Street was also done in the Mission Revival style, with a functional tower designed for hanging wet fire hoses. This building

96. Eddy House, 1923, Dean & Dean
photo by Roger Klemm

replaced the Romanesque-style Old City Hall built in 1892 and later expanded into a fully functioning City Hall.

In addition to schools, churches and public buildings, the Dean & Dean firm was highly regarded for their house designs. In July 1927 the trade journal, *The Architect and Engineer,* praised Dean & Dean's house design talent:

> *Their houses are homes — not residences. A charm prevails or mantles them with an air of refinement which never tires. Simplicity in form and detail is most apparent both in house and garden and such versatility in execution in the work of modern periods from the Colonial to the modern Spanish. Bits of interest sparkle here and there indicating devotion to each problem as it came to them for solution.*

Dean & Dean designed several homes for Woodland residents between 1923 and 1940. The A. B. Eddy home (1923) at 710 First Street captures the essence of the rustic, shingled Cape Cod cottage *(fig. 96)*. A modest wooden Bungalow at 904 First Street owned by Forrest and Lenora Caldwell was remodeled by Dean & Dean into a Mexican style Hacienda with outdoor patio (1924).

97. K. Laugenour House, 1936, Dean & Dean, architects, Del Fenton, builder
photo by Roger Klemm

When Ken and Alice Laugenour decided to build a new home in Beamer Park in 1936, they had clear romantic images of the Old World cottages from travels in the French countryside. They selected Charles Dean to create the charming cottage at 714 W. Keystone Avenue *(fig. 97)*. Dean's drawings for the house, located at the City of Sacramento Archives, specify a large wooden wine barrel on the front porch to capture rainwater from the downspout located on the front facade of the house. Although the wine barrel no longer exists, the romance of the cottage still lingers. Charles Dean's personal residence, a "Hansel & Gretel" cottage at 2221 Markham in Sacramento, is similar in design and scale to the Laugenour house in Woodland. However, Dean went even further with his romantic impulses, creating a turret on his fairytale house.

The Monterey Colonial Revival home at 750 Second Street (1936) was built for Neil and Amelia Dougherty *(fig. 98)*. Charles Dean's design was based upon the Castro-Breen home, built during the Mexican period in San Juan Bautista. That home was owned at one time by Mrs. Daugherty's grandfather, Patrick Breen, Jr., a survivor of the Donner party. The placement of the windows on the house gives the walls a thickened appearance, like its adobe predecessor in Old California. Dean & Dean also designed the impressive Tudor Revival home for William and Meryl Crawford (c.1940) which graces the large corner lot at 106 Bartlett Avenue *(fig. 99)*.

The legacy of the Dean & Dean firm is extensive, and several well-known regional architects began their careers with the firm. William W. Wurster, a very influential Bay Area architect who became Dean of Architecture at U.C. Berkeley (Wurster Hall is named after him) and Harry Devine Sr., a noted Sacramento architect who designed the second phase of Woodland City Hall (1936) and Holy Rosary Church (1949), both worked for Charles Dean.

Nicholas Tomich was hired by Charles Dean in 1931 as an apprentice architect and stayed with the firm for 56 years before retiring in 1987. Tomich grew up in Orangevale and became inspired with architecture as a student at the Dean-designed Sacramento City College campus. When Charles Dean died in 1956 at the age of 71, Nicholas Tomich formed a partnership with Ivan Saterlee to take over the firm. Tomich had various partners with the firm up until his retirement. During his career Tomich continued to work closely with designer Earl Barnett. The two collaborated (along with Robert McLain) on St. Paul's Lutheran Church (1968-69) located at 625 W. Gibson Road in Woodland *(fig. 100)*. This modern style church has a ceiling built at three levels, with the highest level containing skylights that illuminate the chancel of the sanctuary.

Today the old Dean & Dean firm is known as Sheehan, Van Woert. Since its inception in 1922, the firm has been responsible for the design of more than 900 projects throughout Sacramento and northern California. While there were significant Woodland designers who came and went in a flash, making brief contributions, here is a solid, enduring firm that represents quality over time, with many examples in Woodland to honor its reputation. Their achievements demonstrate that top architecture and a town's distinguished history are mutual partners whose vision supports each other, often for a long, long time.

98. Dougherty House, 1936, Dean & Dean
photo by Roger Klemm

99. Crawford House, c.1940, Dean & Dean
photo by Roger Klemm

100. St. Paul's Lutheran Church, 1968-69, Tomich, McLain, Barnett
courtesy Yolo County Museum

Joseph G. Motroni

A Young Italian Immigrant Becomes Woodland's Premier Home Builder

Joseph G. Motroni
courtesy Josephine Motroni Gillette

Joseph G. Motroni's rise to prominence in Woodland as a prolific and high-quality designer and building contractor was born out of an adventurous spirit, a creative nature, and an immigrant's strong will to succeed. Guiseppe Motroni (1890-1950) was born in Montecatini, Italy, near Florence. In 1906, at age sixteen, Guiseppe received permission from his parents to immigrate to San Francisco to join the many Italians who were emigrating to help with the rebuilding.

Once in California, Motroni Americanized his given name and added a middle initial and thenceforth was known as Joseph G. Motroni. He learned English and worked as a casual laborer, lodging in a boarding house owned by the Cecannti family, who took him under their wing. When the Cecannti family moved to Los Gatos in 1908, Joe moved with them. Between 1908 and 1913 Motroni worked odd jobs, mastered the English language, and became a brick mason under the tutelage of a friend of Mr. Cecannti.

When construction work became scarce, Motroni sought work as a laborer for Southern Pacific Railroad, then worked in the mines and lumber mills of northern California. In 1915 Joe Motroni's younger brother, Guido, joined him in California.

In the spring of that year he and Guido, with $5.00 between them, moved to Woodland in search of a future, quickly starting their own contracting business. An advertisement in the 1917 Woodland High School *Ilex* yearbook promotes Motroni as offering *brick, stone, terrazzo and plastering work* and one of Motroni's earliest jobs in Woodland was terrazzo steps that front the Woodland Public Library.

In Woodland Joe Motroni met a fellow Italian plasterer and mason, Vincent Fatta, and the two brothers welcomed a new partner. Soon gaining a solid foothold in the Woodland construction business, Motroni-Fatta's reputation blossomed by completing high-quality subcontractor jobs, such as the Yolo County Courthouse project, the Electric Garage, and homes constructed by Woodland general contractor, William Fait.

World War I put Motroni's budding building career on hold, as he served in the U.S. armed forces in France between 1918-19. Returning from the war, he resumed his partnership with Fatta and his brother.

Motroni also married Ida Louise Nardinelli of Woodland in 1920 and built a modest family home that doubled as his office at 1015 Beamer Street, on the southeastern edge of Beamer Park *(fig. 101)*. Across the street Motroni purchased 1.5 acres of land and built a large shed where he began to manufacture concrete building blocks. A novel idea at the time, this material was slow to catch on in the local building trade.

In the early 1920s Motroni bid successfully on larger contracts for projects outside of Woodland, for example, in May 1922 paving nine blocks of streets in the Butte County town of Biggs. During this time he also did work in Napa County. His partner Fatta also began working independently outside of Woodland.

101. Motroni House & Office, 1920, Joseph Motroni
courtesy Josephine Motroni Gillette

In 1921, Fatta constructed an innovative Italianate style house out of concrete block at 945 North Street for his personal residence *(fig. 102)*. To simulate the stone houses of Tuscany, Fatta formed the base of the house with concrete block, tinted a darker shade to simulate rough-hewn stone, as do the quoins on the corners of the house. For the main body of the house, Fatta used smoother and lighter tinted blocks with horizontal grooves. The vertical rectangular windows have keystones and the windows above the portico have concrete flower boxes cantilevered from the house. The portico has arched openings formed by pilasters with terrazzo steps and a floor designed in a mosaic pattern.

Such unusual styles provide an interesting comparison between this Italianate house, constructed by a native Italian builder, and fanciful Victorian versions built of redwood in the 1870s. Fatta's version is simpler and more authentic, but like the Victorian version it has the flat-hipped roof, a portico with Doric pillars and stone blocks on the corners of the house to simulate quoins. Unlike the redwood free-style American models, this unique look offers no fancy wood carved brackets or cast iron Corinthian capitals and very little window ornamentation. Fatta's style of house was uncommon in the West and remains the only one of its kind in Woodland.

102. Fatta House, 1921, Vincent Fatta
photo by Roger Klemm

Expanding into large commercial projects, in May 1923 Motroni completed a 10,000 square foot auto dealership at 325 Main Street for W.A. Bloodworth. Constructed of brick with several showroom windows with transoms, the building originally housed Bloodworth's Willys-Knight and Overland car showroom, offices and other auto-related businesses. Motroni also was the concrete mason employed by Woodland general contractor, Jacob Witzelberger, to build the Main Street Garage on the southwest corner of Elm and Main Streets for Hiatt and Miller (1923).

By about 1924 Motroni and Fatta went their separate ways. Their skills and reputations had evolved significantly, allowing each to develop successful businesses on their own. In 1924 Fatta opened a temporary office of his own in Oakland where he had secured lucrative contracts. Within a few years he moved permanently to the Bay Area.

Meanwhile, Motroni's work in Woodland flourished as his growing reputation for high quality work led to increasingly prestigious contracts. Motroni was selected to build an interesting Spanish Revival building at 508 Main Street (1924) for the new Fitch's variety store designed by Dean & Dean. Motroni was applauded in an August 25, 1924 article in the Woodland *Daily Democrat* for his building skills:

> *Contractor Motroni gave his undivided attention to the construction of the handsome edifice to a successful business enterprise, with the result that the building throughout, from basement to roof, is conceded to be by all who view it with skilled eyes, the last word*

in convenience and commodious arrangement for a general merchandise store. And in Motroni's favor also let it be known that he has completed the building in 10 days less time than were given him in the contract.

By the mid 1920s Motroni began to contract for complete houses or major remodels. He became the builder of choice for several owners with wealth and taste who hired top flight architects to design artistic homes. From plans drawn by Dean & Dean, Motroni successfully remodeled the Caldwell home at 904 First Street (1924) from a modest wooden Bungalow into a smooth plaster finish Mexican style Hacienda with an outdoor patio *(fig. 103)*. This same year, across from the Caldwell house, Motroni crafted a charming Spanish Revival Bungalow for Don and Bernice Huff at 911 First Street *(fig. 104)*. This project signaled Motroni's coming of age as a designer of houses, even though his construction virtually imitated an existing house in Beverly Hills admired by the owners.

103. Caldwell House, 1924, Dean & Dean, architect
Joseph Motroni, builder
courtesy Josephine Motroni Gillette

104. Huff House, 1924, Joseph Motroni
courtesy Josephine Motroni Gillette

Alpha Draper approached Motroni in late 1924 with her idea to build five small bungalows on Cleveland Street, between Main and Court streets. Draper developed the plans herself to meet the needs of couples who wanted the privacy of a small house, but not the upkeep or expense of a large house. Each bungalow contained two rooms and a kitchenette, adding large windows for plenty of fresh air and sunshine. When Motroni completed the "bungalow court" in January 1925, three newlywed couples immediately moved in. Thus, the *Daily Democrat* dubbed the new housing units the "Bridal Court." Motroni built a second bungalow court of six small houses for J.W. Barr at 717-719 Fourth Street (1930).

In 1927 Motroni constructed the rustic Mission Revival style Kraft Bros. Funeral Chapel at 175 First Street, designed by Dean & Dean. Motroni was the low bidder on this prestigious contract, besting other local contractors, E.L. Younger and William Fait. In 1928 he teamed with Berkeley architect, John Hudson Thomas, to build the romantic Tudor Revival home finished with a rusticated stucco exterior for Dr. Blevins at 742 First Street. One year later he built the lovely Tudor Revival style home at 712 Second Street for the Merritt family. Its designer was Carlton Pierson of Woodland.

About 1928 Motroni built a cabinet shop out of the concrete blocks he manufactured and also began selling lumber and hardware at 1038 Beamer Street. Expanding into the lumber and building supply business assured Motroni of timely supplies of building materials for his own construction projects and alleviated his growing frustration with unreliable dealers.

In 1930 Motroni designed and built an impressive

two-story Mediterranean Revival style home at 520 Cross Street *(fig. 105)* on the former site of the John Stephens mansion. Using the big lot effectively, Motroni set the large house back a considerable distance from the street (near where the Stephens mansion had stood) and constructed a circular driveway leading up to the house. Skillfully placed ballast stone, collected by Motroni when he repaved a portion of Main Street with concrete, made an impressive gateway to the front of the house. Though initially planned as the family residence, the Motronis had second thoughts, and they opted for a more modest home constructed by Joe in Beamer Park at 32 Palm Avenue (1929). The Cross Street home was sold to the Epperson family, owners of a downtown car dealership. Motroni also used ballast stone to construct a wall at the Beamer Park home.

Motroni's range extended beyond residences to embrace Woodland's strong baseball culture. Erecting a fine grandstand at Clark Field on Beamer Street in 1930, he and his partners Charles and Alma Robinson, leased this state-of-the-art baseball park to the Woodland Oaks baseball team of the regional Sacramento Valley League. Professional baseball teams from the Pacific Coast League also rented the facility for spring training, including the San Francisco Missions in 1932. By 1933 Motroni and partners faced financial difficulties with Clark Field when the Oaks could not make lease payments. Though Motroni won community praise for carrying the debt as long as he did, eventually the City of Woodland assumed ownership of the ball field.

The early 1930s was a difficult period for builders since there was little demand for new housing. Taking a risk in 1933, Motroni built a Tudor Revival cottage on a speculative basis at 527 W. Keystone Avenue

105. Epperson House, 1930, Joseph Motroni
courtesy Josephine Motroni Gillette

106. D. Traynham House, 1933, Joseph Motroni
courtesy Josephine Motroni Gillette

in Beamer Park *(fig. 106)*. Brick and rock were used skillfully for the exposed chimney, the corners of the house, and around the windows. Moroni's venture paid off as the house sold quickly to Don and Georgia Traynham. This was the only house Joe built in 1933 during the depths of the Great Depression. To make matters worse, his bank closed its doors in 1933 and Joe's money was frozen.

In spite of these hardships and obstacles, Motroni managed to keep his loyal employees working enough to put food on the table. In 1934, using some of the lumber and building supplies he was not able to sell, Motroni and crew built three modest spec houses at 152, 158 and 164 Cleveland Street. He secured the first three F.H.A. loans issued in Woodland. By 1935 homebuilding picked up and in 1936-37 Motroni became very busy filling in many lots in Beamer Park on W. Keystone Avenue, Hollister Road and Sunset Avenue. By now Motroni was designing almost all the houses he built. One exception was a house he built at 507 Sunset Avenue (1937) designed by Dragon & Schmidts. The majority of the homes were constructed of masonry, cement, or stucco, thus displaying the expertise of Motroni and his crew. Many of these designs demonstrate considerable desire to experiment and expand his craft for homebuilding. The house at 511 W. Keystone Avenue (1937), for example, is constructed of volcanic rock with a tile roof.

Motroni's most playful experiment, known as the *airplane house*, was his last personal residence at 524 W. Keystone (1938). Motroni designed the structure in the shape of an airplane with the nose and wings of the "airplane" facing W. Keystone and the fuselage stretching away from the street. As he had done with his two previous personal residences, Joe crafted a sturdy rock wall along the eastern edge of the property.

To enhance the artistic, personal dimension of homebuilding, Motroni commissioned an art student from San Francisco named A. DeSimone to paint a large mural on a wall inside the octagonal entrance of the house. This pastoral, biographical scene depicts a flowing river in the hill country with a winding trail leading to the top of a bluff. A young man in peasant dress is beginning his walk of life up the steep and precipitous trail. Comfortably perched on the top of the hill in front of an Italian villa is an older man. This was 1939 and Joe Motroni, taking stock of his life, could look back over his 48 years with pride in his impressive and difficult ascent from a poor immigrant to a successful, propertied businessman in the New World.

Current owners, Danielle and Ray Thomas, have restored the mural with the assistance of local artist, Cosme Munoz, who added a ceiling mural of blue sky and puffy clouds and a symbolic small airplane. Softly lit by clerestory windows, this space celebrates Joe's productive and inspired life.

In 1938 Motroni decided to sell the lumber and building material business to his brother Guido and Frank Heard, who began working for the company in 1933. Freed of this part of the business, Motroni could now concentrate on running his busy construction company and cabinet shop.

During the war years from 1942 to 1944, Motroni only built one home in Woodland. Showing his adaptability, he worked mostly in the Sutter Basin building granaries, repairing farm buildings, and constructing concrete irrigation structures. After the war, Joe built many small houses along Bliss Avenue and Sutter and Jackson streets on the east side of Beamer Park, including several more speculative houses. In 1948 Guido decided to go into farming and Joe purchased his half share in the lumber business. When Joe died in 1950 of cancer, his son Douglas became Heard's partner and the business prospered for many years until closing in the 1980s.

All in all, Motroni built over 200 houses and buildings in Woodland. No single builder has constructed more custom homes and Motroni designed most of these houses. He also constructed buildings outside of Woodland in Yolo County, Williams, Robbins, and as far away as Jackson in the foothills. The Woodland houses come in all shapes, styles, and sizes. According to Motroni's daughter, Josephine Motroni Gillette, Joe Motroni personally guaranteed his work and took great pride in crafting sturdy homes that are admirably standing the test of time.

Eugenio Ricci & Sons

Italian Mason Converted Humble Home Into a Showcase of his Craft

Born in Montecatini, Italy (also the birthplace of Joseph Motroni), Eugenio Ricci (1883-1949) descended from a long line of brick and tile contractors. After completing his education he apprenticed in this line of work with his father, Peter. In 1906 he married Asunta Danesi Ricci and the couple had three children, Nella, Remo, and Rismo, all born in Italy.

Like many of his fellow countrymen before him, Ricci immigrated to America in 1913 lured by the knowledge that his building skills were in demand and the prospect of building a prosperous life in a new land of opportunity and wealth. He landed in San Francisco where he went to work as a brick and tile setter for the construction of the San Francisco World's Fair.

In 1915 Eugenio settled in Woodland, likely because of his hometown connection with Joe Motroni. For a short period he was a partner with fellow Italian, Fatta, but he would eventually realize his dream of running his own business.

One of the first jobs Ricci tackled was the intricate cornice work on the Yolo County Courthouse, completed in 1917. Designed by William Henry Weeks, this building is a masterwork of terra cotta ceramic tile construction. Ceramic architectural pieces, molded by skilled artisans (many of them Italian) at the Gladding, McBean terra cotta plant in Lincoln, California, were shipped to Woodland by train and installed by skilled craftsmen like Ricci.

Tragically, Eugenio's whole family never united in America. His wife stayed behind in 1913 to be with their three young children. Eventually, the two boys left Italy to join their father in Woodland. Asunta Ricci and her daughter, Nella, stayed behind because Mrs. Ricci had contracted tuberculosis and was not allowed to immigrate to the United States. Eugenio visited Italy in 1926; this was the last time he saw his wife, who died in 1943. In 1947 Nella joined her father and brothers in Woodland.

In 1927 Eugenio formed a partnership with his newly-arrived sons, Remo (1909-1993) and Rismo (b. 1911), with the company name of E. Ricci & Sons. Thus, the Ricci family carried on the family building tradition in the New World.

In 1930 Eugenio purchased a modest home at 96 Railroad Avenue, which borders East Street along the Southern Pacific railroad tracks. He remodeled the home with architectural features that showcased his Italian artistry *(fig. 107)*. On the front facade of the house Ricci crafted a rounded multiple-arched entryway using earth-tone bricks and rock. These materials were also used in the chimney on the side of the house. A fence in a lace pattern was sculpted out of iron and concrete to surround the front yard where Ricci crafted rock sculptures to embellish his garden. Eugenio Ricci's initials adorn both sides of the garden gate. A round flowerpot house was also constructed in the side yard. This one-of-kind house became a landmark of sorts to the passenger trains and motorists passing along East Street.

E. Ricci & Sons worked on numerous houses and buildings in Woodland as a masonry and plastering contractor, including the Hotel Woodland, City Hall, and Beamer School. In 1937 Ricci was awarded the contract to plaster the new Woodland High School Music Building, located on College Street near Marshall, now used for the Douglass Jr. High School music program. The company also constructed the brick Masonic Lodge in Knights Landing.

In 1936 newlyweds Remo and Erma Morelli Ricci built a modern Mediterranean Revival style house at 19 Pershing Avenue in Beamer Park *(fig. 108)*. The white plaster finish, tile roof, courtyard and small tower adorning the house are reminiscent of the Ricci's

107. Remo (left) & Eugenio Ricci in front of Ricci House
courtesy Erma Morrelli Ricci

Italian roots. The house was constructed by Woodland general contractor Del Fenton and Remo.

During this time Rismo Ricci, who had been living with his father, Eugenio, at the family house on 96 East Street, moved to Davis to pursue his own contracting business. Here, Rismo quickly became established and over a long, successful career helped construct many homes and other noted buildings, including the Davis Community Church and the Bank of Davis. After Rismo moved to Davis, Remo and Erma Ricci decided to move in with Eugenio rather than move into their new house in Beamer Park. Subsequently, they sold the Beamer Park house.

Remo, with the help of Michael Landucci, built a new family home at 216 Marshall (1948) of masonry

108. Ricci House, 1936, Delmus Fenton & Remo Ricci
photo by Roger Klemm

construction. After his father's death in 1949, Remo Ricci continued the family business during a long solo career in Woodland. According to his wife, Erma Morelli Ricci, Remo worked as a plasterer and mason until he was 75 years old. He died in 1993.

C. Carleton Pierson

A Talented Local Designer with a Love of Classic Romantic Styles

C. Carleton Pierson
courtesy Louise Stephens Jones

C. Carleton Pierson (1892-1976) moonlighted as a fine house designer for well-heeled friends and clients in Woodland during the boom times of the 1920s through the onset of the Great Depression while commuting by electric train to Sacramento to a steady day job with the State Division of Architecture. All of his documented houses were done early in his career, possibly when he was working as a relatively low paid draftsman. Known as "Perke" by his friends and co-workers, Pierson was a native of Sacramento. While attending UC Davis and studying agriculture, he overheard a remark by acting State Architect, Maury I. Diggs, that jobs were available with the state architecture program. Deciding against farming as a calling, Pierson acted on Diggs' lead; he was hired by the State Architect's Office in 1911 as an assistant to the office boy, which meant running errands and making blueprints. During the next four decades Pierson steadily worked his way up the office ladder as a draftsman, estimator, inspector, and, finally, became supervising specifications writer.

In 1917 Pierson moved to Woodland and married Dorothy Chiles Ross, then lived in a rented farmhouse near Brown's Corner at 17380 Road 98 (still standing). By the time of his retirement in 1955, Perke Pierson figured his "dual life" meant he had commuted 415,000 miles between Woodland and Sacramento.

Pierson never became a licensed architect. On blueprints of the houses he drew he is listed as a "designer." Nonetheless, his talent as a house designer is evident in the finely crafted homes built in the late 1920s when Old European Revival styles were in fashion.

The lovely Tudor Revival home designed for Dr. William A. Eckart at 902 Elm Street (1929) has a

109. Bruton House, 1927, C. Carleton Pierson, architect
photo by Roger Klemm

110. Robert Huston House, 1928, C. Carlton Pierson
photo by Roger Klemm

wide shingled roofline with flush-faced dormer windows and a tall chimney. A steep gabled front facade frames the simple, porch-less front entrance. The house is set back from the street with a wide lawn and garden featuring an English Copper Beech tree. The home Pierson designed at 415 Bartlett Street (1927)

111. Merritt House, 1929, C. Carlton Pierson, architect
Joseph Motroni, builder
courtesy Josephine Motroni Gillette

for Yolo County Superior Court Judge J. Grant Bruton followed a sketch Bruton brought back from the French countryside as a lieutenant in World War I. The rustic cottage has a side entrance and three French style doors open from the main living area to the outdoors *(fig. 109)*.

Pierson's charming, single story Tudor Revival cottage designed for Robert and Clare Huston at 617 Cross Street (1928) has a "ski slope" sweeping roofline, bay window, simple arched entrance and a lovely garden and courtyard fashioned by Kathy and Ken Trott *(fig. 110)*.

Further Pierson successes are the Merritt House (1929) at 712 Second Street *(fig. 111)* and Lowe House (1931) at 815 College Street *(fig. 112)*, both very fine renditions of the two-story Tudor Revival style with tall, pointed gables, no roof overhang, prominent chimneys, simple entrances without sitting porches, and set within gracious yards. Joe Motroni constructed both of these houses.

The Nannie Stephens House (1927) at 603 College Street is a "Hansel & Gretel" cottage capturing the charm and romance of the dollhouse *(fig. 113)*. A low sloping shingled roof, pierced by a recessed dormer

112. Lowe House, 1931, C. Carlton Pierson, architect
Joseph Motroni, builder
courtesy Josephine Motroni Gillette

113. N. Stephens House, 1927, C. Carlton Pierson
photo by Roger Klemm

114. Arthur Huston House, 1929, C. Carlton Pierson, architect, Brown & Woodhouse, builder
photo by Roger Klemm

window, covers half of the front facade, reducing the scale of the wooden plank front door. Rounding out Pierson's impressive legacy is a Colonial Revival house at 611 Bartlett Avenue built for Arthur and Lorraine Huston (1929, *fig. 114*). The dormer windows and central gable with Palladian window are symmetrically positioned on the front facade, as are the downstairs windows. Jeff and Kelley Morgan upgraded the house with a faux painted front entrance and window shutters and constructed a matching garage.

After his retirement, Carleton Pierson moved to Los Gatos where he died in 1976. He is buried in the Woodland Cemetery.

Delmus Fenton

A Long, Productive Life for Woodland Builder

Delmus Fenton from *History of Yolo County*, William Russell, ed., 1940

Born in Springfield, Ohio, Delmus "Del" Fenton (1876-1973) learned the builder's craft from his father. Coming west in 1906 to help rebuild San Francisco after the earthquake, Fenton bounced between construction jobs in San Francisco, Davis (where his uncle lived), and Berkeley before settling in Woodland in 1909.

In the early days of his career Fenton was active in Davis. He constructed the octagon-shaped Livestock Judging Pavilion (1907), one of the original buildings on the UC Davis campus. Later moved to Old Davis Road, this building is now a theater. In addition, he constructed most of the original commercial buildings on the west side of G Street between Second and Third Streets in downtown Davis, including the Davis Masonic Lodge (1917) located at 221 G Street. Fenton also built the H.J. Hamel House (1920) at 505 Second Street in Davis, now a realty office.

Fenton designed and built many homes in Woodland during a long career. He constructed a classic two-story bungalow at 532 Elm Street for his family (1925, *fig. 115*) and lived here until his death at age 97 in 1973. The Carrow house at 716 Third Street (1928) is a finely crafted home done in the Spanish-Revival style *(fig. 116)*. The house has a large arched entrance flanked by a pair of Palladian windows.

George Cranston, one of the owners of Cranston Bros. Hardware, hired Fenton to construct a large home at 148 North Street (1930). This house was built as somewhat of a twin to the adjoining house owned by his brother, Lester, and constructed by Joseph Motroni in 1929. These two houses literally face each

115. Fenton House, 1925, Delmus Fenton
photo by Roger Klemm

116. Carrow House, 1928, Delmus Fenton
photo by Roger Klemm

118. Florist Shop, Emmet Pugh, designer, Delmus Fenton, builder
photo by Roger Klemm

117. G. Cranston House (left), 1930, Delmus Fenton, **L. Cranston House (right),** 1929, Joseph Motroni
photo by Roger Klemm

other, with front entrances angled away from North Street *(fig. 117)*. The house constructed by Fenton is a Tudor Revival, with a high-pitched roof, flush-faced dormers unusually placed on the side of the house, and two Palladian windows on the ground floor.

In 1936 Fenton constructed two picturesque houses in Beamer Park. The lovely French-style cottage at 714 West Keystone, built for Ken and Alice Laugenour, was built from plans drawn by the noted Sacramento architect, Charles Dean. Fenton also assisted Remo Ricci, a plastering contractor, with a house at 19 Pershing Avenue that harkens back to Ricci's native Italy. The Mediterranean-Revival house has a small tower at the angle of the L-shaped plan, a courtyard, and a white plaster finish with a tile roof.

Further, Fenton completed several commercial projects in Woodland. An Art Deco florist shop at the southeast corner of Main and West Streets designed by its owner, Emmet Pugh, has Egyptian motifs *(fig. 118)*. The large motel complex constructed by Fenton for developer A.H. Weston (1946) at 127 Main Street was converted to a senior housing complex in the 1980s. Del Fenton lived to be over 90 years old and left a lengthy legacy of buildings that significantly contributed to Woodland's rich architectural character.

Gustave Wingblade

He Played in the Eagle Band and Built Bungalows

Gustave Wingblade in Eagle Band Attire
courtesy Yolo County Museum

A native of Sweden, Gustave "Gus" Wingblade (c1873-1938) immigrated to the United States as a boy. He learned the builder's trade in the eastern United States before moving to Yolo County in 1905. In Woodland he was probably employed as a carpenter before he began to purchase lots on the north side of town and build a variety of handsome wooden bungalows. Wingblade was also a musician, playing clarinet in the Woodland Eagle Band.

From 1915 to 1923, Gustave Wingblade and his wife, Mary, lived at 1 First Street. He then built a classic two story Bungalow at 4 First Street (1923), which served briefly as the family home until it was sold in 1925, presumably to raise working capital for his building business *(fig. 119)*. In 1928, when Wingblade may well have gained some financial security, he constructed another Bungalow at 21 First Street where the family resided for many years. Gustave died in the home in 1938 at the age of 65, while Mary Wingblade, who lived to be 97, resided here until the late 1960s.

Wingblade built several homes on north First Street during the boom period of the 1920s, but there are no city building records documenting earlier homes he may have built. The Craftsman Bungalow at 39 First Street (1926) exemplifies his fine homebuilding skills: it is low-pitched, constructed of redwood, with brick accents along the porch and a tall chimney *(fig. 120)*. Lush vine and mature trees on the property complement the organic feel of the house and typify the Craftsman aesthetic of rustic simplicity.

119. Wingblade House, 1923, Gustave Wingblade
photo by Roger Klemm

120. Koch House, 1926, Gustave Wingblade
photo by Roger Klemm

Jacob Witzelberger

A Builder and Distributor of Steam Beer

Jacob "Jack" Witzelberger (1880-1966) was born in Munich, Germany and immigrated to the United States as a young man. After living for a period of time in San Francisco, he settled in Woodland in the early 1920s and constructed his own home, a stucco bungalow at 737 Second Street (1922, *fig. 121*). This house is almost identical to a house he built for H.G. Kennedy, a PG&E employee, at 724 First Street (1922).

121. Witzelberger House, 1922, Jacob Witzelberger
photo by Roger Klemm

At the time he was building these houses, Witzelberger was awarded a contract to construct a one-room United Brethren in Christ church at 900 Lincoln Avenue (1922). This simple structure has a short tower and is clad in shingles, its small scale and rustic appearance making it a good neighbor to the adjoining residential area. Although the building is now surrounded by commercial structures, a small apartment building crafted by Witzelberger at 30 Main Street attracts with its elegant classical symmetry. Constructed of brick, the building has upper bay windows with light brick banding surrounding the lower windows, the double entry doors and under the decorative cornice *(fig. 122)*.

122. Small Apartment Building, Jacob Witzelberger
photo by Roger Klemm

123. Witzelberger (far left) distributed Fredericksburg Beer and Old Joe Steam Beer
courtesy Yolo County Archives

In addition to building houses and churches, Witzelberger also constructed commercial projects in Woodland. He was awarded a $10,000 contract to enlarge the Main Street Garage on the southwest corner of Main and Elm streets (1923) for proprietors Perry Hiatt and N. Lee Miller. Witzelberger subcontracted with Joseph Motroni for the stone and tile work on the building.

In 1934 a fire started at the Yolo Brewery on Main Street (near the location of Nugget Market), spread south along Cleveland Street and destroyed St. John's Evangelical Church. A committee formed to rebuild the church hired Witzelberger to construct the picturesque brick Gothic Revival structure at 434 Cleveland Street (1935) from plans drawn by William Coffman. Witzelberger gained praise for building the new church and adjoining parsonage in 90 days.

Chinese grocer Wong Lee hired Witzelberger in 1939 to build the Streamline Moderne style Yolo Grocery Building at 534 Bush Street. Designed by Berkeley architects Dragon & Schmidts, the aerodynamic-looking building is finely crafted with aqua-blue tile, chrome banding, and glass skylights. Although Witzelberger was the initial contractor for the job, historical records indicate that another builder was hired to finish the project.

Like other builders of his era, Witzelberger was an improviser and diversified into other businesses to compensate for the ups and downs of the construction industry. In 1933, during the depths of the Great Depression, he started the Yolo Colusa Beverage Company as a distributor *(fig. 123).* He also built and operated the 99 Motel at 117 W. Main Street, adjacent to his family house. These buildings were razed by family heirs and redeveloped into the present-day commercial center. Jacob Witzelberger died in Woodland in 1966 at age 85.

Rollin S. Tuttle

He Designed the Church He Preached In

Rollin S. Tuttle
courtesy Lake Merritt United Methodist Church

Rollin S. Tuttle (1886-1931) had the unique Woodland distinction of being both a licensed architect of considerable talent and an ordained minister. Tuttle was educated for the ministry at Wesleyan University in Connecticut and for several years served as a pastor at various churches in the eastern states. Apparently inspired by ecclesiastical architecture he had observed first hand, Tuttle moved to the West Coast to enroll at University of Southern California in the architecture program. After completing his studies, he practiced architecture for a period in Los Gatos before moving to Oakland.

Rollin Tuttle was associated with his brother Paul V. Tuttle for much of his work. Between 1922-24 he had a dual career in Oakland serving as pastor of St. Stevens Methodist Episcopal Church on East 38th Street in Oakland, a church he designed in 1924, while designing other churches in both northern and southern California.

About this time, the First Methodist Episcopal Church of Woodland made plans to build their own new church at Second and North streets. The firm of Tuttle & Tuttle must have seemed like the ideal choice for the building committee with Rollin having a direct connection to the church and a solid architectural track record.

Designed in the Mission Revival style, the Woodland church was similar to Tuttle's parish in Oakland *(fig. 124)*. A tall bell tower flanks the tiled gable roofs of the sanctuary. The Second Street facade of the building has a tall arched, stained glass window with columns above the entrance, which is formed by a tiled arcade with classical columns. There is another arched stained glass window on the North Street facade with circular stained glass above the altar. A series of triplicate arched stained glass windows line both sides of the sanctuary. The interior of the building is quite tall and spacious with exposed elaborate wooden trusses.

124. Woodland United Methodist Church, 1925,
Rollin S. Tuttle
courtesy Woodland United Methodist Church

The blueprints for the project indicate the actual church was smaller than its original design. A two-story section of the church south of the bell tower was never completed, apparently for budgetary reasons. Woodland contractor, William R. Fait, constructed the church, which was dedicated in June 1925.

Specializing in church design, Tuttle promoted himself as an "ecclesiastical architect" through newspaper ads. He designed several other churches in northern California during his brief career, including the Arts & Crafts style Chinese Presbyterian Church on 8th Street in Oakland in 1927 as well as edifices in San Jose, Richmond, Watsonville, and Ukiah.

Newspaper advertisements for the dedication of the Woodland church included sketches of two churches for Long Beach. Tuttle died at a relatively young age in 1931.

Thomas George

English Orphan Finds Success in Woodland

Born in London, England, Thomas George (1886-1972) was an orphan raised by his aunt and uncle. During his formative years, he was placed in a carpentry apprenticeship program to learn a building trade and, as a young man, immigrated to San Francisco via a stint in Ontario, Canada. In 1914 he settled in Woodland, rented a room from a distant relative, and free-lanced as a carpenter for a few years. He married Lillian Alice Mumma in 1917.

Like other contractors of his era, George bought a lot, built a home on a speculative basis, then rented the house to cover his debt or sold the property after its value rose. According to his son, Robert George, Thomas generally drew his own house plans and bought his lumber and building materials from a Mr. Toof, who ran the Diamond Match Lumber Company. Mr. Toof sometimes referred prospective homebuyers to George as part of their business arrangement.

Most of the houses built by George in the '20s and '30s were modest, vernacular homes. The first home he constructed was his family home at 609 Fourth Street (1918-since remodeled). In 1929 George was able to buy the old Usual Shellhammer property west of Woodland and build a new family home at 37179 Highway 16. George continued to build homes until about 1940 when the war halted construction.

The stucco Bungalow constructed by George at 1009 First Street has a single low-pitched gable roof resting on four stout elephantine columns, a wide sitting porch and saw-tooth decorative trim added as a custom touch by the builder *(fig. 125)*. A wooden Bungalow at 736 Fourth Street has no porch, but a stoop entrance protected by a small gable roof *(fig. 126)*.

According to Robert George, his father built over 30 houses in and around Woodland, but not all of these have been documented to date. After World War II, George quit the building business and lived comfortably on rental income from his houses and farmland. He died in 1972.

125. 1009 First Street, Thomas George
photo by Roger Klemm

126. 736 Fourth Street, Thomas George
photo by Roger Klemm

Lester J. Caldwell

World War I Veteran Continues the Family Building Tradition

Captain Lester J. Caldwell
from *Woodland Daily Democrat*, May 8, 1919

Lester J. Caldwell (1887-1940) learned the construction trade from his father, Joseph Caldwell, with whom he was in the contracting business for a number of years. He was the nephew of Samuel Caldwell, a leading Victorian-era builder in Woodland. Lester was born in Woodland, attended local schools, and married Elizabeth Young in 1908. He was a veteran, serving as a captain in local Company F National Guard and in World War I.

During the early years of his building career, both before and just after returning from the War, he was in partnership with Ernest Brown, but eventually became an independent builder.

"Cap" Caldwell, as the press affectionately called him, exploited his status as a returning war hero to promote his home building business in an interview in the Woodland *Daily Democrat* on May 8, 1919:

Many persons of wealth have largely added to their fortunes through the war, even after deduction of income and profit taxes. The present is a favorable period for the use of such gains in the immediate building of new homes, so that the desired increase of comfort or of luxury may be enjoyed at an early date.

Delay may result in the spending or the unwise investment of such savings. It is a part of wisdom to begin promptly the best form of investment for the workingman — a home for himself and his family.

City building records indicate Caldwell built several homes in the '20s and '30s south of Pendegast Street between Second and Third Streets. An inviting Mediterranean Revival home for Fred Weider at 753 Third Street (1927) features two very large leaded glass picture windows, opening the house to the street. The doorway is outlined by plaster quoins, mimicking Italian stone work *(fig. 127)*. His interesting Spanish Revival house for O.D. and Neva Payne, designed by C.A. Walton at 750 Third Street (1927), boasts a flat two-tiered roofline shaped like simple geometric boxes, influences attributed to the noted Southern California architect, Irving Gill.

Lester J. Caldwell's building career was cut short by a fatal heart attack in 1940 at the age of 53.

127. Weider House, 1927, Lester J. Caldwell
photo by Roger Klemm

William E. Coffman

A Picturesque Church Before a Promising Career Tragically Cut Short

On September 8, 1934 a fire started at the Yolo Brewery on Main Street (about where Nugget Market is today) and destroyed not only the brewery but also several houses, St. John's Evangelical Church, and its parsonage on Cleveland Street. The congregation decided to quickly rebuild and selected Sacramento architect, William E. Coffman (1891-1937), to design the new church.

Located at 434 Cleveland Street and now known as St. John's United Church of Christ, the church is Tudor Revival in style constructed in a checkered pattern of light and dark clinker bricks *(fig. 128)*. A steeply pitched gable forms the main structure of the church, with an attic vent shaped like a cross and a large round stained glass window (added during an interior remodel of 1991) on the front facade. There is a side entrance to the church at an adjoining rectangular-shaped tower through a Tudor arch enclosing a pair of wooden plank doors and stained glass window. Several pairs of tall stained glass windows line both sides of the main axis of the church, with side doorways framed with blocks of concrete imitating stone.

The parsonage, built with the church in a matching brick pattern, has two half-timbered gables, one with a flattened rustic shape and a tall chimney. The landscape architects for the project were H. Dana Bowers and P.H. Cushing. Amazingly, construction began in January 1935, a mere four months after the fire, and was completed in just 90 days by Woodland contractor and church member, Jacob "Jack" Witzelberger using a large crew of workers.

William E. Coffman originally hailed from Chico, attended school in Tehama County, studied business and drafting at Heald's Business College in Chico, and worked two years as a draftsman for Diamond Match Company. In 1916 he moved to Sacramento, where he found drafting work for a short period before enlisting in the military. During World War I he served in France, was wounded, and received medals for bravery.

128. St. John's United Church of Christ, 1934, William E. Coffman, architect, Jacob Witzelberger, builder
photo by Roger Klemm

129. **Jones House,** 1932, Brown & Woodhouse
photo by Roger Klemm

130. **Reid Duplex,** 1932, Brown & Woodhouse
photo by Roger Klemm

After the war, Coffman began his apprenticeship by way of drafting jobs for Sacramento architectural firms George Sellon & Co. and Leonard F. Starks & Co. In 1928 the partnership of "Coffman-Sahlberg-Stafford Architects & Engineers" was formed and, among its Sacramento landmarks, are the Eastern Star Hall at 2719 K Street and the Oak Park Library at 3301 5th Avenue.

Coffman became an independent architect about 1930 and in 1935 Coffman and family were living in an upscale Spanish Colonial Revival home that he presumably designed at 1126 46th Street. Tragically, about the time Coffman was coming into his own as an architect, he was killed in an automobile accident in 1937.

Brown & Woodhouse

Creators of Upscale Homes Between the Wars

Howard Brown & Family
courtesy Ronald M. Noble

Howard Brown (1896-1972) and Albert Woodhouse (d.1952) formed the prominent design-build firm, Brown & Woodhouse, in Woodland in 1928. Born in Indiana, Brown's family moved to Del Paso Heights when he was a teenager. After serving in the army during World War I, he became a general contractor and moved to Woodland in 1927 where he probably met Woodhouse. Little is known about Woodhouse, other than he was a highly skilled carpenter originally from England.

Although Brown had no formal training as an architect, he designed many of the upscale houses the firm built between 1928 and World War II. An early example of their craftsmanship is the rectory adjacent to St. Luke's Episcopal Church at 515 Second Street (1928). The Elizabethan half-timbered style complements the grace and old world charm of the 1912 church.

Underneath a majestic valley oak tree at 749 College Street, Brown & Woodhouse built a lovely Colonial Revival home for M.E. "Elmer" Jones, manager of the local J.C. Penny's store (1932, *fig. 129*). This house has an upper story gabled roof and single story gambrel roofline with narrow shed dormers. Brown & Woodhouse also built a single story version of this style of house for Jones at 105 Bartlett Avenue (1940). The quaint Tudor Revival duplex built for Sadie Reid at 151-153 Third Street (1932) has "eyebrow" attic vents on the shingled roof and gabled entrances at both ends of the building *(fig. 130)*.

Between 1938 and 1941 Brown & Woodhouse was

131. Geer House, 1941, Brown & Woodhouse
photo by Roger Klemm

particularly active building homes in its own subdivision in the southwest part of Woodland along the 100 and 200 blocks of Bartlett, Marshall, and Hays. Several of these single story, rectilinear homes are good examples of the Ranch Style, likely inspired by the designs of California architects Cliff May and William Wurster and featured during this period in *Sunset Magazine*.

The Ranch house at 140 Marshall Avenue built for Orvil Geer (1941) is linear, single story, with shuttered windows and an attached garage — all typical elements of houses mass produced in subdivisions after World War II *(fig. 131)*. The house built at 216 Hays Street for Margaret Muhl (1940) is a smaller scale version of the Ranch style.

Brown & Woodhouse dissolved their partnership in 1942 when World War II slowed house construction. Howard Brown moved to San Francisco and then to Florida where he spent his final years. When construction rebounded after World War II, Albert Woodhouse worked independently. During this time Woodhouse resided at 804 First Street in a remodeled Victorian house originally designed and built by Edward Carlton Gilbert in 1893. He had a cabinet shop at the rear of the property. Woodhouse continued to build houses until the time of his death in 1952.

Anton Paulsen

Danish Immigrant Missed the Titanic but Captured the California Dream

Anton Paulsen
courtesy Bessie Paulsen Tufts

Living a long accomplished life in his adopted land, Anton Paulsen fulfilled the immigrant's dream of exploiting economic opportunity and leading a multifaceted life in California, the land of dreams. Born in Hjorring, Denmark, Paulsen (1885-1979) grew up on the family dairy farm. Ambitious and adventurous, he completed his high school education and studied architecture at night classes. As a young man of twenty, he sailed to New York and moved to Chicago where he constructed railroad passenger cars for the Pullman Company. He headed to San Francisco where construction work was plentiful after the 1906 earthquake.

In 1911, perhaps from homesickness or in search of a bride, Paulsen returned to Denmark and resettled. He married Christa Regnar in 1912 and they operated a furniture factory for a short period until returning permanently to the United States. According to Paulsen's daughter, Bessie Tufts, fate may have saved the Paulsens on their return voyage to America. Anton and Christa Paulsen had tickets booked on the Titanic, but delays in selling their furniture factory in Denmark caused them to miss the boat.

After working for a few years in San Francisco, Paulsen became a rice farmer and moved the family to the Willows area. In 1920 the Paulsens settled in Woodland where Paulsen was hired to help build the Woodland Clinic, perhaps working for contractor William Fait. During his long life in Woodland, Paulsen developed a dual career as both a rice farmer and general contractor.

In the early 1930s, Paulsen bought property along the south side of Pendegast Street, between Second and Third Streets. He designed and constructed several charming Tudor Revival homes with brick accents, including the family home at 702 Pendegast Street (1931, *fig. 132*). The houses at 716 and 720 Pendegast Street and at 802 Third Street are similar in style and create a unified grouping of period homes. In 1948 the Paulsens moved to the west side of town to 410 Buena Tierra into a new home built by Paulsen and his son-in-law partner, James G. Adams. This house is basically a one-story version of the old family house on Pendegast.

Between 1930 and 1950, buffeted with major "down" periods caused by the Great Depression and

132. Paulsen House, 1931, Anton Paulsen
photo by Roger Klemm

133. Peckman House, 1939, Anton Paulsen
photo by Roger Klemm

134. Mather House, 1939, Anton Paulsen
photo by Roger Klemm

World War II, Paulsen built a few homes each year to supplement his farm income. The Tudor Revival style house at 5 West Street (1937) makes good use of a corner lot to display a series of Palladian windows, with this pattern repeated at the front entrance to the house. Paulsen constructed a nice rendition of a single story rectilinear Ranch house for R.M. Peckman at 132 Bartlett Avenue (1939, *fig. 133*). Across the street, he built a large picturesque Tudor Revival house for C. Mather at 131 Bartlett (1939, *fig. 134*), which boasts a large lot with many trees.

Engaged in the community, Paulsen served on the Woodland Planning Commission and in 1937 the City Council appointed Paulsen to fill a vacancy on the council. In 1939 he was elected to a four-year term on the Woodland City Council. As an extension of his rice farming interests, Paulsen developed Sunset Rice Dryers during WWII in partnership with his son, B. Regnar Paulsen and Peter Christiansen. This facility, located at the corner of Kentucky Avenue and East Street, was eventually sold to PIRMI and still operates today. Active in the Masonic Order, Paulsen was selected by his peers to build the Masonic Temple located at 228 Palm Avenue (1958) from plans drawn by Woodland architect Robert Crippen. Paulsen's long, inspired life came to an end in 1979. He was 96 years old.

Dragon, Schmidts & Hardman

Critical Talent Behind the Weeks' "Design Machine" Leave Their Own Legacy

Perhaps the most recognizable architect in Woodland lore is William Henry Weeks, the celebrated architect of small town California. Yet behind the marquee name of Weeks were many top design professionals working behind the scenes at Weeks' large Bay Area offices.

One of the top staff architects for the prestigious Weeks firm for many years was Paul Lewis Dragon, Sr. (c.1882-1949). Born in Kansas City, Missouri, Dragon graduated from Stanford University and settled in Berkeley in 1919. As a staff architect, Dragon spent considerable time in Woodland with various projects and was involved with the designs for the Porter Building (1913), Yolo County Courthouse (1917), and Hotel Woodland (1928). After many

135. Vickery House, 1937, Dragon & Schmidts, architect
Joseph Motroni, builder
photo by Roger Klemm

136. Yolo Grocery, 1939, Dragon & Schmidts, architect,
Jacob Witzelberger, builder
photo by Roger Klemm

137. Christian Church, Disciples of Christ, 1949
Dragon, Schmidts & Hardman
photo by Roger Klemm

productive years of working for Weeks, Dragon and another employee of Weeks, Carl R. Schmidts, quit the Weeks firm in 1931 to form their own partnership in Berkeley.

Dragon & Schmidts designed three structures in Woodland. A modest Ranch style house designed for J.M. Vickery at 507 Sunset in Beamer Park was constructed by Joe Motroni (1937, *fig. 135*). Built of brick, the facade has a large gable with extended flush-faced chimney and a large picture window flanked by casement windows. The entrance to the house is level with the yard and there is no sitting porch.

In 1939 the firm was commissioned by the Lee family to design the Streamline Moderne style Yolo Grocery Building at 534 Bush Street *(fig. 136)*. Reflecting the "less is more" philosophy of the 1930s and the aerodynamics of aircraft, the building has rounded corners and aqua-blue tile horizontal banding along the upper part of the structure. The broad marquee of the building has chrome banding. The Lees operated their grocery store into the 1980s.

The enlarged firm of Dragon, Schmidts & Hardman also designed the picturesque Mission Revival style Christian Church, Disciples of Christ at 509 College Street (1949, *fig. 137*). The elegantly proportioned facade of the church has a deeply recessed arched entrance with classical columns and capitals. Period light fixtures, recessed windows mimicking thick adobe walls, and a traditional interior courtyard evoke the California Mission ambience. A small chapel fronting the courtyard connects the church to the Educational Building constructed by Motroni (1927).

The Spanish Colonial Revival style Davis City Hall (1938), at 226 F Street in downtown Davis is a familiar Yolo County building designed by this firm.

Noted for expertise in school design, following mentor Weeks, the Dragon firm designed the Art Deco/Moderne style Whittier School in 1939, now a Berkeley historical landmark. Paul Dragon died in Berkeley in 1949 at the age of 67.

Younger Bros. Inc.

The Purity Market Story

Jack Younger from *San Francisco Focus*, July 1993, p.27

Woodland contractor Earle E. Younger's nephews, Don and Jack Younger, principals of Younger Bros. Inc., a general contracting company based in San Francisco, built approximately 80 Purity Markets throughout northern and central California, including the store in Woodland at 528 Bush Street (1939, *fig. 138)*. An older brother, Dwen Younger, a self-taught structural engineer, developed the signature arch-shaped design for Purity Market, thus visually distinguishing them from traditional box-shaped groceries.

Purity Market's first few stores were constructed in a more traditional design. However, Younger Bros. demonstrated that Dwen Younger's prototype "air-

138. Purity Market, 1939, Younger Bros., Inc.
photo by Roger Klemm

plane hanger" design could be built cheaper and was structurally sound. Consequently, a long-standing business partnership was consummated between builder and grocery store chain. Today, many of these "funny looking" Purity stores are instantly recognizable in small towns throughout northern California. Today, many have been cleverly adapted to other uses, including a two-story City Hall in the City of Willits.

In addition to his success as a builder, Jack Younger is a well-known philanthropist. In 1972 he visited a Guatemalan mountain village, Nuevo Progreso, and was moved by the critical need for a medical clinic. He proceeded to raise funds in the Bay Area to build a hospital in the small village. Younger's vision and commitment to the project resulted in the creation of 45-bed hospital, staffed by volunteer doctors, nurses, and dentists who fly to Guatemala at different times during the year.

William B. David

A Dashing Figure and Creator of Art Deco Movie Theaters

William B. David *courtesy Richard Mann*

In 1937 a large "movie palace" named the State Theatre opened at 322 Main Street in Woodland, and its designer was William B. David (1905-1985). The Art Deco theater created a stir in town, with its glamorous marquee and tower, 1,000 seats, and refrigerated air conditioning *(fig. 139 & 140)*. Redwood Theatres of San Francisco developed the theater for a total cost of $175,000.

The State Theatre was the

139. State Theatre, 1937, William B. David, designer *courtesy Richard Mann*

140. State Theatre – Interior
courtesy Richard Mann

second theater developed in Woodland by Redwood Theatre group. In 1936 the Porter Theatre opened at 327 College Street, behind the Porter Building. This non-descript building grew out of a post office constructed in 1924 by Woodland builder, Earle L. Younger. The Porter Theatre was remodeled into an office building in 1959 and the building was substantially upgraded in appearance in the 1990s.

In a June 25, 1937 front-page spread on the grand opening of the State Theatre, the Woodland *Daily Democrat* summarized the appeal of the design:

Architecturally, it follows the colonial theme, with bold, modern strokes that almost obscure its basic form. Innovations in design and color have been skillfully blended by architects working under the direction of W.B. David, supervisor of architecture for the two theatre men, and converted into reality by the workmen of Moore and Roberts, San Francisco contractor . . . true to its note of ultra modernism, the State Theatre utilizes glass in many forms and novel methods. It is incorporated in the exterior design to illuminate the marquee and vertical sign, which present the only design of their kind in the United States.

The main auditorium is arranged in the new and

increasingly popular stadium style, in which there is no balcony, and every seat has an unobstructed view of the screen . . . Developing the theme of Colonial architecture upon which the lines of State Theatre is based is a mural on the wall of the lounge . . . Principals in the painting are a colonial lady and her escort, executing one of the graceful figures of the stately minuet. The mural was prepared by R.A.Eckels of the Eckels Studios, with offices in San Francisco and Los Angeles.

William B. David, the man in charge of the creation of the State Theatre, had a very colorful, flamboyant career in the creative arts. He was born in Brockton, Massachusetts in 1905 and moved to Pasadena with his parents. As a young man he worked his way through college, graduated from UCLA and worked as a Hollywood set designer for the movie studios of William Randolph Hearst. He also was employed by Hearst to help with interior design of his castle at San Simeon.

Much to Hearst's displeasure, David quit working for him to join the offices of nationally known theater architect, Sim Charles Lee of Los Angeles. Here, under the tutelage of Lee, David received his training as a cutting-edge designer of movie palaces. Never a licensed architect, David worked as a "registered building designer" who collaborated with licensed architects and engineers to get his plans approved by local building departments. In fact, a citation in the *Daily Pacific Builder* on September 2, 1936 cites S. Charles Lee as the "official" architect for the State Theatre project in Woodland.

In the 1930s, the Redwood Theatre Group, headed by George Mann, retained David to design several new theaters. Those theaters in northern California designed by David include the State Theatre in Modesto (1934), the Tower Theatres in both Marysville and Sacramento, the Esquire Theatre in Sacramento, the Noyo Theatre in Willits, a surviving theater in Eureka, and the State and Porter Theatres in Woodland. William David eventually became Vice President of the Redwood Theatre group and was part owner of the State Theatre in Woodland until his death.

During World War II, David parted ways with George Mann and returned to Hollywood to make several movies with his company, Golden Gate Pictures. After the War, when building resumed, David returned to San Francisco to pursue architecture, commercial development opportunities, and his favorite recreational pursuits: horses, aviation, and sports car racing. At one time, David was president of the Sports Car Club of America and was a member of the Motion Picture Pioneers of America.

In 1956, David designed the "million dollar" Woodland Shopping Center, developed by Joseph Blumenfeld Enterprises of the Bay Area. As Woodland's first automobile-oriented shopping center, it was located on Main Street, just a few blocks west of the State Theatre on the old site of Holy Rosary Academy, which partially burned in 1952 and was demolished in 1956. J.C. Penney's moved from its downtown location into a much larger store as the anchor tenant at David's new shopping center, along with F.W. Woolworth.

The Woodland Shopping Center was one of many shopping centers designed by William B. David & Associates. One of David's largest clients was the Blumenfeld Corporation, the developer of many theaters and shopping centers throughout northern California, including Country Club Center in Sacramento. In addition to designing the Woodland Shopping Center, David was a part owner of the project.

In the latter part of his career, David returned to work as a designer for George Mann's son, Richard Mann, who took over the theater empire of his father and continued to develop movie theaters throughout northern California. William B. David died in San Francisco in 1985 at the age of 80.

As of 2002, Richard Mann still owns the State Theatre building in Woodland and leases the building to a theater operator. The original elegant marquee and tower of the State Theatre were taken down several years ago by order of Caltrans when Main Street was designated part of State Highway 16. Caltrans claimed the marquee encroached on the highway.

William I. Stille

The Food Market that Grew and Grew

William I. Stille
courtesy Gene Stille

A commercial icon in Woodland, Nugget Market is the lone surviving grocery store that originated in a small storefront in the historical core of downtown. Nugget Market was founded in 1926 at 416 Main Street in the Gibson Block (1889). (Although most of the Gibson Block was demolished, the Nugget storefront still remains). The market was co-founded by father William I. Stille (1877-1953) and son Mack N. Stille.

In 1946 William designed and built a modern, freestanding Nugget Market at 157 Main Street *(fig. 141)* on a vacant lot formerly occupied by the Yolo Brewery, which burned down in 1934. Built with iron posts and trusses and concrete block, this first store, having been enlarged several times, is today hidden within the greater footprint of the modern superstore. Woodland architect Robert Schaefer supervised a large store expansion in the early 1970s that included the tile mural with a Gold Rush theme.

Born in Indiana, William Stille grew up helping his father in the general construction trade. The family moved to Missouri where William and his father built a small chapel in Georgetown that is still standing. William married in Missouri and his son Mack was born there. The family migrated west in search

141. Nugget Market, 1946, William I. Stille
courtesy Gene Stille

142. J.H. Laugenour House, 1940, William I. Stille
photo by Roger Klemm

of greener pastures with stops in Colorado, Portland and Dunsmuir. After Mack Stille moved to Woodland to work for Diamond Match Company as a draftsman, his father joined him to open the grocery store in 1926. William and Mack Stille co-owned Nugget Market until William sold his interest to his son in 1940.

During the 1930s and '40s William built several houses in Woodland. The family home he constructed at 144 Park Avenue (1937) is a modest stucco bungalow. The Ranch style house he built on a wide lot for J.H. Laugenour at 920 Elm Street (1940) is a classic rendition of the style, built low to the ground, long and rectilinear, with shuttered windows and attached garage *(fig. 142)*.

Keehn Keehn & Lucchesi

Home, Commercial and Ag Contractors

Formed in 1935 by Alfred V. Keehn (1908-1980) and Leo Lucchesi (d.1980), this general contracting firm built homes, grain dryers and silos, and swimming pools in the Woodland area through 1955. Keehn and Lucchesi worked for Brown & Woodhouse builders in Woodland prior to starting their own building company. Alfred's brother, John A. Keehn, Jr. (1910-2002), joined the firm in 1939. Alfred and John Keehn Jr. were sons of John Keehn Sr., of the Keehn Brothers contracting firm.

Alfred Keehn oversaw the business end of the company and did job estimating, bidding, and drafting of plans. As a young man Alfred overcame two severely broken ankles suffered from a fall through the roof of a warehouse on a job site. During his recuperation he studied construction at a trade school in Berkeley. Leo Lucchesi specialized in cement and brick masonry, including stucco and plaster work. John Keehn was an all-around carpenter who served as foreman of the construction crews for the company. A third Keehn brother, Joseph T. Keehn, worked as a laborer and carpenter for his older brothers for several years while learning the building trade, but never became a partner in the business. He eventually went to work for UC Davis.

Construction work was scarce in the mid-1930s with the country still in the throes of the Great Depression. In the late 1930s, KK&L built several homes in Woodland, the first of which was built on a speculative basis at 443 Grand Avenue (1938). Two similar vernacular homes at 51 Second Street (1939) and 118 Second Street (1940) followed. A house at 144 Bartlett Avenue (1940) has large picture windows and an unusual round stoop porch *(fig. 143)*.

143. House at 144 Bartlett Avenue, 1940, Keehn Keehn & Lucchesi
photo by Roger Klemm

144. Quonset Hut Storefront, 1949, Keehn Keehn & Lucchesi
courtesy Joe T. Keehn

During World War II, because of difficulty in procuring building materials for home construction, KK&L survived by diversifying into specialty agricultural structures. John Keehn learned to prepare bids and build farm and ranch structures with the help of U.C. Davis and the Yolo County Building Department. Noted agricultural projects that KK&L completed in rural Woodland included large dairy milk sheds for Herb Schuler (1942) along Kentucky Avenue (now demolished), farm worker housing for Frank King (1944), a rice drier at Tindle Mound outside of Knights Landing, and a rice drier and storage bins for Howard Beeman west of Brown's Corner.

After the war, KK&L built several large facilities using Quonset hut designs. First developed in Quonset, Rhode Island, a Quonset hut is a prefabricated building made of corrugated metal, shaped like a longitudinal half of a cylinder. A large Quonset hut warehouse was constructed by KK&L for Heidrick Bros. (1946) on road 97 just south of Highway 16 and the firm also erected a Quonset hut building with a storefront at 660 Sixth Street (1949) to be used as the company's business office and retail hardware and lumber yard establishment *(fig. 144)*.

In 1948 the Keehn & Lucchesi subdivision was developed on the outskirts of Woodland along the east side of West Street between Elliot and Clover Streets. After annexation into the city and the installation of curbs and gutters and city utilities, the property was sold to general contractor Gerhard Klinkhammer, newly arrived from Oregon, who built the houses in the subdivision.

KK&L also built several large swimming pools for wealthy clients during this period, including one for Dr. Nichols at 520 Woodland Avenue. The company consulted with Woodland City Engineer, Asa Proctor, on the structural design for the reinforced concrete construction techniques used in the building of the pools.

After a twenty-year partnership, Keehn Keehn & Lucchesi dissolved in 1955. Alfred Keehn continued as an independent contractor until 1961, finally working for Yolo County as a building inspector. In 1969 he joined the Yolo County Sheriff's Department and was a deputy until his retirement in 1975. He died in Woodland in 1980 at the age of 71. Leo Lucchesi worked for the City of Woodland, using his construction knowledge until his retirement. He also died in 1980. John Keehn Jr. remained in the local construction business for a few years then worked as a union carpenter for several large contracting firms in the Sacramento area. John Jr. lived at the home he built at 753 W. Gibson Road until his death in 2002.

Klinkhammer Construction Company

A Brief Stop, A Land Purchase, and a Family Career

A Minnesota native, Gerhard Klinkhammer (1878-1959) moved to Woodland in 1947 at the age of 69 and started a general contracting business. Before settling in Woodland, he and his family lived for about twenty years in Klamath Falls, Oregon where he farmed and started a building business with one of his

145. Tract Housing on Eunice Drive, c1950, Klinkhammer Construction Company
photo by Roger Klemm

sons. Prior to that he lived and farmed in Idaho and Grand Junction, Colorado and Kansas.

According to his son, Earl Klinkhammer, the family was driving through Woodland on their way back from the Bay Area to Oregon in 1947 and decided to stop and investigate real estate. A few hours later, Gerhard had bought 11 undeveloped lots in the South Land Park subdivision from Fred Shaffer. The family returned to Oregon, packed their belongings, and moved to the warmer climate of Woodland to begin a new life.

The Klinkhammer Construction Company was a partnership of Gerhard, his son Earl, and Chet Willey. In 1947 they built homes on the 11 lots they had purchased in the new South Land Park subdivision on Buena Tierra and Fremont Streets. In 1948 Klinkhammer purchased the Keehn & Lucchesi subdivision and constructed many modest single story homes during the post-World War II building boom.

Beginning about 1950 Klinkhammer developed 70 lots in the Klinkhammer subdivision. This addition to Woodland was located in the southwest corner of the city bounded by Gibson and West Streets and included Eunice Drive named in honor of Gerhard's wife. The layout of this subdivision featured wide streets without planting strips for trees, and tract housing with standard Ranch style designs featuring prominent attached garages. This style of neighborhood design would come to dominate post WWII Woodland as the town grew steadily *(fig. 145)*. In contrast with the tract version of the style, a small custom Ranch house built at 21 Casa Linda Drive by the company (1950) captures more of the essence of the style by retaining a functional sitting porch, a rustic ambience, and setback garage *(fig. 146)*.

146. Ranch House at 21 Casa Linda, 1950
Klinkhammer Construction Company
photo by Roger Klemm

Gerhard Klinkhammer died in Woodland in 1959 at the age of 81, but Earl Klinkhammer and Chet Willey continued the contracting business. Earl Klinkhammer was born in 1922 in Kansas, but grew up in Klamath Falls, Oregon. He joined the Marine Corps during WW II, then settled in Woodland and went into partnership with his father as a hands-on builder.

Between 1956 and 1976 during a period of steady growth and expansion of Woodland's boundaries,

Klinkhammer and Willey built many homes in Woodland, including several upscale Ranch style homes along Toyon Drive and Cedar Lane in the Gibson Park Subdivision on land purchased from James Adams. One notable house built by the company at 210 Toyon Drive was designed by Dean Unger for Orville Geer. Klinkhammer and Willey also constructed the brick Ranch style house appropriately sited on a very wide lot at 75 W. Gibson Road for Dan Best, Jr.

Branching out to commercial development, Klinkhammer constructed Alderson's convalescent hospital at 124 Walnut Street in three phases as well as St. John's Retirement Village and Stollwood homes on the north side of Woodland. In 1989, Earl Klinkhammer formed a partnership with his son, Robert Klinkhammer. Now in its third generation, Klinkhammer Construction Company has been actively building in Woodland for over fifty years. A recent project completed with Robert Klinkhammer at the helm of the company is the Spanish Revival style Orick Building at 194 W. Main Street.

Harry J. Devine

Sacramento-born Designer of Public Buildings and Catholic Churches

A native of Sacramento, Harry Joseph Devine (1894-1963) attended Christian Brothers School. His graduation from the University of California at Berkeley in 1919 was delayed by his 1917 enlistment and a Navy tour of duty in Europe during World War I. Prior to his military service he worked for a short period as a draftsman at the State Engineer's Office. After college graduation he returned to Sacramento where he trained with the prominent architects Dean & Dean. Devine opened his own office in Sacramento in 1926 and steadily rose to prominence as a respected architect and civic leader.

Although the Great Depression years were tough on architects, Devine secured several commissions funded by the federal Works Progress Administration (WPA). In 1936 Devine designed the Woodland City Hall addition, which complemented the initial phase of the building designed by Dean & Dean in 1932. The two-story addition created an arched front entrance on First Street adorned in Mexican tile with city council chambers on the second floor.

Devine's WPA work carried over to the Sacramento City College campus where he designed the Moderne style library building. This beautiful building was demolished in the 1990s and replaced by a larger structure, despite a lengthy battle by preservationists to save the building. Another well-known building of Devine's in Sacramento is the Art Deco style Roos-Atkins Building at 1011 Tenth Street near the K Street mall.

As the principal architect for the Sacramento Catholic Archdiocese for several years, Devine designed a number of Catholic Churches in Sacramento, including Sacred Heart, Our Lady of Guadalupe, St. Rose, St. Ignatius, and Christian Brothers High School.

By the late 1940s, Holy Rosary Church in Woodland prepared to build its fifth church to replace the abandoned Gothic stone church designed and built by Fedele Costa in 1912. Harry Devine was selected as the architect for the new church, located at 301 Walnut Street, one block north of the abandoned church. Completed in 1949, the style of the church building is Romanesque, constructed of reinforced concrete with a tile roof. The tall building became an instant Woodland landmark with its majestic 108-foot bell tower *(fig. 147)*.

In addition to his work as an architect, Devine was very active in the Sacramento community where he served on the city planning commission. A leading Catholic layman, Devine's work for the church and the community earned him high honors. In 1953 and 1955 he received awards from Pope Pius XII, and in 1957 he was the recipient of two National Catholic Education Association awards for his work on St.

147. Holy Rosary Catholic Church, 1949, Harry J. Devine
courtesy Yolo County Archives

Ignatius Catholic Church. Devine also had a life-long interest in baseball and was a majority stockholder of the Sacramento Solons Pacific Coast League baseball team between 1948 and 1950. Devine died in 1963, leaving an impressive portfolio of attractive buildings in the Sacramento region. His son Harry J. Devine, Jr. took over the business and practiced architecture until he retired in 1990.

Howard F. Terhune

Rediscovering Treasures:
A 1950s Restoration Expert
Pioneers a Woodland Trend

When Howard Terhune (b. 1915), a trained interior designer, purchased a run-down Victorian Italianate house at 648 College Street in 1953 and began a 15-year restoration effort, he heralded a sustained, grass-roots preservation movement in Woodland's historic neighborhoods that continues to the present day.

Woodland's historic restoration is distinguished both by the great number of homes preserved in a concentrated area and by the fact that it was privately financed, without government subsidies.

Born in Hackensack, New Jersey, Terhune studied interior design at the Art Students League and the American School of Design in New York City. During his New York years, Terhune worked in art galleries and was an "antique scouter" for several top design professionals. He traveled throughout New England and the South Central States hunting antiques and objects of art.

In the 1930s, Terhune was introduced to historic preservation through his work on historic buildings along the Hudson River, including a major interior design job for the Broadway actress Helen Hays at her estate in New Jersey. This experience resulted in his selection to restore other historic homes in California in the 1950s.

During World War II Terhune was stationed at Camp Beale, near Marysville, and became acquainted with the Sacramento area. He relocated to California in 1950, settling in Woodland while working as a buyer and decorator for Breuner's Furniture in Sacramento. He married Sylvia Santoni of Woodland in 1951.

Two years later the couple purchased an 80-year old Victorian at 648 College Street and spent the next fifteen years remodeling the interior of the home while preserving its exterior. Many of the ornate brackets on the cornice of the house needed replacement and Terhune sought out Bay Area artisans to replicate this solid wood ornamentation.

Around 1964 the Terhunes learned the Italianate Victorian house at 640 College Street, a twin to their adjacent residence, would be sold to a developer who planned to raze it and build an apartment complex. To Woodland's great fortune, Terhune managed to buy the house, then preserved and remodeled the interior into a duplex with top and bottom flats *(fig. 148 & 149)*. In the 1990s this home was lavishly remodeled into a single-family residence by Jeff and Starr Barrow and now stands as a local landmark, one of the most charming and striking Victorians in town.

Well received by the Woodland community, Ter-

148. 648 & 640 College Street before Howard Terhune's restoration, from *Communicator,* National Clean Up-Paint Up-Fix Up Bureau, (Washington, D.C., June 1968)
courtesy Howard Terhune

149. College Street Houses After Restoration, c.1967, from *Communicator,* National Clean Up-Paint Up-Fix Up Bureau, (Washington, D.C., June 1968)
courtesy Howard Terhune

hune's preservation projects were spotlighted locally as part of the "National Clean Up, Paint Up, Fix Up" program *(fig. 150)*. On the strength of his work and vision in the field of historic preservation, Terhune joined the Society of Architectural Historians, a national organization.

During the 1960s Terhune ran a successful interior design business, serving wealthy clients throughout Woodland and the northern part of the state. His studio was located in a building he remodeled at 605-607 North Street. Here, Terhune employed upholsterers and drapery makers to execute his designs.

As the 1960s came to a close, a growing preservation movement had visibly taken root in Woodland's core area. Rather than reside in a tract house in the newer housing subdivisions encircling the old part of Woodland, several young, adventuresome couples followed Terhune's lead and began purchasing historic houses at bargain prices and restoring them.

150. Howard Terhune (left) receives award for home restoration from Jim Lingberg of Woodland Chamber of Commerce.
from *Daily Democrat,* September 19, 1967

In 1969 Terhune purchased two Bungalow homes on First Street adjacent to his office and shop on the corner of North Street. He joined these small houses, creating office space by adding a modern facade constructed of glass and rough-hewn redwood planks. Terhune designed wrought iron gates leading to the rear of the property where he constructed a secluded brick patio with a pergola. The intent of the project was to foster commercial revitalization of this transitional area, located between the downtown and the residential neighborhoods. The preservation of the exterior architecture of the small homes was de-emphasized in favor of opening the buildings up to the street through the expansion of the front facades of each building. The scale, natural colors, and rustic ambience of the project fit in well with the adjacent residential area.

Shortly after the completion of the North Street commercial project, Terhune moved to Palm Springs, where he became a fine art appraiser and owner of an art gallery. As of 2002, Howard and Sylvia Terhune reside in Desert Hot Springs.

Grant F. Cloud

Experimenting with Adobe

A Woodland native, Grant Franklin Cloud (1918-1965) began building homes in Woodland after World War II using adobe bricks. His inspiration for adobe construction came from an architect in Carmel who was successfully using the building material. Adobe brick has several properties that make it appealing for house construction: it is fireproof, has a high insulation value, and is very durable. One of the local promoters of adobe was former Woodlander Harrison Fait, son of Woodland builder William R. Fait. Harrison owned an adobe brick plant on Howe Avenue in Sacramento during the 1950s.

In 1948 Grant Cloud constructed the first of several adobe homes in the region at 731 First Street for his parents, Franklin and Genevieve Cloud. This is a Ranch style house built level to the ground with a second story loft and an attached garage. The adobe brick used for this two-story house was left its natural color *(fig. 151).*

Other adobe homes built by Cloud in the 1950s are at 4 Westway Place and 3 Rancho Place. Several adobe homes were crafted by Cloud outside of Woodland, for example, a large adobe house near Esparto

151. F. Cloud House, 1948, Grant Cloud
photo by Roger Klemm

for Carl Giguiere and other examples in the Yuba City area. Cloud's building career was relatively short, for adobe houses did not grow in popularity. After building a few homes, he left the contracting business to take a job with the state, dying at a relatively young age in 1965.

Dreyfuss & Blackford

Sacramento Innovators Create Stylish Casa Linda Home

Knights Landing residents Marietta and Phil Leiser moved to Woodland in 1954 so their young children could attend city schools. They purchased a lot in the new Casa Linda subdivision at 409 Casa Linda Drive. Although they were country folks, they were interested in modern architecture. In fact the family house in Knights Landing was a relatively modern house built in the 1930s. Seeking out new house styles in Sacramento, the Leisers were attracted to the work of the young Sacramento firm of Albert M. Dreyfuss and Leonard D. Blackford. The Leisers wanted a large house for their growing family, but beyond that parameter the architects were given free reign on the design.

The resulting composition was cutting-edge modern *(fig. 152).* From the street, the house is a series of

152. Leiser House, 1954, Dreyfuss & Blackford
photo by Roger Klemm

masonry walls, with some extending from the structure and providing enclosure. A flat roof slopes towards the front entrance with an overhang that shades small horizontal windows. As private and protected as the front of the house is, the living areas facing the back yard have an open view through floor-to-ceiling windows. A large copper fireplace separates the living room and kitchen. The long house is about 3,500 square feet with a rear garage that is accessed from a long driveway entered from College Street. The Leisers planted the grouping of ginkgo trees in their front yard in the 1950s.

Now a Sacramento institution, Dreyfuss & Blackford Architects is a firm with a distinguished history. During the last forty years the firm has designed many well-known and admired buildings throughout the Sacramento region. A few of these noted buildings include: the Nut Tree and Coffee Tree buildings in Vacaville, Lincoln Plaza, a terraced and heavily landscaped office building in downtown Sacramento, the original SMUD headquarters building (visible from Highway 50 in Sacramento and featuring an exterior mural by Wayne Thiebaud), and the Herman Miller, Inc. furniture manufacturing facility in Rocklin, which won the prestigious AIA National Honor Award for 1991. A recent project of the firm is the new terminal at Sacramento International Airport.

Joseph Esherick

A Distinctive Early Work from a Nationally-Known Innovator

Joseph Esherick
courtesy Esherick Homsey Dodge & Davis
© Mark Darley/Esto

When Daniel G. and Bernice Best commissioned up-and-coming Bay Area architect, Joseph Esherick, to design a large sweeping Ranch style house on their large lot at 303 West Gibson Road in Woodland in 1958, little did they know that one day he would be famous in architectural circles. Dan Best was introduced to the work of Esherick through his friend, Harry Holt. These two men were long-time friends, their families having merged their respective tractor manufacturing businesses to create the world-famous Caterpillar Company. The Bests liked the house that Esherick designed in Stockton for Harry Holt and decided to hire him to design their new house on the edge of Woodland.

Joseph Esherick (1914-1998) graduated with a degree in architecture from the University of Pennsylvania in 1937. An early influence on his approach to building was his uncle, Wharton Esherick, a well-known sculptor and builder. After a trip to Europe, Joseph Esherick moved to San Francisco in 1939 and began studying the works of Bernard Maybeck and William Wurster to gain a better knowledge and appreciation of the Bay Area style of residential design.

Esherick worked for Gardner Dailey's influential

architectural firm for two years, refining his ideas about house design, before opening his own office in San Francisco in 1945. His firm became a leader in residential design in the Bay Area and branched out into commercial and office design by the 1960s. In 1952 he joined the faculty of the College of Environmental Design at the University of California, Berkeley where he taught architecture for over 40 years. In 1957 he designed the Pelican Building on the UC Berkeley campus.

For the Woodland project, the Bests presented Esherick with a paradoxical design concept: to create a house with "high ceilings and a low roof." Actually, this idea meshed well with Esherick's design philosophy of "packing the box," which involves fitting living requirements into a hierarchy of spaces, with the living area given the greatest volume through height rather than floor area. Like his mentors, Wurster and Dailey, he believed that buildings should be designed from the inside out, encouraging the natural elements of light and views to dictate form.

The Best house orients around a tall central living area with extra high ceilings formed by a side-gabled roof with exposed rafter tails, reminiscent of the Craftsman style of architecture. The placement of the gable across the long axis of the house opens the tallest area to light and air. The low-slanted shingled roof provides protective covering for ceiling-to-floor windows in the front and rear of the house as well as providing soothing natural light, a gracious interior space, and a strong connection to the spacious yard.

The roof forms an outdoor room at the front entrance to the house and a patio to the rear for the enjoyment of outdoor living *(fig. 153 & 154)*. The service and sleeping quarters, extending from the central living area, are built lower to the ground. There is no garage, but a carport to the rear of the house. The overall shape of the house is influenced by Esherick's attraction to the California barn, a rural form that appears in other houses he designed.

The house is encircled by a large yard designed by the internationally known landscape architect, Thomas Church (1902-1978). A native Californian, educated at the University of California, Berkeley, with a graduate degree in landscape architecture from Harvard University, Church designed residential gardens in the

153. Front Entrance, Best House, 1958,
Joseph Esherick
photo by Roger Klemm

154. Rear Garden and Patio, Best House
photo by Roger Klemm

thirties for Wurster, Dailey and other prominent architects. He later consulted for architects throughout the country. A generous assortment of trees and spacious lawn complement the relaxed feeling of the house. The brick wall fronting the property along Gibson Road is not original, but a privacy barrier added when Gibson Road was widened to four lanes.

By the 1960s Esherick was a rising star in the profession as his people-friendly commercial projects received critical and popular acclaim. In 1967 Esherick & Associates completed The Cannery at Fisherman's Wharf in San Francisco, a very successful historic preservation and redevelopment project that became a national destination spot for tourists and helped revitalize the San Francisco waterfront. In 1972 the firm expanded to become Esherick, Homsey, Dodge, and Davis. The firm was chosen to design the Monterey Bay Aquarium, completed between 1977-84. This is a complex of both old and new buildings that blend with the industrial buildings of Cannery Row.

Other important projects that Esherick's firm designed include Wurster Hall for the College of Environmental Design at the University of California, Berkeley, Stevenson College at the University of California at Santa Cruz, and the Secretary of State/Golden State Museum in downtown Sacramento in 1997. This interesting public building was designed around an interior courtyard with a monumental wall sculpture depicting thought-provoking words from the State Constitution.

In recognition of Joseph Esherick's distinguished career and major contribution to American architecture, he was awarded the prestigious Gold Medal by the American Institute of Architects in 1989. Only 47 architects have received this award since 1907, including Louis Sullivan, Frank Lloyd Wright, and Bernard Maybeck. He was cited by the AIA as "an outstanding designer, and educator steeped in the arts, and a humanist with a deep concern for the betterment of the profession and our society."

Robert E. Crippen

A Jazzman & Woodland's First Licensed Architect

Robert E. Crippen
courtesy James Crippen

A passionate jazz musician-turned architect, Robert Crippen was a prolific designer of Woodland buildings in the 1950s and '60s. He moved to Woodland from Chico, California as a boy and graduated from Woodland High School in 1940. After high school graduation, Crippen attended the University of the Pacific in Stockton in 1941 and studied music. A saxophone player and jazzman, Crippen was a classmate of jazz great, Dave Brubeck. Between 1942-46 he served in the U.S. Army and was assigned to play music for the troops as a member of the European Command ("E.C.") Aces, a big band that was featured on BBC radio.

After the war Crippen remained in Paris for a short period playing music and absorbing the city's immense architectural resources before returning to California. The exposure to European architecture stimulated Crippen's interest in the profession. Returning home, he worked for a short period for Woodland designer Carleton Pierson, before enrolling at the University of Oregon in the Architecture program. After completing his academic training in architecture in 1951, Crippen returned to Woodland, serving his apprenticeship from 1954 to 1956 with the Sacramento firm of Cox & Liske (the forerunner of the present-day firm of Lionakis Beaumont Design Group). He served on the Woodland Planning Commission from 1953 to 1958.

In 1956 Crippen started his own architectural firm in Woodland. The Crippen firm represented a milestone in the architectural history of Woodland: the

155. Yolo County Jail and Sheriff's Office, 1968, Robert Crippen & Alfred Graff
courtesy Yolo County Museum

first local firm headed by a licensed architect. (Crippen's early mentor, Carleton Pierson, practiced design part-time in Woodland for several years before the Crippen firm, but Pierson was a specifications writer employed in Sacramento, not a licensed architect).

Robert Crippen practiced architecture in Woodland from 1956 to 1968. During this time his firm employed up to seven members and completed many buildings in a wide range of types, including commercial, government, churches, housing, and industrial to meet the functional needs of a growing community. Most of Crippen's buildings are modest in scale and budget and conservative in design, perhaps reflecting the ethos of Woodland at this time.

His major government project was the Yolo County Jail and Sheriff's Office at Third and North streets (1968), with simplified columns inspired by the classical columns of the neighboring Yolo County Courthouse *(fig. 155)*. Alfred Graff, a Winters-based architect, assisted Crippen on this project. Crippen's design for the Woodland City Hall Annex (1961) was a glass and aluminum addition that clashed with the original Mission Revival style of the older part of the building. Crippen also designed the branch Fire Station for the City of Woodland on East Street.

156. Pepsi Bottling Plant, 1957, Robert Crippen
photo by David Wilkinson

The Wells Fargo Bank at 444 Court Street (1963), an example of Crippen's commercial work, is a tilt-up concrete structure with exposed-aggregate walls. The Pepsi Bottling Plant (1957) on Fourth Street, just

157. Yolo County YMCA, 1960, Robert Crippen
courtesy Yolo County YMCA

south of Main Street, was an industrial building of corrugated metal with a "saw tooth" style facade and large window space that allowed the general public to view the bottling operation *(fig. 156)*. This structure was demolished in 1995 after Pepsi vacated the premises. A large tilt-up concrete warehouse (now remodeled) is all that remains of the Pepsi complex.

Crippen's buildings were typically constructed of economical, mass-produced building materials, like concrete block and aluminum windows. For the Yolo County YMCA, located at 1300 College Street (1960), Crippen used concrete blocks to form a series of multilevel rectangular masses with a flat roof. The front facade has tall aluminum windows and ceramic tile to add color and visual interest to the building *(fig. 157)*. The American Legion Hall at 523 Bush Street (1964) is a smaller scale version of this style of building.

In the field of housing, Crippen teamed with the well-known Bay Area firm of Campbell & Wong to design the Yolanda Village public housing complex on Lemen Avenue for the Yolo County Housing Authority. He was also the architect for St. John's Retirement Village at 135 Woodland Avenue (1966).

In 1967 the Crippen firm drew up plans for an interesting house built for Dr. Lynn Keys (now owned by Tom and Meg Stallard) at 10 Toyon Drive *(fig. 158)*. The design concept for the house was based upon a plan Dr. Keys mail ordered from an Arizona architect

158. Dr. Lynn Keys House, 1967, Robert Crippen
photo by Roger Klemm

inspired by the work of Frank Lloyd Wright. The massing of the house is horizontal, in the Prairie tradition, with masonry walls. The front of the house has a carport adjoining the entrance and, with the exception of a row of clerestory windows, there is no glazing, for maximum privacy. The house opens wide to the rear garden and to an indoor swimming pool built between the living and bedroom wings.

Towards the end of his career in Woodland, Crippen became a partner with Robert Schaefer. He moved to Reno in 1969 where he practiced architecture for two years until opening his own office in Truckee in 1970. Crippen played jazz and designed buildings in both California and Nevada until 2000 when he was 78 years old. When he stopped work due to a stroke, he was the oldest licensed architect working in Nevada.

Gary Wirth & Bill McCandless

Award-Winning Designs Linking the Present With the Past

Gary Wirth
courtesy Gary Wirth

Bill McCandless
courtesy Bill McCandless

Born and raised in Woodland, Gary Wirth spent his lengthy career as an architect in his hometown making a major contribution to Woodland's contemporary built environment. His work spans the period from about 1966 to 2000 and, as a small town generalist, his portfolio includes all types of new buildings and many quality historic preservation projects. He began working as a draftsman in Robert Crippen's architectural firm in Woodland while in high school and, after graduation, attended Sacramento City College where he studied engineering. Crippen was influential in Wirth's decision to attend his mentor's alma mater, the University of Oregon, where he received his architecture degree in 1965. As a student he toured Europe, viewing all the great monuments and nurturing a love of international travel and study that he pursued throughout his career.

After his college years, Wirth returned to Woodland and went to work for Crippen-Schaefer & Associates as an apprentice. From a young age, Wirth was an ambitious and inspired architect who knew he would one day run his own firm. He cut his teeth in the profession as the lead designer for Crippen-Schaefer on several large projects. One of the first projects he designed was the Martin Luther King, Jr. Library in Sacramento. In Woodland, Wirth was given major responsibility for the design and project management of Dr. Keys' house at 10 Toyon Drive (1967) and the Yolo County Jail and Sheriff's Office, at Third and North streets (1968).

Shortly after Crippen moved to Nevada in 1968, Wirth became Schaefer's junior partner. The firm tackled two large historic preservation projects in the mid-'70s that were key contributors to downtown Woodland's early revitalization. In 1974, in need of larger office space, the partners remodeled the upstairs of the Richardsonian Romanesque style Diggs building, originally constructed in 1894, into a spacious office with adjoining small office suites unified by a central sky-lit atrium. Hereafter, the firm listed its office at 666 Dead Cat Alley, no doubt an easy address for the firm's clients to remember and a humorous link to the town's folklore.

Schaefer-Wirth's remodel of Woodland City Hall (1976), successfully integrated several additions to the building (including, ironically, Crippen's unsympathetic 1961 glass and aluminum addition) into a cohesive design in the Mission Revival style of the original building *(fig. 159)*.

In 1979 Keith Long, a graduate of U.C. Berkeley, joined the growing firm which by this time employed about 14 people. With many commissions in the greater Sacramento area during this period, Schaefer-Wirth opened a second office in Citrus Heights headed by Robert Schaefer. Eventually, Schaefer-Wirth split into two independent businesses. The Schaefer firm remained in the Sacramento area, while Gary Wirth ran his own Woodland office. Long moved to Hawaii, leaving the Woodland firm in 1981.

159. Woodland City Hall Remodel, 1976, Schaefer & Wirth
courtesy Wirth & McCandless

In 1983 Gary Wirth & Associates hired Bill McCandless as an associate architect. A native of Pennsylvania, McCandless received his architecture degree from the University of Arizona in 1979. After working in Sacramento for a short period, he joined the Wirth firm. In 1988 McCandless became a partner and the firm became Wirth & McCandless.

Some of Wirth's most interesting work is in the field of residential design, beginning in the late 1960s. This was a period of sustained growth in the town with large subdivisions and mass-produced tract housing drowning out variety and innovation. With a few exceptions, housing tastes and choices, even among the more affluent that could afford an architect-designed house, were conservative. Typically, a custom home meant a large version of the ubiquitous ranch house or a pumped-up colonial revival.

The innovative Sea Ranch style did make inroads into Woodland and this uniquely California aesthetic is evident in some of Wirth's houses of the '60s and '70s. The Sea Ranch style evolved out of the prototype Sea Ranch Condominiums built in 1965 on the California coast south of Mendocino designed by Charles Moore & Associates of Berkeley. This style

160. House at 9 W. Monte Vista Drive, c1970, Gary Wirth
photo by David Wilkinson

emphasizes simple, angular, juxtaposed forms with a lean-to or shed appearance. The original wooden Sea Ranch houses were partially inspired by California's weathered barns. A house that Wirth designed for himself at 4 Sequoia (1969) shows this influence. It is tall and shaped like a shed, clad in wooden shingles (since painted) with minimal glazing. Wirth designed another variation of this style at 9 W. Monte Vista Drive (c1970) on a large corner lot *(fig. 160)*. Here he

161. Wirth House, 1998, Gary Wirth
courtesy Wirth & McCandless

162. 932 Jordan Circle, 1994, Gary Wirth
photo by Roger Klemm

juxtaposed several shed structures with varying heights for dramatic interior effect, lit with tall narrow windows or clerestory glazing. In a departure from the traditional woodsy look, the exterior of the house is light colored stucco.

When Wirth built a second personal residence at 936 Jordan Circle (1998) he returned to his fascination with shed style forms *(fig. 161)*. He describes the shape of the house as "wings of a butterfly," referring to the two tall, uneven shed forms devoid of front windows that form the massing of the residence. A front entrance with glass block sidelights connects the wings of the house. The tall angled ceilings create interesting variations in height throughout the interior of the house and many windows provide views to the beautifully landscaped rear garden. The garage is hidden to the rear and does not detract from the sculpted look of the house.

At a neighboring house at 942 Jordan Circle (2000), Wirth also used shed massing combined with an imaginative use of glass. The lower floor has bay windows and a recessed window grid, with round windows and glass blocks on the porch, while the second story shed dormer has a row of small square windows.

Other noteworthy Wirth houses include a Ranch style home at 25 W. Monte Vista Drive from the early 1970s, featuring a gabled post and beam front entrance with rock posts and fireplace. The landscape berm settles the house into the site and exposed rafters on the gables enhance the organic, natural feel of the house. A house at 622 Fairview Drive (1985) has a high-pitched roof in the French style with a large chimney and corner quoins. Wirth crafted another French style house at 205 Monte Vista Circle. At 932 Jordan Circle (1994), Wirth created a rarity for Woodland: a Prairie style house with blocky columns and a hipped roof with a large overhang affording protection to the ribbon windows *(fig. 162)*.

Wirth's love of the Sea Ranch form was also used skillfully in commercial and school buildings. In a masonry rendition for the Bank of America at 50 W. Main Street (1980), two shed-shaped masses at off-

163. Bank of America, 1980, Gary Wirth
photo by Roger Klemm

setting heights are joined together creating a very voluminous central lobby, softly lit by clerestory windows *(fig. 163)*. Diagonal wood siding and a shake roof add to the informal aesthetic, with light brown brick used for the lower walls. Zamora School at 1716 Cottonwood and Greengate School at 285 W. Beamer Avenue are institutional variations of the Sea Ranch style, as is the Parsons Seed Certification Center (1985) located on the U.C. Davis campus behind Hunt Hall.

Wirth was also active in the City of Davis adapting historical buildings for modern uses. After the new high school was built, the old Davis Joint Union High School on Russell Blvd. (1927) was converted into city offices and a freestanding City Council chamber was added to the rear of the property (1981). The old City Hall on 226 F Street, designed by Dragon & Schmidts (1938), was converted into the city Police Station. Two other prominent Davis projects completed by Wirth are the Davis Senior Center at 646 A Street (1983) and the Yolo County Health and Justice Center at 600 A Street (1989), both done in a similar Spanish style.

For the Woodland Opera House, restored in several phases during the 1980s, Wirth was the lead architect on all but the last phase, involving interior design and the construction of the Opera House Plaza. Of major importance to this top-flight project was a sensitive new addition to the original structure that distinguished a new era, but was compatible with the old. Wirth created a new three-story annex (1980) in unadorned brick with a short slanted section to an otherwise flat roof. A large arched segmented window echoes the entrance to the main building *(fig. 164)*.

Wirth & McCandless have also completed several quality historic preservation projects in Woodland. The rehabilitation of the 1891 landmark Jackson

164. Opera House Annex, 1980, Gary Wirth
courtesy Wirth & McCandless

165. Beeman House Addition, c1989, Gary Wirth
courtesy Wirth & McCandless

Building at 426 First Street (1986, *see fig. 34*) headed by local developer Mark Ullrich, creatively converted the unused attic space into an upscale restaurant. During the installation of a new slate roof on the building, the venerable turret was lowered to the ground, re-sheathed, and reinstalled to its familiar position. This outstanding project received a Citation Award from the Central Valley Chapter of the AIA.

In collaboration with owner, Steve Venables, Wirth & McCandless rehabilitated the Excelsior Building (1875) at 522-24 Main Street. The facade of the building was restored and an interior walkway was created lined with shops including the new home of Woodland Travel.

Wirth & McCandless also completed several outstanding renovations of historic homes for owners who have demonstrated a strong commitment to preserving and elevating Woodland's architectural heritage. During the late 1980s, Wirth was the lead on a large addition to the Italianate Victorian Beeman farmhouse at 20123 East Street *(fig. 165)*. The addition seamlessly blended a large first floor veranda with an upper balcony into the Victorian style of the house. The owners created a very picturesque, pastoral setting by also upgrading several farm outbuildings surrounding the house. This scenic farmhouse is a visible reminder of Woodland's prosperous agricultural history to the many motorists who travel along old tree-lined Highway 113 to and from Woodland.

Wirth designed a new conservatory, garage, and gazebo to enhance the Italianate Victorian at 640 College Street restored from a duplex to a single family residence by Jeff and Starr Barrow in the early 1990s. The Barrows later purchased the Gable Mansion at 659 First Street and Wirth also consulted for this ambitious project. Although a new structure, the Blue

166. Hotel Woodland Courtyard, 1996, Bill McCandless
courtesy Wirth & McCandless

Shield office building designed by Wirth at 435 East Street (1993) borrows California Bungalow imagery from the neighboring Woodland Train Depot constructed in 1913.

Bill McCandless was the lead architect for the impressive restoration of the Woodland Hotel at 436 Main Street (1996). Layers of old paint and grime were removed in the ornate lobby and local artists, Cosme and Yvonne Munoz, restored the original vibrant colors of the wood beams and stenciled ceilings. This beautiful space is now used by the community for a variety of social functions. The lobby is expandable to the building's rear courtyard that McCandless designed with a wall enclosure *(fig. 166)*. Clarksburg artist, Roger Barry, designed the fountain. The old hotel rooms were converted into affordable apartments by Davis non-profit developer, Community Housing Opportunities Corporation, while Woodlander Mark Engstrom developed the ground floor of the building. The California Preservation Foundation recognized the design excellence of this meticulous restoration of the original 1928 William Henry Weeks building.

In the field of commercial design, McCandless has shown verve and flair in improving the quality of Woodland's new shopping centers. In the late 1990s he designed attractive Food for Less and Big 5 Sporting Goods buildings at the Sycamore Point center at East Main and Pioneer streets. The basic warehouse structures are built of polychrome concrete block with elegant decorative canopies of exposed steel supports and aluminum sign grids *(fig. 167)*. In 1998 McCandless remodeled a drab building on Pole Line Road

167. Sycamore Point Shopping Center, 1997, Bill McCandless
courtesy Wirth & McCandless

168. Yolo Community Bank, 1998, Bill McCandless
courtesy Wirth & McCandless

169. Red Cross Building, 1999, Bill McCandless
courtesy Wirth & McCandless

in Davis into an eye-catching Art Nouveau style Nugget Market, transforming this mundane shopping center into an inviting and elegant beacon for the surrounding neighborhood. The design is based upon a French Market concept with iron canopies and oversized statuary on the exterior of the building.

McCandless has completed several other imaginative commercial remodels. He converted a banal realty office at 624 Court Street into the stately Yolo Community Bank (1998, *fig. 168*). The gable roof was removed and brick veneer and cast stone trim were used on the exterior of the building to create a more symmetrical look, consistent with the traditional formal style of banks. The front facade is constructed of dark aluminum with two large picture windows and clerestory windows with decorative grillwork.

The Red Cross Building at 120 Court Street is another example of a successful remodel of a modest small building by McCandless (1999, *fig. 169*). To a simple single story gabled structure, he added a two story gabled central tower. The extended rooflines have elbow brackets creating a relaxed Craftsman look. A tasteful polychromatic color scheme adds visual interest to the project.

In addition to his long productive architectural career, Wirth pursued several other interests. He was a founder of the Bank of Woodland, serving on its Board of Directors. He also cultivated a serious interest in archeo-astronomy, an interdisciplinary profession researching ancient astronomical sites and cosmic beliefs. This hobby took him to Easter Island where he collaborated with scholars in the formation of the Easter Island Foundation, an educational and research facility to promote the study of this ancient culture and the advancement of its native people.

When Gary Wirth retired in 2000 from the firm he had been associated with for over thirty years, Bill McCandless became the principal of the Woodland architectural institution now named McCandless & Associates.

Gerald S. Anderson

An Innovative Collaboration between San Francisco Designer and Woodland Family

In the late 1960s realtor Gary Schafer subdivided a large tract of land in west Woodland called the Monte Vista subdivision, running south of Gibson

Road along Midway Drive and W. Monte Vista Drive, with short cul-de-sacs built along these feeder streets. The lots were relatively deep and wide, each about one-half acre in size, tailor made for the many large and long Ranch houses to be built by affluent owners on these parcels.

Pauline and Wim Van Muyden were one of the first families to build in the new housing tract at the end of the cul-de-sac at 3 Loma Vista Place, and they were decidedly not Ranch house-type people. They wanted something different that matched their yearning for a woodsy retreat to complement their love of gardening and growing trees plus interior spaces that enhanced close interaction with their young children. They were not interested in a big house, only an interesting house built within a modest budget.

After interviewing several architects, the Van Muydens connected with a young, creative architect from San Francisco, Gerald S. Anderson (b. 1938), who shared their design enthusiasm and patiently spent many hours with the couple learning of their lifestyle and values to design an innovative house they "could live in." From west Texas, Anderson studied engineering at Rice University before transferring to the University of Oklahoma where he studied under mentors Herb Green and David Arnold, protégés of the influential architect, Bruce Goff. Anderson moved to California in 1962 and started his own firm in 1966.

The Van Muyden house (1969) was unique, bold, experimental for its time, and to this day, over thirty years later, deeply loved by its owners. The relatively small 2,400 square foot house was shaped by a studied analysis of the ecology of the site *(fig. 170 & 171)*. With the realization that western sun exposure is intense during the hot months, Anderson located a focal point roughly midway on the parcel, thus encouraging house and landscape to radiate from the center. All of the windows, except the tall narrow glazing on

170. Van Muyden House, 1969, Gerald S. Anderson
photo by Roger Klemm

171. Van Muyden House, Rear View
photo by Roger Klemm

a second floor library, are turned towards the focal point, facing southeast. This decision gives the two-story house its tilting appearance. In a preference characteristic of the era, the owners sought privacy from the street, and the house faces inward. Anderson concurred with this orientation, influenced by his Texas roots and many Mexican style houses with exterior walls sheltering private interior patios and outdoor living areas. The house and site were closely planned as an integrated whole, with the grounds a place to work and play and the house a private gathering place for family and friends.

The multi-tiered roofline is a function of the interior rooms, each with a different volume and shape. The living area in the center of the house has as its focal point a large stone fireplace and a tall ceiling that reaches its zenith. A bridge forms a backdrop to the fireplace and spans the two parts of the second story. The floor plan is open, designed for interaction between rooms for the close-knit family. The exterior of the house was originally to be clad in natural wood shingles, but the Van Muydens opted for stained wooden siding to stay within budget. However, several years later, they shingled the house.

The unusual appearance of the house made the Van Muyden's banker nervous. So much so, in fact, that had granting the loan been solely his discretion, he would have surveyed the entire neighborhood to see if people were comfortable with the house style! Compare such conservative tastes and skittish lenders, which thwarted progressive design in Woodland during this period, to the earlier risk-taking and sense of adventure! Fortunately for both the Van Muydens and architectural enthusiasts, the approval of the loan was made out of town by the regional bank office.

Unlike the innovative John Hudson Thomas, whose radical design for the Stephens house on First Street in 1916 led to two other commissions in the same neighborhood, Gerald Anderson never got a second call from Woodland. He moved to Healdsburg in 1976 to specialize in design-build projects as both a designer and general contractor. His other interests have included breeding Arabian horses and viticulture.

Brocchini Architects

Modern Woodland Again Turns to Top Bay Area Artists: A Residence and the Opera House Interior and Marquee

172. Millsap House, 1967, Brocchini Architects
photo by Roger Klemm

Based in Berkeley, Brocchini Architects is headed by the husband-wife team of Ronald G. Brocchini and Myra Mossman Brocchini. The Brocchinis both received masters degrees in architecture at U.C. Berkeley. Over the course of a forty-year career, the Brocchinis have completed many new buildings and historic preservation projects. Historical projects completed by the firm include the YWCA Building designed by Julia Morgan in San Francisco, several buildings on the U.C. Berkeley campus, and historic homes designed by Morgan and Bernard Maybeck. Other well-known projects of theirs are the Emeryville Public Market, an adaptive reuse project that integrates a brick warehouse with a new complex, and Merrill College at U.C. Santa Cruz.

At the start of their careers, the Brocchinis both worked for the prestigious San Francisco firm of Campbell & Wong. After working independently for a short time, Ron Brocchini formed a partnership with Worley K. Wong from 1968 until Wong's death in 1987. Myra also worked for this firm. In 1987 the Brocchinis formed their own firm.

When Beth and Russell Millsap decided to build a new house at 816 First Street, they were drawn to the house designs of Campbell and Wong featured in *Sunset Magazine*. The Millsaps contacted this firm, but Campbell and Wong were tied up with large projects and they were referred to the Brocchinis who designed the house. The Millsap house (1967) shows the influence of the rustic "Sea Ranch" style, in vogue during this time *(fig. 172)*. The house is clad in wooden shingles and the angular form resembles lean-to sheds. The sides of the house are almost solid masses, broken by very narrow tall windows. The front facade is symmetrical, with evenly spaced, large shingled chimneys. The house is tall and spacious with sixteen-foot ceilings on the first floor. Overhanging roofs afford summer protection to the front and rear porches. The eight, simple, front columns are a nod to the Georgian Revival style. Recessed double doors leading to a wide hallway and stairs are painted brightly to contrast with the overall dark appearance of the house. A similarly shaped studio above a garage was built to the rear of the property in 1984.

The ornate front porch lantern was originally part of the Victorian Gable Mansion just up the street. At some point the lantern was removed from the Gable Mansion, then turned up years later as a collector's antique when the Millsaps purchased it. When the Gable Mansion was rehabilitated a few years later Robert McWhirk had a replica made of the original lantern, based on the design of the prototype hanging on the Millsap's house.

In the late 1980s, the Brocchini firm was selected by the Woodland Opera House Board to complete

173. Interior Design of Woodland Opera House, c1988, Brocchini Architects
courtesy Ron Brocchini

the interior restoration of the theater, the final phase of the nine-year project. A State Historic Park and registered California State Landmark, the Woodland Opera House is a rare example of a functioning, small town Victorian performing arts center with a horseshoe balcony. The elegant interior restoration of the theater includes interior antique lighting, historic paint colors, and Bradbury & Bradbury Arts and Crafts wallpapers that recreate an authentic interior design *(fig. 173)*. The interior restoration project received an Award of Merit from the California Preservation Foundation and a Citation Award from the League of Historic American Theaters.

The Intermission Garden brick marquee and entrance, also designed by the Brocchinis, was added in 1990.

Dean F. Unger

New Faces for Woodland Integrating the Old and the New: Homes, the County Administration Building and Courthouse

Dean F. Unger
courtesy Dean F. Unger, AIA, Inc.

The Unger name is a familiar one in building circles in the Sacramento region. Charles Unger was a well-known Sacramento contractor who built the 1936 addition to the Woodland City Hall. Dean F. Unger, Charles' son, opened his architectural office in Sacramento in 1959 and has designed many quality buildings in Yolo County. Born and raised in Sacramento, Unger graduated with a Masters Degree in architecture from U.C. Berkeley. He served in the Air Force and then worked a few years for the architectural firm of Rickey & Brooks before starting his own firm. Unger has resided

174. Geer House, c1964, Dean F. Unger
photo by Roger Klemm

for many years in El Macero, near South Davis. Dean Unger's son, Bruce, also studied architecture at U.C. Berkeley, and works for the firm.

Unger's first projects in Woodland were houses. The long, elegant Ranch style house at 212 Toyon Drive (c.1964) was designed for Orville Geer *(fig. 174)*. This interesting house has a grand gabled entrance of post and wooden beam construction. The Payne House at 201 W. Monte Vista Drive (c.1970) is a large Ranch house graciously situated on a spacious corner lot.

Unger's plan for the Yolo County Administration Building at 625 Court Street (1984) responded to the need for expanded office space for county government and a new meeting space for the Board of Supervisors *(fig. 175)*. A portion of north Second Street was used for the project. In contrast with the Renaissance

175. Yolo County Administration Building, 1984, Dean F. Unger
courtesy Dean F. Unger, AIA, Inc.

Revival style of the Courthouse, Unger's design for the Yolo County Administration Building is contemporary, with Spanish design elements inspired by City Hall and the adjacent United Methodist Church. The building is constructed of steel framing with a brick exterior. Low-pitched gable roof sections, covered in tile, have exposed wooden beams with generous overhangs. Wide, flowing brick steps lead to a large patio entrance covered with a pergola, constructed of large masonry posts and wooden beams.

The building is constructed on three levels. The first floor was built below ground level for energy efficiency and to make the height of the building above ground consistent with the neighboring buildings. This space has an atrium with clerestory windows that provide soft natural light. The cantilevered stairways facing the atrium are built of rich natural wood and a glass elevator is centrally located in the atrium space, used throughout the year for community events *(fig. 176)*. In 1985 the Central Valley Chapter of the American Institute of Architects recognized Unger for the design excellence of the Yolo County Administration Building.

176. Atrium, Yolo County Administration Building
courtesy Dean F. Unger, AIA, Inc.

By the 1980s, the terra cotta exterior of the Yolo County Courthouse Building (1917) had lost its alluring luster and glow and some sections were loosening and deteriorating. Using local and state historic preservation funds, Yolo County hired Dean Unger in 1984 to rehabilitate this landmark in several phases over a ten-year period. The exterior terra-cotta tile surface of the building was meticulously cleaned and repaired, revealing the original color and sheen of the terra cotta. Parts of the gargoyles were recast using the original molds at Gladding, McBean.

The interior of the building was converted to courtroom use only. The existing rooms were refurbished and two new courtrooms were added, including one in the round, which places the jury and witnesses in closer proximity.

Unger also designed a commercial building in Woodland, the Heart Federal Savings building at 115 Main Street (1971). The building is rectangular with glazing on the eastern half of the building and slumpstone masonry on the other half. The roof is flat and cantilevered with exposed beams.

In addition to his work in Woodland, Dean Unger has contributed several important projects in Yolo County. The Davis Veterans Memorial Center (1974) is a woodsy, shed-shaped complex inspired by the Sea Ranch style. Other Davis projects include the Sudwerk Microbrewery (1989), of which Unger is a part owner, the Fifth and G Street Plaza (1998), a downtown office and theater complex, and the UC Davis Medical Group professional offices at 2660 W. Covell Blvd. Aspen Village, a 112 acre subdivision in west Davis, features a wildlife refuge used for storm water retention and contains the U.S.'s first co-housing project.

At Highway 113 and Road 29 north of Davis, Teichert Construction built new offices designed by Unger (1999) in an appropriate Prairie style, with blue metal roofs that hover above the flatlands of the Yolo countryside.

East Street Court

A Creative Mixed Use Project Defining the Future of Downtown Woodland

An innovative and visionary adaptive reuse of an old industrial complex, East Street Court demonstrates how uniquely interesting historical structures can be recycled for modern day uses that enrich local culture. Constructed in 1904 at the northwest corner of East and Court streets for the Woodland Grain & Milling Company, the rice mill and warehouses were built sturdy and fire proof because fire destroyed the previous mill on the site *(fig. 177)*. The main three-story structure was constructed almost entirely of concrete, steel, and brick, including steel stairways and a metal roof. It was known as the Globe Rice Mill for many years and then sold to the Rice Grower's Association of California in 1950, which operated the facility until its closure in 1981 *(fig. 178, next page)*. During the next ten years the site was prepared for a new life. A large warehouse on the western side of the property was demolished to make room for a parking lot and the milling machinery was removed from the tall building. By 1990 part of the enormous space was rented to artists for studios, while the owners looked for a buyer to develop the complex.

When Santa Cruz developer and art collector, Leland Zeidler, drove to Woodland to purchase art work at the rice mill, he fell in love with the site, envisioning a dynamic complex transformed into live-work spaces for artists, restaurants and offices. Zeidler had already completed a similar project in downtown Santa Cruz that was contributor to the successful revitalization of the beach community and was ready to tackle a new project. Soon he recruited a team of investors, including San Francisco architect Jack Reineck and Woodland real estate broker Rick Elkins, and purchased the property. Reineck designed Zeidler's Santa Cruz project that included live-work space, an innovative concept at the time. A native of

177. Globe Rice Mill, c1920
from *Yolo in Word & Picture, Woodland Daily Democrat* 1920, *courtesy Yolo County Archives*

178. **Rice Mill and Warehouses Before Adaptive Reuse**

southern California, Reineck received his architecture degree from Cal Poly San Luis Obispo in 1967. After a short period in the Los Angeles area where he met Zeidler and collaborated on a project, Reineck moved to San Francisco in 1972.

Completed in 1991, Renick's innovative design for East Street Court was interesting and visionary and a model for future development in the downtown area. It combined several different uses for the three large buildings and demonstrated that live-work space is a viable option in converted industrial buildings. Reinick split the large warehouse to the rear of the property into two separate wings, divided by a courtyard *(fig. 179)*. The two buildings were converted to a series of loft units used as living quarters with

179. **Courtyard and Live Work Studios, East Street Court,** 1991, Jack Reineck

180. East Street Court
All photos courtesy Jack Reineck

downstairs commercial uses. The walls facing the courtyard are new with windows and doors, but the rest of the building is original. A courtyard also connects the live-work spaces to the three-story main building that is used for office space *(fig. 180)*.

The third structure facing Court Street received minimal interior treatment. The shell of the voluminous building was left wide open, including the exposed brick walls and metal trusses spanning the very tall ceiling, preserving the industrial ambience. It became the new home of an independent bookstore and café attracting a crowd that values a downtown offering unique and uplifting spaces and a respite from the monotony and depersonalization of chain stores.

Epilogue *Woodland's Legacy as Guide for Our Future*

The story of Woodland's architects and builders illustrates the remarkable achievement of the crafting of a beautiful valley jewel, filled with a wide diversity of architectural styles. The builders were resourceful, hard working and took great pride in their work. Several immigrants, in fact, achieved the American Dream for themselves while building dream houses for prosperous, often adventurous Woodlanders.

The exceptional architecture, mostly developed before World War II, is visible proof the community not only cultivated wealth, but good taste and the eagerness to seek out competent, often progressive architects to create attractive buildings with character and style. With excellence fueling excellence, a tradition developed early in Woodland's history for fine homebuilding, the town identified with its achievements, and promoted the beauty and diversity of its homes and buildings through local and area media.

Architectural Excellence and Community Values

The crafting of Woodland, mirroring the rich diversity of architectural styles across the Golden State, did not come by chance. Nor was it the offspring of a boomtown mentality, fashioned around a single family, group or industry so typical in California and the west. An industrious, diverse group of people produced Woodland's architectural legacy and consciously shaped a gracious and livable town. This inheritance carries its own responsibilities for this (and future) generations both to understand and to revitalize the tradition.

For the value of interesting architecture and a preservation ethic goes far beyond aesthetics, impacting the town's future economic prospects. Leading-edge research, in fact, links the quality of life in a town, defined in part by the existence and adaptive reuse of historical architectural resources, to its ability to attract new "creative classes," the artists and entrepreneurs who drive the local economic engine and expand its culture.[1] Creative people flock to certain places for good reasons, including the availability of interesting downtown housing choices, such as live-work studios and lofts, either new or crafted from historic buildings. Woodland's history exemplifies how high architectural expectations can lead to one interesting building inspiring the next. Similarly, lack of appreciation and interest in progressive architecture and the inability to develop exciting uses for aging historic buildings, leads to mediocrity, even a loss of competitive edge for a community.

Thus, with this modern perspective, we can begin to understand the lessons and context that explain why Woodland is special — that rare coming together of the right people with the right resources — especially craftsmanship and capital — at the right time. Certainly, the fertility of land provided the initial economic underpinnings, augmented by an early California sense of limitless possibility, where one could make (or remake) a new world. Healthy competition

---

[1] Richard Florida, "The Rise of the Creative Class," Washington Monthly magazine, May 2002.

among the town's economic winners played a clear role, as homeowners strove to show off their achievements, assets, and good taste. However, what this history demonstrates above all is that the determining factor driving architectural excellence is real-world decisions by real people — imagining exceptional neighborhoods, schools, and public buildings, placing high value on attractive buildings and public spaces (and willingness to pay), and recruiting the right talent to give substance to those dreams.

The Creative Heroes

As the book's subtitle implies, heroes in Woodland's architectural legacy are a wide range of talented people — beginning with the local builders/designers — and including the forward-looking architectural talent "imported" from Sacramento, San Francisco, and Berkeley that kept Woodland abreast of current architectural fashions. Furthermore, throughout much of Woodland's history, visionary business and political leaders, plus distinguished homebuilders, valued quality and fresh design — thus qualifying as important community heroes.

What galvanized in Woodland by the 1880s were a set of socio-economic values — encompassing private enterprise, entrepreneurship, aesthetics, enhanced quality of life — and a progressive, open attitude towards current fashions in architecture. In the early 20th century, citizens demonstrated civic entrepreneurship by passing bond measures for several modern, attractive schools and an expensive, elegant courthouse, as investors helped fund a fine downtown hotel. Well-capitalized local banks developed top-notch buildings on several street corners and Woodland's beauty, refinement and character were applauded, advancing pride of place. There were setbacks along the way, including two world wars and major economic downturns in the 1890s and during the Great Depression of the 1930s, when building materials were scarce or people could not afford to build homes. Yet Woodland always rebounded from these setbacks. During the mid-thirties until the early-forties attractive homes in a variety of styles were the fashion: throughout Beamer Park by Motroni and along Hays Street and Marshall Avenue by Brown & Woodhouse.

However, in the 1950s and '60s in Woodland and throughout much of California, traditional neighborhood design gave way to large subdivisions, with wide streets, no planting strips for shade trees, and mostly mass-produced housing with trivial variations in style. Viewed from the lens of history, there were several reasons for this shift in the way neighborhoods were designed. Explosive population growth led by the baby boom generation created a strong steady demand for housing throughout California's job centers. Low interest government mortgages made available to returning World War II veterans also stimulated the housing industry. Importantly, more middle-income families achieved the American Dream of homeownership.

The single story L-shaped ranch style house with a protruding two-car garage dominated the new housing tracts. The proliferation of air conditioning powered by cheap energy diverted attention away from the ecological benefits of shade trees lining city streets. Planting strips were typically eliminated in favor of wider streets and as a way to economize on subdivision costs. Alleyways and hidden garages fell out of fashion. Houses exhibiting some individuality, with sitting porches that were inviting to the street, became fewer in an era marked by conformity, electric garage openers, and low architectural expectations. New housing here was indistinguishable from so many newer, less storied California cities.

A New Generation Redeems the Past

By the late 1960s a new wave of families, valuing the architectural character, variety, and craftsmanship of historic Woodland, began to rehabilitate aging historical houses and buildings. This new cultural trend represented a conscious lifestyle choice by these "weekend warriors," attracted to the individuality and personality of the older, aging housing stock, rather than the monotony and sameness of tract housing. Similarly, committed entrepreneurs restored commercial buildings, drawn to the irreplaceable history and character of the structures and the personal desire to preserve a sense of place on the verge of being lost forever. For thirty-five years now, older neighborhoods have been reborn through heroic and inspired efforts by a generation who value Woodland's special legacy.

Today, having 140 years of architectural history by which to judge, we observe a dimming of Woodland's historical distinction as a cohesive architectural jewel. Although a few visually interesting houses in outlying areas were built in modern times, on the whole the design of post-WWII neighborhoods are inferior to the tree-lined neighborhoods, with inviting houses in a variety of styles and sizes, that preceded them. And, despite excellent downtown preservation efforts during the last twenty-five years by inspired local entrepreneurs, there has been very little new commercial architecture in progressive, modern styles reflecting a contemporary understanding and approach to design. Mediocrity, rather than excellence, became more the norm as Woodland policy makers failed to aggressively tackle redevelopment of the town center with in-fill development featuring high quality contemporary architecture. The proliferation of banal strip malls and big box warehouse stores increasingly distant from the historic core has eroded Woodland's character, compactness and sense of place.

Not surprisingly, Woodland has not fared very well in the competitive economic development arena, largely failing to attract high-tech entrepreneurs or top-flight, innovative companies with highly educated, creative employees whose energy, civic involvement and new ideas advance community culture. These key ingredients — quality of life, cultural and intellectual diversity, even a sense of collective adventure — are essential to sustain Woodland as a great place to work and live.

Woodland is still an affluent, fiscally healthy town, with low debt, and can thus afford exceptional buildings. Other nearby cities, such as Suisun City, set a good example, refashioning in the 1990s its downtown and old industrial area into beautiful, inviting public spaces and residential areas. In addition to a formulating a strong planning vision and commitment to design excellence, Suisun City willingly floated bonds to achieve distinction. Woodland can do the same, though great projects take strong, visionary leadership, measured risk taking, and civic entrepreneurship. The responsibility for developing good public buildings and a first-class community rests not only with elected leaders with passion and vision, but also with voters who must be willing to approve bond and tax measures to implement the vision. Recent school bond approvals and tax increases to pay for a new police station and community center are positive indicators that the community cares about Woodland's future.

Significantly, the exciting conceptual design for the new police station at Fifth and Lincoln streets by LPA architects reflects modern, progressive architecture with a brick exterior that blends with the historic industrial context of the area and includes environmentally responsible "green" design features. When built, this project will not only revitalize a blighted transitional area, but also demonstrate the city is inspired about elevating the standard of public architecture, establishing a benchmark for the private sector to match.

Taking the 2103 Perspective

How will Woodland's architectural history be recorded and evaluated 100 years from now? The choice is ours. Do we settle for mediocrity and sameness, or do we use the past for inspiration and expect and encourage more attractive, progressive designs? We can start by re-affirming a strong, committed public policy that emphasizes quality civic buildings, parks, plazas and schools designed by talented architects. A strong, unwavering commitment to a quality community vision, embodied in the current *General Plan*, *Downtown Specific Plan*, *East Street Corridor Plan*, *and Spring Lake Specific Plan,* will elevate the future aesthetics of the community. We should endorse and foster high quality, new development from the private sector, respectful of Woodland's architectural legacy, and not settle for less. Starting with the impending Spring Lake development in the southeast part of town, firm neighborhood design guidelines need to be adopted and enforced. These guidelines, derived from principles of the New Urbanism and inspired by the "old urbanism" of Woodland's inviting core neighborhoods, should stipulate some or all of the following:

- house designs for large tracts be designed to achieve variations in style, floor plans, and elevations;
- builders be encouraged to hire talented architects to design fresh, progressive style houses, with less reliance on "stock" designs;
- neighborhoods be less segregated by high and low incomes, achievable by avoiding uniform housing sizes and types;
- Lot sizes be conducive to building houses with detached garages;
- non-profit builders and housing cooperatives, using these design guidelines, be assisted by the public sector to construct tasteful multi-family housing, bungalow courts, and live-work structures for low and moderate income families next to market-rate housing.

These New Urbanism design concepts offer the best way to honor Woodland's marvelous building heritage. The vision is for Woodland's new development to bridge the best we have now, thus creating the kind of unified framework that Woodlanders, 100 years hence, will look upon with pride.

Finally, inspired and smart community development means taking advantage of opportunity. California's dynamic economy and steady growth will provide ample opportunity for polishing Woodland's luster as a valley jewel for this generation and those to follow. As it was for pioneering families, our destiny is in our hands. We all gain by using the best of Woodland's architectural legacy, not as static museum pieces or for mechanical imitation, but as inspiration and incentive for crafting a larger town that will justify another such historical survey within a generation. If we commit to excellence, this initial exploration into Woodland's architectural history will be the first of others to follow.

Appendices

Researching Woodland's Architectural Past: *Archives and Record Offices Consulted*

Many thanks to the librarians, staff, and volunteers at the following institutions and records centers for their assistance during the course of researching the book:

- The Archdiocese of San Francisco, Chancery Archives
- Bancroft Library, University of California, Berkeley
- Berkeley Architectural Heritage Association
- California Historical Society
- California State Library Newspaper Microfilm Collection
- Christian Church of Woodland Archives
- Foundation for San Francisco's Architectural Heritage
- Genealogy Library, Sacramento & Woodland, The Church of Jesus Christ of Latter-Day Saints
- Holy Rosary Church of Woodland Archives
- Napa County Historical Society
- Oakland Cultural Heritage Survey
- Oakland Public Library
- Sacramento Archives and Museum Collection Center, History and Science Division
- St. John's United Church of Christ Archives
- St. Luke's Episcopal Church Archives
- Spokane Public Library
- United Methodist Church of Woodland Archives
- University of Washington, Department of Architecture
- Woodland City Library Newspaper Microfilm Collection
- Woodland City Cemetery Burial Records
- Woodland City Hall, Building Permit Records
- Woodland City Hall, City Council Minutes
- Woodland City Hall, Historic Maps and Tax Assessment Records
- Yolo County Archives and Record Center
- Yolo County Historical Society
- Yolo County Library Newspaper Microfilm Collection
- Yolo County Museum

Oral Interviews

The following individuals were interviewed for the book and I wish to thank them for their stories and information:

Gerald Anderson, Daniel & Bernice Best, Ronald Brocchini, Ray Columbara, Robert Crippen, Mrs. William David, Eleanor Fait, Terry Garcia, Bob George, Josephine Motroni Gillette, Frank Heard, Julianna Inman, Louis Stephens Jones, Joseph T. Keehn, Earl Klinkhammer, Marietta Leiser, Bill McCandless, Richard Mann, Pat Noble, Harold Parker, Jack Reineck, Erma Morelli Ricci, Peter M. Saucerman, Gene Stille, Howard Terhune, Nicholas A. Tomich, Bessie Tufts, Dean F. Unger, Pauline & Wim Van Muyden, Gary Wirth, Barbara Woolsey, Gladys Younger, and Jack Younger.

Sources

Architect and Engineer periodicals (1905-1919). San Francisco: Architect & Engineer Company.

Baird, Joseph A., Jr. 1962. *Time's Wondrous Changes: San Francisco Architecture, 1776-1915.* San Francisco: California Historical Society.

Bernhardi, Robert. 1979. *The Buildings of Oakland.* Oakland: Forest Hill Press.

Boorstin, Daniel J. 1993. *The Creators: A History of Heroes of the Imagination.* New York: Vintage Books.

Cerny, Susan Dinkelspiel. 1994. *Berkeley Landmarks.* Berkeley, CA: Berkeley Architectural Heritage Association.

Cox, Don. 2000. *History of 2120 V Street, Sacramento, CA.* unpublished.

Davis, Ellis. A., editor. 1911. *Commercial Encyclopedia of the Pacific Southwest.* Berkeley, CA.

Davis Community Development Department. *Cultural Resources Inventory.* 1996. Davis, CA: City of Davis.

Downing, Andrew Jackson. 1981 (reprint of original 1842 edition). *Victorian Cottage Residences.* New York, N.Y.: Dover Publications.

Duany, Andres, Elizabeth Plater-Zyberk, and Jeff Speck. 2000. *Suburban Nation: The Rise of Sprawl and the Decline of the American Dream.* New York: North Point Press.

Fait, Harrison. 1988. *A Biography of William Fait.* Yolo County Historical Society collection.

Gilbert, Frank T. 1879. *The Illustrated Atlas and History of Yolo County*. San Francisco: DePue and Company.

Gregory, Thomas Jefferson. 1913. *History of Yolo County*. Los Angeles: Historic Record Company.

Gebhard, David, Eric Sandweiss, Robert Winter. 1985. *The Guide to Architecture in San Francisco and Northern California*. Salt Lake City: Peregrine Smith Books.

Hunt, Marguerite and Harry Lawrence Gunn. 1926. *History of Solano and Napa County, California*. Chicago, S.J. Clarke Publishing Co.

Kirker, Harold. *California's Architectural Frontier*. 1960. Salt Lake City: Gibbs M. Smith, Inc., Peregrine Smith Books.

Kurutz, Gary F. *Architectural Terra Cotta of Gladding, McBean*. 1989. Sausalito, CA.: Windgate Press.

Larkey, Joann L. and Shipley Walters. 1987. *Yolo County Land of Changing Patterns*. Windsor Publications, Inc.

Lewis, Betty. *W.H. Weeks, Architect*. 1985. Fresno, CA: Pioneer Publishing Company.

Lofland, John. *Old North Davis: Guide to Walking a Traditional Neighborhood.* 1999. Woodland, CA: Yolo County Historical Society.

Lowell, Waverly B., editor. *Architectural Records in the San Francisco Bay Area: A Guide to Research.* New York: Garland, 1988.

Marinovich, Charles S. "*The Durant — A City Landmark*". Berkeley, CA: Berkeley Architectural Heritage Association Newsletter, Spring 1998.

McAlester, Virginia & Lee. 1990. *A Field Guide to American Houses.* New York: Alfred A. Knopf, 1990

Martinez, Larry. May 1998. *History of Clark Field.* Series published in *Daily Democrat* newspaper.

Miller, Donald L., editor. 1995. *The Lewis Mumford Reader.* Athens, Georgia: University of Georgia Press.

Mumford, Lewis. 1961. *The City in History.* New York: Harcourt, Brace & World, Inc.

______ 1971 (reprint of 1931 edition). *The Brown Decades: A Study of the Arts in America 1865-1895.* New York , N.Y: Dover Publications, Inc.

Oakland Planning Department. *Oakland Cultural Heritage Survey.* Oakland, CA: City of Oakland.

Ochsner, Jeffrey Karl, editor. 1994. *Shaping Seattle Architecture.* Seattle, WA: University of Washington Press.

______ 1982. H.H. Richardson: *Complete Architectural Works.* Cambridge, MA.

Powell, John Edward. 2001. *Biographies of Prominent Historic Architects, Designers, and Builders in Fresno and the Central Valley: Ira Wilson Hoover.* Unpublished.

Russell, William Ogburn. 1940. *History of Yolo County.* Woodland, CA.

Sacramentan. August 1955. "*Perke" Pierson Retires After 43 Years in Architecture.*

Sacramento Heritage, Inc. *Historic Architecture of Sacramento — Walking Tour Guides.*

Sacramento Pioneer Association. 2001. *Gone to Rest: Biographies of Sacramento Pioneers Buried in or nearby Pioneer Grove of the Old Sacramento City Cemetery.*

Scully, Jr., Vincent J. 1969. *American Architecture and Urbanism.* New York: Frederick A. Praeger Publishers.

______ 1971. *The Shingle Style and the Stick Style.* New Haven: Yale University Press.

Snyder, John W. 1975. *Index of the California Architect and Building News*. Davis, California. University of California, Davis M.A. Thesis.

Starr, Kevin. 1973. *Americans and the California Dream 1850-1915*. New York, N.Y.: Oxford University Press.

_______ 1985. *Inventing the Dream: California Through the Progressive Era*. New York, N.Y.: Oxford University Press.

St. Luke's Church, Woodland, CA. *Historical Summary*.

Sunset Magazine and Books Editorial Staff. 1958. *Western Ranch Houses by Cliff May*. Menlo Park, CA: Lane Books.

Traveler's Hotel National Register Application. 1974. Sacramento, CA.

University of California, Davis. 1987. *U.C. Davis Historical Resources Inventory*.

Ver Planck, Christopher P. 1997. *Building by the Book: John Cotter Pelton's "Cheap Dwellings" of San Francisco, California 1880-1890*. M.A. Thesis submitted to University of Virginia.

Walters, Shipley. 1995. *Woodland City of Trees*. Woodland, CA: Yolo County Historical Society.

Welsh, Patricia Ann. 1993. *Thomas John Welsh, Architect 1845-1918*. San Francisco, CA: PAW Productions.

Western Neighborhoods Project. 2003. "Mark Daniels" www.outsidelands.org/daniels

Wilkinson, David, Marcia Cary, Ron Pinegar, Jack Potter. 1992. *Historical Downtown Woodland Walking Tour*. Woodland, CA: Woodland Downtown Improvement Association, Inc.

Withey, Henry F. & Elsie Rathburn Withey. 1970. *Biographical Dictionary of American Architects*. Los Angeles: Hennessey & Ingalls, Inc.

Wolfe, James E. and George Wolfe, editors. (1879-1900). *The California Architect and Building News*. San Francisco: San Francisco Architectural Publishing Co.

Woodbridge, Sally B., John M. Woodbridge, FAIA, Chuck Byrne. 1992. *San Francisco Architecture*. San Francisco, CA: Chronicle Books.

Woodbridge, Sally, editor. 1988. *Bay Area Houses*. Layton, Utah: Gibbs M. Smith, Inc.

Woodbridge, Sally. 2002. *John Galen Howard and the University of California*. Berkeley: University of California Press.

Woodland Community Development Department. *Woodland Historical Resources Inventory*. 1981-82. Woodland, CA: City of Woodland.

Woodland Historical Preservation Commission. 1997. *Walking Tour of Historic Woodland*. Woodland, CA: City of Woodland.

Yolo County Historical Society. 1971. *Historic Homes of Woodland, CA*. Woodland, CA: Yolo County Historical Society, Booklet #4.

Location and Dates of Construction of Buildings by Woodland Architects and Builders

* denotes builder only
** denotes designer only

George Barber

Leake House (1903)	547 Second St.
Cranston House (1906)	610 First St.

Albert A. Bennett

Yolo County Hospital (1863)	121 First St.
Yolo County Court House (1864)	Courthouse Square (demolished)

Brocchini Architects

Woodland Opera House Interior Design (1989)	340 Second St.
Milsap House (1967)	816 First St.

Brown & Woodhouse

Brown & Woodhouse (1928)	539 Third St.
C.G. Gawantka House (1928)	340 Lincoln Ave.
M. Farlee House (1928)	Cross St.
F. Acedo House (1928)	First St.
St. Lukes Rectory (1929)	515 Second St.
A.C. Huston House* (1929)	611 Bartlett Ave.
W.A. Eckart House* (1929)	902 Elm St.
J. Ruppert House (1930)	152 Third St.
D.L. Wightman House (1931)	922 Second St.
Brown & Woodhouse (1931)	401 Bartlett Ave.
M.E. Jones House (1932)	749 College St.
Sadie Reid Duplex (1932)	153-55 Third St.
Mrs. C. Whitehouse House (1932)	914-918 Second St.
Charles Frey House (1932)	218 Cross St.
Gloria Montgomery House (1935)	304-316 Walnut St.
W.E. Bush House (1935)	160 Pendegast St.
W.P. Boyce House (1935)	310-309 Lincoln Ave.
Brown & Woodhouse (1936)	335 Oak St.
Elizabeth Duncan House (1936)	445 Bartlett Ave.
Mrs. William Johnston House (1936)	625 Walnut St.
William Johnston House (1936)	621 Walnut St.
Neil Daugherty House (1936)	750 Second St.
W.A. Dozier House (1937)	303 Clover St.
Lillian White House (1937)	148 Park Ave.
John James House (1937)	552-554 Walnut St.
John James House (1937)	215-219 Oak St.
Frank Rook House (1937)	120 Fifth St.
G. Miller House (1938)	223 Marshall Ave.
M.E. Jones House (1940)	105 Bartlett Ave.
C.J. Celoni House (1940)	164 Bartlett Ave.
Dr. P.F. Phares House (1940)	916 Cleveland St.
H. Lamoree House (1940)	145 Marshall Ave.
Margaret Muhl House (1940)	216 Hays St.
Orville Geer House (1941)	144 Marshall Ave.
H.H. Brown House (1941)	144 Hays St.
B.J. Stephens House (1941)	135 Marshall Ave.
Robert Emler House (1941)	138 Hays St.
E.E. Olsen House (1941)	217 Marshall Ave.
William Crawford House* (c1940)	106 Bartlett Ave.

Joseph Caldwell

Brown House (1885)	422 Lincoln St.
Byron Ball House (1885)	427 North St.
Joseph Caldwell House	1003 Court St.
House	326 Lincoln St. (attributed)
House	539 Second St. (attributed)
R.I. Pierce House (1910)	325 Lincoln St.

Lester J. Caldwell

House (1927)	750 Third St.
House (1927)	753 Third St.
House (1928)	Second & Pendegast Sts.
House (1928)	922 Third St.
House (1928)	Third & Bartlett Ave.
House (1928)	757 Pendegast St.
House (1929)	715 Bartlett Ave.
House (1930)	11 Court St.
House (1936)	909 Second St.
House (1936)	933 Second St.
House (1937)	905 Second St.
House (1937)	915 Second St.
House (1938)	710 Bartlett Ave.
House (1938)	829 Third St.
House (1938)	10 Third St.
House (1939)	828 Third St.
House (1939)	925 Second St.

House (1940)	705 Marshall Ave.
House (1940)	715 Marshall Ave.

Samuel Caldwell

Samuel Caldwell House	College & Laurel Sts. (demolished)
John D. Laugenour House (c1875)	Cross St. (demolished)
Richard H. Beamer House (1876)	19 Third St. (attributed)
House (c1879)	33 Third St. (attributed)
Old First Baptist Church (1881)	First St. (demolished)
Muegge House (1882)	547 First St.
Holy Rosary Academy* (1884)	Main St. (demolished)
Walnut St. Primary School (1885)	Walnut St. (demolished)
Traughber House (1886)	163 Second St.
House (c1889)	25 Third St. (attributed)
"Triple House" Townhouses (1893)	165-169 College St.
Yolo County Hospital* (1892)	Beamer & Cottonwood Sts. (demolished)
Marshall Diggs House* (1892)	619 College St. (burned)

William Henry Carson

Byrns Hotel (1883)	College & Main (demolished)
Douglas House (1884)	67 Third St.
Thomas House (1885)	745 First St.
Prior House (1885)	620 Second St.
Lowe & Hollingsworth Block (1883)**	411-425 Main St.
McConnell-Fielding House (1886)	709 First St.
Episcopal Church (1887)	435 Second St. (demolished)
Esperanza Hotel (1889)	Esparto (demolished)
Pond House (1886)	552 College St.
House	525 North St.
Hord House (1885)	434 Walnut St.
House	442 Walnut St.
Ritchie House (1887)	Main & Cleveland Sts. (demolished)
Oak St. School** (1889)	Oak & Elm Sts. (demolished)
Armstrong & Alge Building (1890)	604-606 Main St.

Bryan Clinch

Holy Rosary Academy (1884)	Main St. (demolished)
Holy Rosary Rectory (1891)	demolished

Grant F. Cloud

Cloud House (1948)	731 First St.
House	4 Westway Place
House	3 Rancho Place

William E. Coffman

St. John's United Church of Christ (1934)	434 Cleveland St.

Colley & Lemme

City Hall (1892)	300 First St. (demolished)

Fedele Costa

Holy Rosary Church (1912)	Main & Walnut Sts. (demolished)

Levi Craft

Holy Rosary Church (1869)	Main St. near Walnut (demolished)
Odd Fellows Hall/ Bank of Woodland (1870)	540 Main St.
Town Hall/ Fire Engine House (1882)	702 Main St.
Lowe & Hollingsworth Block (1883)	411– 425 Main St.

Robert E. Crippen *(partial list)*

Pepsi Cola Bottling Company (1957)	Fourth St. (demolished)
Masonic Temple (1958)	228 Palm Ave.
St. John's Church of Christ Education Building (1960)	Cleveland St.
Yolo County YMCA (1960)	1300 College St.
Woodland City Hall addition (1961)	300 First St.
Wells Fargo Bank (1963)	444 Court St.
American Legion Hall (1964)	523 Bush St.
St. John's Retirement Village (1966)	135 Woodland Ave.
Woodland Branch Fire Station	East St.
Dr. Keys House (1967)	10 Toyon Dr.

Yolo County Jail and Sheriff's Office (1968)	Court St.
Yolo County Housing Authority-Yolanda Village	1224 Lemen Ave.
Central Valley Bank	Location Unknown
Calvary Baptist Church	506 Cottonwood
Woodland Ave. Church of God	Location Unknown
Church of the Nazarene	100 Woodland Ave.
United Church of the Brethren	Location Unknown
Holy Rosary Parish House	318 Court St.
Holy Rosary School	505 California St.
Plainfield Elementary School	County Rd. 97

Cuff & Diggs

Rasor House (1912)	555 College St.

William Henry Curson

Woodland Opera House* (1885)	Second & Main Sts. (burned)
Oak St. School* (1889)	Oak & Elm Streets (demolished)
Woodland Public Library* (1905)	250 First St.
Odd Fellows Hall* (1905)	723 Main St.
Primary School* (1915)	175 N. Walnut St.

William B. David

Porter Theater (1936)	327 College St. (remodeled)
State Theater (1937)	322 Main St. (altered)
Woodland Shopping Center (1957)	120 Main St.

Dean & Dean

Eddy House (1923)	710 First St.
Lowe House (1923)	County Rd. 98
Fitch's Variety Store (1924)	508 Main St. (remodeled)
Caldwell House (remodel, 1924)	904 First St.
Daily Democrat Building (1925)	Second & Court Sts.
Kraft Bros. Funeral Chapel (1927)	175 Second St.
Woodland Fire Station/Jail (1932)	300 First St.
Laugenour House (1936)	714 W. Keystone
Daugherty House (1936)	750 Second St.
Crawford House (c1940)	106 Bartlett Ave.

Harry J. Devine, Sr.

Woodland City Hall Addition (1936)	300 First St.
Holy Rosary Catholic Church (1949)	301 Walnut St.

Dodge & Dolliver

Woodland Public Library (1905)	250 First St.

Dragon & Schmidts

J.M. Vickery House (1937)	507 Sunset
Yolo Grocery Building (1939)	534 Bush St.

Dragon, Schmidts & Hardman

Christian Church, Disciples of Christ (1949)	509 College St.

Dreyfuss & Blackford

Leiser House (1954)	409 Casa Linda Dr.
Bank building (1971)	203 Main St.

Harrison Ervin

Diggs Block (1891)	514-516 Main St.
Jackson Apartment Building (1891)	426 First St.
Beamer Place (1892)	708-712 Main St.

Joseph Esherick

Best House (1958)	303 Gibson Rd.

William R. Fait

Asa Morris House (1911)	Location unknown
Fait-Hiatt House (1913)	448 Pendegast St.
Bailey House (1912)	421 Pendegast St.
Brink House (1913)	405 Pendegast St.
Payne House (1913)	110 First St.
E. A. Bullard House remodel (1913)	County Rds. 99 & 27
Cranston's Hardware Building (1914)	618 Main St.
Woodland High School Manual Arts Building* (1914)	College St. (demolished)
Brink House (1914)	411 Pendegast St.
Hays Gable House (1914)	650 Second St.
Fait House (1915)	765 Third St. (remodeled)
E. R. Campbell House (1917)	720 First St.
C.E.Byrns House (1916)	Location unknown
Boyce House (1917)	907 First St.
H.E. Gray (1917)	"4 miles west of Woodland"
Schluer House	4 Third St.
A.B. Welch ("country house")	Location unknown

Harry Strickland House	Location unknown
Annie Martin House	Location unknown
Osborne-Morris House (c1917)	31 Palm Ave.
Karl Giguiere House (c1917)	43 Palm Ave. (remodeled)
Fait-Minnie Jacobs House (1917)	19 Palm Ave.
Fait House (1918)	25 Palm Ave.
W.H. Arata House (1919)	55 Pershing Ave.
Dan Jacobs (1919)	Beamer Park
Willis House (1919)	41 Palm Ave.
Willis Country House (1919)	Location unknown
Dickey House	220 Cross St.
Woodland Clinic Hospital*(1920)	Third near Cross (demolished)
First National Bank* (1920)	Knights Landing
Meier Ford Dealership (1921)	Bush & College Sts.
Yolo Fliers Club (1921-22)	County Rd. 94B
North St. Apartments	504-506 North St.
Minnie Stevens (1922)	Location unknown
Leon Campbell Apartments (1922)	902 Court St.
High School Agricultural Mechanics Building* (1924)	910 College St.
United Methodist Church* (1925)	212 Second St.
Williams House (1929)	39 Pershing Ave.

Vincent Fatta

Fatta House (1921)	945 North St.

Del Fenton

Fenton House (1925)	532 Elm St.
A.R. Lee House	Location unknown
F.V. Stening House	Location unknown
H.E. Norton House	Location unknown
O. Howard House	Location unknown
E. Snavely House	Location unknown
Bray House	Location unknown
Alice Ralls House	Location unknown
George A. Zane House (c1912)	East St. & County Rd. 25A
J.J. Keene House	Location unknown
John Dole House	Location unknown
H.J. Hamel House (1920)	505 Second St. (Davis)
J.G. Bruton House* (1927)	415 Bartlett Ave.
G. Rassmussen House (1928)	817 Cross St.
J.W. Crank House (1929)	617 Clover St.
Robert Harling (1929)	433 Cross St.
H. Carrow (1929)	716 Third St.
George Cranston (1930)	148 North St.
Nettie Anderson (1930)	420 Court St.
S.P. Jull Cottages (1930)	125-129 College St.
J.A. Sowash (1930)	649 A&B Fifth St.
W.H. Curson (1930)	50 Third St.
Ken C. Laugenour* (1931)	714 W. Keystone
W.J. Huerger (1931)	224 Cross St.
C.G. Gawantka (1931)	342 Lincoln Ave.
Duplex (1931)	508 Elm St.
Jacob Snider (1932)	124 First St.
Remo Ricci (1936)	19 Pershing Ave.
A. Nurenberg (1936)	12 Lincoln Ave.
William Dahler (1936)	418 Cross St.
R.W. Woods (1936)	7 Third St.
Fred Meeker (1937)	1107 Second St.
T.E. Hooper (1938)	27 ? College St.
Paul Gould (1938)	158 Park Ave.
B.F. Coehn (1941)	147 Elm St.
Margaret Porter (1941)	719 Second St.
Carolyn Gregory (1941)	407 Bartlett Ave.
A.H.Weston Motel (1946)	127 Main St.
B.W.Whitmire (1948)	314 Maedell Way
J. Leathers (1949)	922 Elm St.
House (1951)	224 Marshall Ave.
House (1953)	134 Elliot St.
Garrette House	511 Woodland Ave.
Pugh Florist Shop*	2 Main St.
House	159 Third St.

Elmer H. Fisher

Lowe House (1890)	458 First St.

Thomas George

Thomas George House (1918)	609 Fourth St.
Harry N. Carrow House (1921)	731 Third St.
House (1920)	604 Fourth St.
Andrew Bobb House (1923)	650 Fifth St.
House (1924)	733 Third St.
Thomas & Vivian McCoy House (1925)	731 Third St.
Frank B. Elston House (1927)	646 Fifth St.
Dr. F.W. Wells House (1926)	700 Block Third St.

Helena & J.C. Stitt House (1927)	745 Third St.
J.F. & Beatrice Hendley House (1927)	724 Third St.
Mumma House (1929)	530 Fourth St.
Thomas George House (1929)	37179 Highway 16
House	730 Third St.
House	736 Fourth St.
Lester Johnson House	526 Fourth St.
House	1009 First St.
Richard Willet House (remodel)	1212 Churchhill Downs

Gilbert & Sons (Edward Carlton Gilbert)

Jackson House "Yolanda" (1884)*	County Rds. 99 & 25A
George Armstrong House (1884)	Third & Cross Sts. (demolished)
Gable Mansion (1885)	659 First St.
John Daniels House (1885)	Fifth & North Sts. (demolished)
Harlan House (1885)	638 Fourth St.
YMCA Building (1886)	Second St. (demolished)
Methodist Episcopal Church South (1886)	Second & Court Sts. (demolished)
Lack House	537 Walnut St.
Old Primary School**	Walnut St. (demolished)
Minnis Building (1889)	315-317 Second St.
Yolo County General Hospital** (1892)	Beamer & Cottonwood (demolished)
Nicholas A. Hawkins House (1893)	804 First St. (remodeled)

Glenn & White

Pendegast-Demment House (1883)	728 College St.
North Methodist Church	North St. (demolished)
A.D. Porter Mansion (1886)	Main & Walnut (S/W corner (demolished)
Porter Carriage House (1886)	435-37 Walnut St.
Gibson Block (1886)	Main & Elm Sts. (S/E corner) (demolished)
Charles White House (1888)	554 Elm St.
Pond House (1887)*	552 College St.
George K. Glenn House	458 Walnut St.
Laugenour-Hershey House (1891)*	Main/Walnut (N/W corner) (demolished)
C. White House (c1892)	604 Elm St.
Will Porter House (1892)	427 Walnut St.
W.S. White House	503 Walnut St.

Nathaniel D. Goodell

Exchange Hotel (1882)	Main & Second (N/E corner)(burned)

Gould & Colley

Jackson Building (1891)	428 First St.
Diggs Building (1891)	514-516 Main St. (altered)

Olin S. Grove

Fairchild House (1913)	914 First St.

Joseph Johnson Hall

Marshall Diggs House (1892)	619 College St. (burned)
Spaulding House (1892)	638 First St.
Farmers & Merchants Bank (1893)	Second & Main Sts. (demolished)
Diggs-Leithold Building (1893)	619-21 Main St.
Jackson-Armfield Building (1893)	617 Main St.

Willam C. Hays

St. Luke's Episcopal Church (1912)	515 Second St.

Keehn Bros.

Keehn Family House (1897)	327 Sixth St.
James Campbell House	Davis (demolished)
Van Zee House (1902)	Rd. 16 (demolished)
German Lutheran Church Parsonage (1902)	Cleveland St. (burned)
George Hollingworth House (1903)	Plainfield (burned)
Joseph Coopers House (1903)	County Rds. 16A & 98B
Edward E. Leake House (1903)*	547 Second St.
J.J. Brown House (1904)	804 College St.
Black House (1904)	813 First St. (attributed)
House (1904)	1310 West St.
Thomas B. Gibson (1905)	311 Gibson Rd.
Fred Sieferman House (1905)	County Rd. 95

Yolo Town Hall (1905)*	Yolo
Rueben B. Cranston House (1906)*	610 First St.
Zamora Catholic Church (1907)**	Zamora
Aldo Baccei House	106 Main St.
H.E. Coil House	Churchhill Downs Rd.
Z. Kinchloe House	Location Unknown
Fred Miller House	Location Unknown
Charles T. Laugenour House addition	Hwy. 113 (partially burned)
George Merrit House	Location Unknown
Fred Fairchild House (1910)	754 College St.
Dr. T.J. Alexander House (1910)	152 First St.
Inez Ford House (1911)	699 Third St.
Alge House (1911)	429 First St.
Frank Bullard House remodel (1912)	County Rds. 27 & 99
Electric Garage (1912)	801 Main St.
Holy Rosary Academy Auditorium (1912)	Main St. (demolished)
W.B. Collins House (1913)	237 Cross St.
Dan Jacobs House (1913)	211 Court St.
William Germeshausen House	127 Court St.
Edward Germeshausen House	141 Court St.
Edward I. Leake (1914)	622 Second St.
French Laundry Building (1914)	927 Main St.
William Johnston House (1914)	630 Elm St.
Primary School (1915)	175 N. Walnut St.
Bertha Weber House	West St. (demolished)
Frank Meyers House	County Rd. 101 north of Davis
Ben & Ida Keehn House	827 Court St. (demolished)
Frank Kaufmann House — second story	803 College St.
Lester & May Germeshausen House	County Rd. 100B (attributed)
Laugenour House	E. Main St. (demolished)
Alfred Marconi House (1924)	19(?) College St.
J.H. Orendorf House	(1927) 149 Park Ave.

Keehn Keehn & Lucchesi

House (1938)	443 Grand Ave.
Toof (1939)	51 Second St.
Guy Baccei (1939)	117 North St.
Theo Dumars (1940)	140 Bartlett Ave.
House (1940)	144 Bartlett Ave.
House (1940)	118 Second St.
Hermele (1940)	911 Grafton St.
House (1949)	215 Buena Tierra
Quonset Hut (1949)	660 Sixth St.

Gerhard Klinkhammer

Houses (1947)	510-14-20 Buena Tierra
Houses (1947)	1306-10-14-18 Fremont
Houses (1947)	1322-26-30-34 Fremont
Houses (1948)	11-15 Elliott St.
Houses (1949)	7-15-18 Central Place
Houses (1949)	12-20 Clover St.
House (1949)	213 Palm Ave.
House (1950)	210 Buena Tierra
Houses (1950)	1208-10 McKinley
Houses (1950)	1021-1207 West St.
Houses (1950)	1208-12-20-24 Eunice Dr.
House (1950)	21 Casa Linda Dr.

Klinkhammer & Willey

Geer House*	210 Toyon Dr.
Best House	75 W. Gibson Rd.
Alderson's Convalescent Hospital	124 Walnut St.
St. John's Retirement Village*	135 Woodland Ave.

Robert Klinkhammer

Orrick Building	194 W. Main St.

Daniel McPhee

Lowe House (1890)*	458 First St.
Farmers & Merchants Bank (1894)*	Second & Main (N/W corner) (demolished)
Armory Building (1895)	Bush St. (demolished)
Yolo Savings Bank (1903)*	435 Main St.

Meyer & O'Brien

Lowe-Blevins House (1905)	618 First St.

Harold D. Mitchell

Jackson-Hecke House "Yolanda" (1884)	County Rds. 99 & 25A

Morgan & Hoover

Bank of Yolo (1907)	500 Main St. (remodeled)

Joseph Motroni

Motroni Office and Residence (1920)	1015 Beamer St.
House (1920)	1017 Beamer St.
Payne (1922)	750 Third St.
Rademaker (1922)	755 Second St.
Huff (1923)	716 Third St.
Reed (1923)	753 Third St.
Bloodworth Car Dealership (1923)	333 Main St.
Fitch Commercial Building* (1924)	508 Main St.
Caldwell* (1924)	904 First St.
Draper Bungalow Court (1925)	317 Cleveland
Cruson (1925)	53 Palm Ave.
Montgomery (1925)	633 Third St.
Elks Lodge* (1926)	500 Bush St.
H. Traynham (1927)	701 W. Keystone Ave.
Dr. Blevins* (1927)	742 First St.
Motroni (1927)	158 North St.
F. Lawhead (1927)	440 Pendegast St.
Kraft Bros. Funeral Chapel* (1927)	175 Second St.
Christian Church Education Building (1927)	507 College St.
Tillotson (1927)	126 North St.
Buchingnani (1928)	Clover & Elm Sts.
Haskell (1928)	Clover & Beamer Sts.
Cunningham (1928)	349 Court St.
Wilson (1928)	909 College St.
St. Luke's Guild Hall* (1929)	515 Second St.
Roth (1929)	6 Keystone Ave.
Motroni (1929)	32 Palm Ave.
Crawford (1929)	901 College St.
Eckart* (1929)	902 Elm St.
Holmes (1929)	753 First St.
E. Niclas (1929)	47 Palm Ave.
J. Barth (1929)	51 Pershing Ave.
J. Merritt*(1929)	712 Second St.
H.O. Cummings (1929)	666 First St.
Wm. Peck (1929)	Second St.
Lester Cranston (1929)	144 North St.
E. Conger (1929)	728 First St.
Geer (1929)	704 Elm St.
M. Shone (1930)	709 W. Keystone Ave.
F. McGrew (1930)	5 E. Keystone Ave.
C.E. Babcock (1930)	Court St.
Clark Field (1930)	Beamer St.
K. Lowe* (1930)	815 College St.
A. Praeger (1930)	Third St.
R.W. Barr (1930)	717-719 Fourth St.
H.R. Jacobs (1930)	27 Pershing Ave.
R.H. Carter (1930)	5 Cross St.
L. McDonald (1930)	826 College St.
Barth Sheet Metal (1931)	423 First St.
J. Motroni (1931)	14 North St.
A. Jensen (1931)	132 North St.
J. Volonti (1931)	103 First St.
J.D. Musgrove (1931)	605-607 Fourth St.
J.G. Motroni (1931)	520 Cross St.
F.L. West (1931)	1013 Second St.
Louis Ebel (1932)	211 Cleveland St.
City Hall/Fire Station* (1932)	300 First St.
Mrs. C.A. Webber (1932)	66 Second St.
A.B. Brownell (1932)	135 Oak St.
Mrs. F. Brauner (1932)	5 Lincoln Ave.
D.P. Traynham (1933)	527 W. Keystone Ave.
R.S. Spaulding (1934)	Walnut St.
Phipps (1934)	745 Third St.
G.C. Grady (1934)	202 Cross St.
J.G. Motroni (1934)	152 Cleveland St.
J.G. Motroni (1934)	158 Cleveland St.
J.G. Motroni (1934)	164 Cleveland St.
Charles Noble (1935)	716 First St.
L.Abele (1935)	159 North St.
J.Hanson (1935)	163 North St.
Lynch (1935)	325 Lincoln Ave.
Heney (1935)	829 Third St.
Isabelle Wright (1935)	601 Woodland Ave.
Perry Lawson (1935)	133 North St.
J.G. Motroni (1936)	137 North St.
K.Laugenour* (1936)	714 W. Keystone Ave.
Lido Tozzi (1936)	12 Pershing Ave.
J.G. Motroni (1936)	144 Elliott St.
J.G. Motroni (1936)	55 Third St.
C.H. McDonald (1936)	604 Third St.

Henry Anderson (1936)	550 Walnut St.
Nello Tozzi (1936)	16 Pershing Ave.
E. Stowe (1936)	725 Hollister Rd.
F. Duncan (1936)	140 Elliott St.
J. Darnielle (1936)	142 Elliott St.
Vickery (1936)	605 W. Keystone Ave.
J.G. Motroni (1936)	132 Elliott St.
J.G. Motroni (1936)	138 Elliott St.
J.G. Motroni (1936)	524 W. Keystone Ave.
Fortna (1936)	511 W. Keystone Ave.
Borba/Edson (1937)	503 W. Keystone Ave.
Dahnke (1937)	603 Hollister Rd.
Vickery/Jones*(1937)	507 Sunset Ave.
Morris (1937)	516 W. Keystone Ave.
Rossi (1937)	526 W. Keystone Ave.
J.G. Motroni (1937)	521 Sunset Ave.
D.B. Kinney (1937)	602 W. Keystone Ave.
J.G. Motroni (1937)	16 Fourth St.
D.H. Humphrey (1938)	525 W. Keystone Ave.
Cossman (1938)	525 Sunset Ave.
Archer (1938)	529 Sunset Ave.
J.G. Motroni (1938)	130 Elliott St.
Farrington (1938)	124 N. College St.
J.G. Motroni (1940)	13-15-17 Sutter St.
A.E. Baccei (1940)	136 Bartlett Ave.
W. Nardinelli (1940)	18 Jackson St.
J.G. Motroni (1941)	726 Woodland Ave.
Morconi (1941)	44 College St.
Wademan (1941)	20 Jackson St.
Mabel Dozier (1941)	731 Fourth St.
Felix Rossi (1941)	521 W. Keystone Ave.
J.G. Motroni (1941)	9 Sutter St.
J.G. Motroni (1941)	Third St.
J.G. Motroni (1941)	726 Woodland Ave.
J.G. Motroni (1941)	614-616 Hollister Rd.
C.H. Clements (1942)	9 Fourth St.
W.F. Sanborn (1945)	116 Bruton St.
Wm. Delonais (1945)	616 Woodland Ave.
Gregg Van Zee (1945)	910 Hollister Rd.
G. Miller (1945)	28 Jackson St.
A. Fissell(1945)	1006 Hollister Rd.
G. Stotts (1945)	32 Jackson St.
C. Johanson (1945)	1010 Hollister Rd.
J.G. Motroni (1945)	33 Sutter St.
J.G. Motroni (1945)	107 E. Keystone Ave.
L.A. Fritter(1945)	108 Bruton St.
C.A. Nook (1945)	812 Hollister Rd.
R.A. Wolff (1945)	508 W. Keystone Ave.
J.G. Motroni (1946)	1038 Beamer (office)
Cox (1946)	29 Sutter St.
Wm. Simms (1946)	13 Jackson St.
D.E. Wyly (1946)	10 Bliss Ave.
J.C. Dixon (1946)	103 E. Keystone Ave.
R.E. Humphrey (1946)	24 Jackson St.
T.B. Mitchell (1946)	18 Sutter St.
Dr. Nichols/Copeland (1947)	500 First St.
Dr. Railsback (1947)	215 Oak St.
Parkhurst (1947)	1015 Hollister Rd.
Gillette (1947)	27 Sutter St.
J. Lombardi (1947)	25 Sutter St.
J.G. Motroni (1948)	19 Jackson St.
J. Espigares (1948)	811 Hollister Rd.
Others (dates unknown):	
Hickman	607 Hollister Rd.
M.O. Harling	715 W. Keystone Ave.
J.G. Motroni	20 Pershing Ave.
Nurse's Residence	201 W. Beamer St.
Caneda	9 Bliss Ave.
Stafford	24 Bliss Ave.
Sprouse/Reitz Remodel	524 Main St.
Baccei Apt. Building	106 Main St.
J.G. Motroni	149 North St.
E. Leutwien	156 North St.
Modern Cleaners	704 Elm St.
Sieber	656 McKinley Ave.

Arthur D. Nicholson

Northern Electric Train Depot (1912)	Second & Main Sts. (S/W corner) (demolished and rebuilt)

Anton Paulsen

A. Paulsen House (1931)	702 Pendegast St.
House	716 Pendegast St.
House	720 Pendegast St.
House	802 Third St.

H.B. Sells (1933)	37 Elm St.
A. Datchler (1936)	113 Lincoln Ave.
A. Paulsen (1936)	705 Bartlett Ave.
T. Hansen (1937)	71 West St.
C. Hansen (1937)	5 West St.
H. Saunders (1937)	647 Third St.
S.R. Turner (1938)	702 Marshall Ave.
G.E. Schlosser (1938)	818 Second St.
C. Mather (1939)	131 Bartlett Ave.
R.M. Peckham (1939)	132 Bartlett Ave.
R. Paulsen (1945)	1008 Cleveland St.
Wm. Crawford, Jr. (1946)	213 Marshall Ave.
J. Adams (1947)	426 Buena Tierra
A. Paulsen (1948)	410 Buena Tierra
J.G. Adams (1948)	417 Casa Linda
Masonic Temple (1958)	228 Palm Ave.
Sunset Rice Dryers	845 Kentucky Ave.

John C. Pelton, Jr.

Welges House (1881)	Second & Court Sts. (demolished)

C. Carleton Pierson

Stephens House (1927)	603 College St.
Bruton House (1927)	415 Bartlett St.
Huston House (1928)	617 Cross St.
Guild Hall, St. Luke's Church (1929)	515 Second St.
Merritt House (1929)	712 Second St.
Huston House (1929)	611 Bartlett Ave.
Eckart House (1929)	902 Elm St.
Lowe House (1931)	815 College St.

Eugenio Ricci & Sons

Ricci House	96 Railroad Ave.
High School Music Building (1937)	College St.
Masonic Lodge	Knights Landing
Remo Ricci	
Ricci House* (1936) — with Del Fenton	19 Pershing Ave.
Ricci House (1948)	216 Marshall Ave.
Schaefer-Wirth	
Diggs Building remodel (1974)	666 Dead Cat Alley
Woodland City Hall remodel (1976)	300 First St.

Shea & Shea

Laugenour-Hershey House (1891)	Main & Walnut (N/W corner) (demolished)

William I. Stille

Wm. Stille (1937)	144 Park Ave.
F. Murphy (1939)	141 North St.
J.H. Laugenour (1940)	920 Elm St.
M.N. Stille (1941)	445 Elm St.
D. McWilliams (1941)	756 Cleveland St.
R. Farley	750 Cleveland St.
Mrs. K. Hardwig (1941)	111 Pendegast St.
M.N. Stille (1945)	525 McKinley Ave.
F. Shaffer	524 McKinley Ave.
Nugget Market (1946)	157 Main St.

Howard Terhune

House	648 College St.
House	640 College St.
Commercial Building	605-607 North St.
Office Building	177-179 and 185-189 First St.

John Hudson Thomas

Stephens House (1916)	756 First St.
Thomas House (1920)	515 First St.
Blevins House (1927)	742 First St.

Nicholas Tomich

St. Paul's Lutheran Church (1968-69)	625 W. Gibson Rd.

Rollin S. Tuttle

United Methodist Church (1925)	212 Second St.

Luther M. Turton

Unitarian Church (1910)	417 Lincoln St. (remodeled)
Woodland Sanitarium (1911)	Third & Cross Sts. (demolished)

Dean F. Unger

Geer House (1964)	210 Toyon Dr.
Payne House (1970)	201 W. Monte Vista Dr.
Heart Federal Savings Bank (1971)	115 Main St.
Yolo County Administration Building (1984)	625 Court St.

Yolo County Courthouse Restoration (1980s)	725 Court St.

William Henry Weeks

Yolo Savings Bank (1903)	435 Main St.
Woodland High School (1913)	Hays & College Sts. (demolished)
Porter Office Building (1913)	511 Main St.
Woodland Public Library Addition (1915)	Court St.
Primary School (1915)	175 N. Walnut St.
Yolo County Jail (1915)	Third St. (demolished)
Yolo County Courthouse (1917)	Court St.
McConnell House (1919)	705 First St.
Woodland Clinic Offices/ Hospital (1920,1928)	Third & Cross Sts.
Yolo Flyers Club (1920)	County Rd. 94B
Grammar School (1924)	Elm St.(demolished)
Elks Lodge (1926)	500 Bush St.
High School Auditorium and Gymnasium (1925)	College St. (demolished)
Hotel Woodland (1928)	436 Main St.

Thomas J. Welsh

Woodland Opera House (1885)	Second St. (burned)
McIntryre Building (1885)	Main St. (burned)
Holcom House (1886)	715 First St.
Yolo County Hall of Records (1889)	Court St. (demolished)
Beamer Place (1892)	712 Main St.

William S. White

William S. White House (1882)	609 Third St.
Clanton House (1904)	627 North St.
William S. White House (1905)	437 Walnut St. (remodeled)
Hyman House (1908)	639 First St.
Unitarian Church (1910)*	417 Lincoln St. (remodeled)
J.H. Dungan House	637 Second St.
Dexter-Henshall House (1912)	626 Elm St.

Gustave Wingblade

Wingblade House	1 First St. (demolished)
Wingblade-Kramer House (1923)	4 First St.
Wingblade House (1928)	21 First St.
Koch House (1926)	39 First St.
House	45 First (attributed)
House	115 College St.
House	5 College (attributed)

William H. Winne

Congregational Church (1874)	450 First St. (attributed)
Exchange Hotel (1882)*	Main & Second (N/E corner) (burned)
German Lutheran Church (1892)	Cleveland St. (burned)
Episcopal Church (1887)	Second St. N of Lincoln (demolished)
Rebuilt Woodland Opera House (1895-96)	340 Second St.
Holcom-Holmes House (1886)	715 First St.
Steiner House (1890)	632 First St.
Julian Hotel (1894)	Main & Second (N/E corner) (demolished)
Winne Fourplex (1904)	440-442 College St. (attributed)

Gary Wirth *(partial list)*

Wirth House (1969)	4 Sequoia
House (c. 1970)	9 W. Monte Vista Dr.
House (c1972)	18 W. Monte Vista Dr.
House (c1972)	25 W. Monte Vista Dr.
Bank of America (1980)	50 W. Main St.
Opera House Annex (1980)	340 Second St.
House	205 Monte Vista Circle
House	1404 Midway
House	9 Amherst Court
House (1985)	622 Fairview Dr.
Jackson Building Restoration (1986)	426 First St.
Farm Credit Building	283 Main St.
Commercial Building	350 Court St.
Hoppin Office Building Addition	800 Court St.
House (1990)	719 Fairview Dr.
House (1990)	801 Fairview Dr.
House (1994)	932 Jordan Circle

Wirth House (1998)	936 Jordan Circle
House (2000)	942 Jordan Circle

Wirth & McCandless *(partial list)*

Excelsior Building Rehabilitation	522-24 Main St.
Barrow House Remodel	640 College St.
Beeman House Addition (c1990)	20123 East St.
Blue Shield Building (1993)	435 East St.
Woodland Hotel Rehabilitation (1996)	436 Main St.

Bill McCandless *(partial list)*

Food For Less/ Sycamore Point (c1998)	Pioneer & E. Main Sts.
Yolo Community Bank Remodel (1998)	624 Court St.
Red Cross Building Addition(1999)	120 Court St.

Jacob Witzelberger

Witzelberger House (1922)	737 Second St.
Kennedy House (1922)	724 First St.
United Brethren Church (1922)	900 Lincoln Ave.
Main St. Garage Addition (1923)	346 Main St. (demolished)
Parish Hall-Catholic Church (1925)	315 Walnut St.
St. John's United Church of Christ (1935)	434 Cleveland St.
Yolo Grocery (1939)	534 Bush St.
Apartment Building	30 Main St.
Apartment Building	26 Main St.
99 Motel	117 W. Main St. (demolished)
Rominger House (c1940)	County Rd. 19

Albert Woodhouse

Ray Williams (1946)	126 Hays St.
R.A. Blum (1946)	150 Marshall Ave.
Elwood Roth (1946)	215 Hays St.
W.B. Tretton (1946)	132 Hays St.
Mary Kaupke (1948)	1124 Elm St.
E. Reed (1952)	435 Buena Tierra

Earle L. Younger

Porter Building (1913)	Main & College Sts.
Electric Garage Remodel/ Expansion (1918)	801 Main St.
I.H. Gregg House (1919)	15 Palm Ave.
E. Praet House (1919)	74 Third St.
Charles F. Thomas House (1920)*	515 First St.
Boyd & Littlefield Building Car Dealership (1920)	917 Main St.
Granada Theater (1922)	Main & Elm Sts. (demolished)
J.I. McConnell House (1922)*	705 First St.
Russell J. Lowe House (1922)	County Rd. 98
Wilson/McNary Funeral Home (1924)	458 College St.
Post Office (1924)	327 College St. (remodeled)
Daily Democrat Building (1925)*	702 Court St.
Hiatt & Miller Garage (1927)	333 Main St.
George Luck House (1929)	Grand Ave.
Round House Restaurant	41 Main St. (demolished)
Sanitary Dairy (1940)	Lincoln & Sixth Sts.
Esparto Grammar School	Esparto

Younger Bros.

Purity Market (1939)	528 Bush St.

Index

J

K

L

M

U

V

W

Y

Z

About the Author

Woodland resident David Wilkinson balances his two-decade career in professional community development with passions for revitalizing and beautifying his hometown. A civic leader and community activist, David's architectural writing, including two detailed walking tours of Woodland, urges that regional economic development be integrated with local commitments to restore and enhance one's neighborhood, even backyard.

While serving two terms on the Woodland Historical Preservation Commission, which spearheaded the creation of a downtown historic district, David co-founded Woodland's annual Stroll Through History in 1989. The Stroll is a popular, one-of-kind event whose daylong, educational walking tours have introduced thousands to Woodland's special architecture. A committed advocate for redevelopment programs sensitive to human needs, David's successful grants helped save the Woodland Train Depot. In 2000 David co-founded the Woodland Tree Foundation and serves as Board President.

Professionally, David works in the non-profit sector as a financial consultant to local governments, spanning economic development, historic preservation, housing and community facilities. He takes considerable satisfaction in helping create historic districts and restoring historic buildings across Sacramento Valley, including Winters, where he co-developed the Cradwick Building on Main Street.

David's academic training includes graduate work in economic development at UC Davis, which supplemented his 1979 M.A. in economics from San Francisco State University. After moving to Woodland in 1985, he contributed early on to the town's impressive movement to preserve its historic resources by restoring his own Victorian house — thus initiating a marriage between career focus, local and regional architecture, and public service.

About the Photographer

Roger Klemm grew up in the Bay Area and studied architecture at Cornell University. He worked for many years for large architecture firms in San Francisco before starting his own company in 1988. Based in Placerville, he specializes in the adaptive reuse of historic buildings. He has been an active participant in the Woodland Stroll Through History for many years as a walking tour guide and is co-developer of the historic Cradwick Building in Winters. He pursues photography as a serious and enjoyable hobby.

David Wilkinson (on steps, left) and Roger Klemm
at Woodland Stroll Through History
photo by Gary Peters

Publications of the Yolo County Historical Society

Clarksburg: Delta Community
by Shipley Walters
84pp., 1988, ISBN: 1-892626-01-2

Knights Landing: The River, The Land, The People
by Shipley Walters, with Tom Anderson
69pp., 1992, ISBN: 1-892626-03-9

Old North Davis: Guide to Walking a Traditional Neighborhood
by John Lofland
192pp., 1999, ISBN: 1-892626-05-5

West Sacramento: The Roots of a New City
by Shipley Walters
53pp., 1987, ISBN: 1-892626-00-4

Winters: A Heritage of Horticulture, A Harmony of Purpose
by Joann Leaach Larkey
126pp., 1991, ISBN: 1-892626-02-0

Woodland, City of Trees: A History
by Shipley Walters
50 pp., 1995, ISBN: 1-892626-04-7

Order from:
Yolo County Historical Society
P. O. Box 1447
Woodland, California 95776